Economic Diplomacy, Trade and Commercial Policy

To Hanneke, Doris and Vera

Economic Diplomacy, Trade and Commercial Policy

Positive and Negative Sanctions in a New World Order

Peter A. G. van Bergeijk

Edward Elgar

Published by
Edward Elgar Publishing Limited
Gower House
Croft Road
Aldershot
Hants GU11 3HR
England

Edward Elgar Publishing Company
Old Post Road
Brookfield
Vermont 05036
USA

British Library Cataloguing in Publication Data
Bergeijk, Peter A. G. Van
Economic Diplomacy, Trade and Commercial Policy: Positive and Negative Sanctions in a New World Order
I. Title
382

Library of Congress Cataloguing in Publication Data
Bergeijk, Peter A. G. van, 1959–
Economic diplomacy, trade and commercial policy : positive and negative sanctions in a new world order / Peter A. G. van Bergeijk.
p. cm.
Includes bibliographical references and indexes.
1. Economic sanctions. 2. Commercial policy. 3. International economic relations. 4. International cooperation. I. Title.
HF1413.5.B47 1993
337—dc20   94–6035
                                                                          CIP

ISBN 1 85278 893 3

Printed and bound in Great Britain by
Hartnolls Limited, Bodmin, Cornwall

Contents

PART III INSTITUTIONAL CHANGE

Figures and Tables

Acknowledgements

This book reports on a sustained research programme on economic sanctions and the politics of international trade. The aim of the book is to provide a unifying framework for relevant material on the relationship between diplomacy and international economics that is presently scattered in time and journals. The project covers the period 1986 to 1994. During these years I worked at Algemene Bank Nederland NV in Amsterdam, the University of Groningen (where I completed a Ph.D thesis on the subject) and at the Ministry of Economic Affairs in The Hague — first at the Directorate General for International Economic Relations and later at the Economic Policy Directorate's Research Unit. The usual caveat applies: the ideas expressed in this book should not be attributed to the government of the Netherlands.

Obviously such a project can only become a success with the (critical) support of employers and collegues. Henk de Haan and Ger Lanjouw supervized my work at Groningen University. Several articles and research memoranda were written in close collaboration with Charles van Marrewijk and Harry Oldersma. Charles and Harry also read and commented on parts of the book. Jarig van Sinderen stimulated this undertaking at the Dutch Ministry of Economic Affairs. I am indebted to Jan Pen both for stimulating discussions on my Ph.D thesis, for his help with clarifying a number of issues related to the present book and for his kindness in writing a preface to the book. Useful comments on parts of the manuscript were given by Shane Bonetti, Steven Brakman, Richard Gigengack, Robert Haffner, Dick Kabel, Pieter Karsdorp, Ruud de Mooy, Pieter Waasdorp and Ed Westerhout. I also benefited a lot from the comments of participants of the World Conferences of the Peace Science Society (International) (University of Maryland, 1988, and Erasmus University Rotterdam, 1992), the Eastern Economic Association's 15th annual meeting (Baltimore, 1989), the Tinbergen

Institute's lustrum congress 'Economics of International Security' (The Hague, 1992), several workshops on international economics of the Foundation for the Promotion of Research in Economic Sciences (ECOZOEK Wageningen, 1989 and Amsterdam, 1991) and the workshop on economic sanctions of the Research Center for Economic Policy (OCFEB) (Rotterdam 1993). Bettina Hoogeboom typed several drafts of the manuscript and assisted in the preparation of the index. Astrid Kampen provided valuable research assistance both in redoing the econometrics and in providing library services.

Material from the following sources is either edited, updated or partially reprinted and appears by kind permission of the editors of *De Economist* and *Kyklos*:

P.A.G. van Bergeijk, 1987, 'A Formal Treatment of Threats: A Note on the Economics of Deterrence', *De Economist* **135** (3), pp. 298—315.

P.A.G. van Bergeijk, 1989, 'Success and Failure of Economic Sanctions', *Kyklos* **42** (3), pp. 385—404.

C. van Marrewijk and P.A.G. van Bergeijk, 1990, 'Trade Uncertainty and Specialization: Social versus Private Planning', *De Economist* **138** (1), pp. 15—32.

P.A.G. van Bergeijk and H. Oldersma, 1990, 'Détente, Market-oriented Reform and German Unification. Potential Consequences for the World Trade Regime', *Kyklos* **43** (3), pp. 599—609.

P.A.G. van Bergeijk, 1992, 'Diplomatic Barriers to Trade', *De Economist* **140** (1), pp. 44—63.

Nieuw Vennep, February 1994
Peter A.G. van Bergeijk

Preface:
Harmony and Conflict
in International Relations

Jan Pen

Economists are trained to analyse the benefits of international trade. Actual developments support their arguments: the international division of labour has increased substantially since the days of Ricardo. Modern products embody contributions by different people who are widely dispersed around the globe: many of our suppliers and customers are foreigners. The free movement of goods and people favourably influences culture as well — exchange and trade prove very beneficial for civilization. It is praiseworthy that such international harmony is accentuated in political recommendations, because the temptations of nationalism should always be resisted. The resulting bias towards the beneficial effects of trade has helped shape the economist's point of view. Hence, it is hardly surprising that economic theory keeps the common interests of nations especially in mind. Economists have a peaceful view indeed on international relations.

This presumption, however, carries a cost: conflict among nations is rarely analyzed. Economists have no clear perspective on 'war': they neither understand Hitler nor Saddam Hussain. The traditional economist answers the question of why Napoleon went to Moscow with a shrug: 'My degree does not qualify me in the analysis of such decision-makers.' Consequently, a substantial facet of reality is a lost domain for economic theory. Historically, international relations are also characterized by combat, oppression, colonialism, exploitation and attempts to oust other nations from the seas. Trade and piracy have always been close relatives. Economists, however, defer the analysis of these facts of life to historians, political scientists or to dissenters, such as mercantilistic writers, Marxists, and adherents of *dependencia* theories. Indeed trade policy, in which harmony and conflict are subtly intertwined, is often reduced in textbooks to a mere description of traditions, procedures and international organizations. The even more circumspect struggle for power, with its negotiations and — often veiled — threats remains outside the scope of traditional economic analysis. Unfortunately, political scientists do not always fill these gaps in our knowledge either.

In this book Peter van Bergeijk acknowledges these gaps and attempts to bridge them. His analysis both combines and confronts economic and political themes. The disappearance of the Iron Curtain promises the benefits of more liberal trade. At the same time, however, the impact of economic sanctions makes itself felt as a strong negative influence. In our times, antipodal forces are at work, with an uncertain outcome. The analysis which Van Bergeijk presents can help one come to grips with this uncertainty.

Jan Pen

1. Introduction: Economic Limits to Modern Diplomacy

In the early 1990s Mikhail Gorbachev's programme of *perestrojke* triggered two developments that will prove to be of major importance to the world trade system in the 1990s. First, the collapse of the Berlin Wall and the Iron Curtain meant the end of a very substantial distortion of intra-European trade flows. This distortion was not only the result of physical barriers to trade, but also, and especially of psychological and political barriers. Second, the end of the Cold War gave birth to the idea of a New World Order in which military supremacy and especially military force are considered to be less appropriate instruments for solving international conflict. Unless the need for conflict resolution is reduced, this implies the need to use economic sanctions more often as an instrument of modern diplomacy, increasing the probability of political trade frictions. In its turn the increasing potential for political trade frictions stresses the importance of a proper design of the major international institutions that are needed to underpin a world order in which military conflict plays a minor part.

The principal aim of this book is to analyse the impact of these two counterbalancing forces. So a central theme will be the trade-off between on the one hand the beneficial trade impulse of the demolition of political trade barriers and on the other hand the discouragement of trade due to the increased trade uncertainty that is associated with the new international diplomatic setting. The developments on the European continent constitute the most clear and appealing example and, as we will see, the European case may have a more general bearing on the topic of the trade—diplomacy relationship. This twentieth century European renaissance contains important lessons both for other countries and for the architects of the international economic system.

1.1 Trade and Politics in Post-Wall Europe

The normalization of trade between East and West clearly has had a concrete and positive impact on the world's trade potential. According to data compiled by the Organization for Economic Co-operation and Development (OECD, 1993) the trade flows of central and eastern European countries *vis-à-vis* the OECD-area showed double digit annual growth rates in the early 1990s. Most interestingly, this increase in essentially intra-European trade was able to conquer a combination of three adverse demand shocks: the production decline due to radical economic reforms in eastern and central Europe; the collapse of the Council for Mutual Economic Assistance (CMEA or COMECON), implying that the trading arrangements amongst the reforming countries broke down; and finally, the sluggish growth in the OECD countries, which meant a relatively low level of import demand in the OECD.

The speed of the recuperation of old East—West and West—East trade relations reflects the importance of the political trade barriers which had seriously distorted the European trade pattern. Indeed, according to the Centre of Economic Policy Research (CEPR, 1990) the isolation of Eastern Europe after the Second World War was in sharp contrast with rapidly expanding trade in the *interbellum*. The revival of the pre-communist trade patterns showed both the importance of political variables in economic relationships and the potential benefits of the economic integration of central and eastern Europe in the world economic system. Actually, the trade dividend of *détente* may be substantial: the annual global costs of the Cold War in terms of trade potential forgone have been estimated at more than 3 per cent of world production (Van Bergeijk and Oldersma 1990).

The possibilities, however, of reaping the trade dividend of improving diplomatic relationships are certainly not limited to the European continent. Many other instances exist where regional, political, ethnic and social differences have for long stood in the way of the international division of labour. In Southern Africa the end of apartheid offers prospects of political stability and increasing trade and investment flows both for South Africa and for Pretoria's neighbouring states. Hayes (1987), for example, calculates that a 10 per cent change in South Africa's capacity to import from the West may pass through in a 1—2 per cent change in Zimbabwe's merchandise export earnings. In the Middle East a successful peace process could increase intra-regional trade to a large extent, as shown, for example by the analysis of *non*-trade between Israel and 'Palestine' by Denters and Klijn (1991). Table 1.1 illustrates for the cases of West—East and East—West trade flows that the increase of trade potential may be enormous once former antagonists start to co-operate. Moreover, the table shows that such co-operation will improve the trade prospects for East and West. Consequently, this will be economically advantageous to both sides.

Table 1.1 Trade of central Europe with the OECD area (1990—1992)

	1990 level $ million	1990	1991	1992
	Exports to OECD-area	Percentage change over year earlier		
Czechoslovakia	4,865	17.7	35.7	39.6
Hungary	5,698	26.6	17.8	9.8
Poland	8,878	44.9	11.2	13.6
	Imports from OECD-area	Percentage change over year earlier		
Czechoslovakia	4,867	33.0	29.0	71.4
Hungary	5,416	16.2	22.8	18.0
Poland	7,711	24.7	63.7	7.9

Source: OECD (1993), Table 25, p. 122

At the same time, however, difficulties arose due to the full economic and political integration of the former German Democratic Republic (GDR) and the Federal Republic of Germany (FRG) into one country, giving an important warning that political decision-making should not neglect economic logic. In its first annual *Economic Survey of Germany* following the signing of the Treaty creating a monetary, economic and social union of the GDR and the FRG, the OECD secretariat warned those who are used to reading between the lines of official documents that the 1:1 conversion rate between East and West Marks was a compromise between conflicting political and economic considerations. Probably economic logic had to bear the larger part of the compromise (see, for example, Murphy 1992). A more realistic conversion rate 'would have helped eastern German competitiveness as the country was opening up to international (and western German) competition' (OECD 1991, pp. 32—3). The 1993 economic turn-down in the German economic pace, however, illustrates that such economic limits to political aspirations often act as decisive constraints and cannot be ignored in the long-run.

1.2 Peace Dividend versus Trade Dividend

The New World Order (NWO), a political innovation by Brent Scowcroft that was most visibly introduced by the former US president George Bush, is also a spin-off of East—West *détente*. The NWO, however, may have an adverse impact on the world trade system, because it will have to rely more often on economic sanctions, whereas coercion in the international system was until now essentially a military task. The benefits of the NWO (the so-called peace dividend) have been well understood by economic policy-makers. Next to the substantial savings that can be achieved on government budgets if an arms build-down can be staged, a lot of military destruction can simply be avoided if the need for military intervention can be reduced. Pointing out that average military spending worldwide is some 4.5 per cent of Gross Domestic Product (GDP), the managing director of the International Monetary Fund (IMF) Michael Camdessus estimated an annual peace dividend of some $140 billion if the high defence spenders would reduce their military expenditures to the world average.[1] The costs related to the NWO, however, have not been so obvious. The message of this book is that the NWO may to some extent become a threat to the international economic exchange system. Hence the opportunity costs of the NWO may be summarized as the potential gains from trade that might have to be foregone in the course of defending the international legal order.

This 'trade dividend' is substantial: the efforts to integrate countries in the East, West, North and South into one open global economic system that is based on multilaterally agreed rules and principles of the General Agreement on Tariffs and Trade (GATT) are not just motivated by charity. Enlightened self-interest is also a very powerful driving force for international efforts to provide world-wide economic integration and trade liberalization. It is not so much the question whether a potential to develop trade exists; rather the question is how to develop the existing trade potential. Recently, Stoeckel et al. (1990) estimated the opportunity costs of existing quotas, tariffs and other trade barriers at some two to three hundred billion dollars in Japan, the United States and Europe. This is about 5 per cent on average of the annual production in the OECD area. The Third World, moreover, could profit enormously from world-wide trade and investment liberalization. Integration into the world economy would yield additional annual export growth of some 2—3 per cent for developing countries, offering their populations the prospects of an additional per capita income growth of 1—2 per cent a year.[2] So the trade dividend is substantial indeed and the extra growth that could be generated by trade liberalization may provide the funds to cover the capital requirements in central and eastern Europe and the Third World.[3]

An important difference exists between the trade dividend — which essentially pertains to efficiency in transaction — and the peace dividend, as the latter entails adjustment costs because it requires conversion of the production structure. Actually, reaping the trade dividend may be a necessary condition for the existence of any peace dividend at all as international trade may reduce the reallocation costs of restructuring the defence sector from military to civilian production. An important similarity is that both the trade dividend and the peace dividend require stability and peaceful international relations as necessary conditions. A NWO is an important step in achieving this kind of international stability and security.

This movement towards a 'better' world is, however, not a free lunch. The economic instruments that are needed to underpin the NWO carry a cost and have to be carefully designed. Trade-related measures will have to be used with restraint. Only very serious infractions against international rules should be considered as a potential case for the use of sanctions. Most importantly, boycotts and embargoes should only be used when other non-military measures have failed or could be expected to fail. This is so because enhanced reliance on economic sanctions, embargoes and boycotts, may be triggered by the greater ease with which grand coalitions are formed. Such coalitions are usually a prerequisite for successful economic sanctions. Moreover, greater effectiveness of threats due to greater political and economic linkage may increase demand for boycotts and embargoes. Enhanced reliance on economic sanctions, however, also entails some hidden costs. Using sanctions too often may decrease the potential effectiveness of economic leverage and this would deprive the NWO from its ultimate non-violent instrument and, consequently, might trigger military interventionism. Such developments clearly cannot be in support of international security and so it is very important that the demand for politically inspired trade barriers should be the focus of further analysis. Hence the need for restraint and careful design.

1.3   Five Reasons to Expect an Increase in Political Trade Frictions

Government has always interfered in trade flows, balancing, for example, the protection of an advantage in key military systems against the promotion of economic vitality and trade. Adam Smith ([1776] 1976, vol. I, p. 487) was very outspoken in his advice on this evergreen subject: 'Defence is much more important than opulence'. At present, however, the choice between trade and defence is not simply a matter of a trade-off between an economic and a non-economic interest. Trade has become a decisive determinant indeed of military and political power, as shown by, for instance, the growing importance of exports for the economic vitality of the United States and, consequently, for its military base. Hence the impact of trade on potential adversaries also has become of more interest to politicians, the military and diplomats.

Economic variables are not only inputs for the military power equation; economic relationships themselves may constitute sources of power. Although both economic conflict and economic co-operation are not merely political acts, economic warfare and economic peace-keeping are real instruments of foreign policy as well. To restate Von Clausewitz's ([1832] 1988, p. 119) *dictum*: 'economic diplomacy is a mere continuation of policy by other means.' Indeed, politically inspired trade barriers are a phenomenon of growing importance. This is not to say that the number of actually implemented boycotts and embargoes will increase. Rather the contention is that the probability of politically inspired disruption of trade and investment relationships will increase. There are essentially five reasons for this expected global increase in the demand for economic leverage.

The reduced role of the military
First, both the end of the Cold War and the movement towards the New World Order reduce the role of the military instrument in the world system. Indeed, the very idea of the peace dividend is tantamount to the reduction of military expenditures. The decrease in the availability of defence funds is an additional (supply side) reason for today's tune, next to the lower demand for military protection due to *détente*. The upshot is that diplomacy will more often have to use economic peace-keeping and economic warfare (positive as well as negative economic sanctions).

The possibilities for the skilful *non*-use of military and economic force have increased since the superpower conflict ended. Before the present *détente* it was almost customary that differing interests rendered many diplomatic efforts a priori useless, because in a bipolar world countries can always turn to the other superpower for economic, political or military support. Moreover, the role of the United Nations and other international organizations became more and more important, increasing the potential scope of essentially non-violent approaches to diplomatic conflict, such as arbitrage and financial compensation. Finally, the World Bank and the International Monetary Fund (IMF) became increasingly willing to include non-economic elements, for example, with respect to the maximum level of defence spending, in the conditionality attached to their development and balance of payments support programmes.

Invisibility of diplomatic trade barriers
Second, Non Tariff Barriers (NTBs) in general have become
increasingly important as tariffs have been significantly reduced
worldwide in successive GATT rounds. The World Bank (1991, p.
37) assesses that average tariff rates for manufactured goods in
industrial countries amounted to more than 30 per cent in the 1930s.
This average halved to about 16 per cent in the 1950s. Thirty years
later the average tariff stood at 7 per cent only. This reduction in
trade barriers was, however, partly substituted for by the increased
use of NTBs. The consequence was substitution of tariffs by the
increased use of NTBs. Economic NTBs, such as quotas, voluntary
export restraints and technical and legal standards, became the subject
of the analysis of many students of international economic relations
(see, for example, IMF 1992b for a review of recent findings).

Table 1.2 The EC's anti-dumping instrument (1980—1990)

| | Anti-dumping cases | | Import | Relative |
| | No. | % | share | application |
	(1)	(2)	(3)	(2)/(3)
OECD	445	49	60	0.8
Eastern bloc	220	24	10	2.4
Others	238	27	30	0.9
Romania	36	4	0.7	5.7
Czecho-Slovakia	41	5	0.8	8.3
Yugoslavia	43	5	1	5.0

Source: Calculations based on Eymann and Schuknecht (1991), p.23

The *diplomatic* NTB, however, has been neglected by most students
of international economic relations. Essentially unnoticed, the extent
of diplomatic NTBs reached a very substantial level during the 1980s.
As an illustration, Eastern Europe, at the outset of the political
revolutions was confronted by some 5,600 non-tariff restrictions on
its exports to the OECD area, while the EC's anti-dumping measures
of the last decade were disproportionally directed at the eastern bloc
countries (see Table 1.2). Essentially these trade disturbances reflect

political motives, as, for example, Western governments have subjected East—West trade to their domestic political and strategic ends (Van Ham 1992).

Strategic trade policy demands

Third, strategic trade policy considerations may increase the demand for foreign trade sanctions. The so-called 'new' trade theories, introduced amongst others by Brander, Dixit, Helpman, Krugman and Spencer, deal with economic conditions of increasing returns under oligopoly.[4] The 'new' approach shows that government intervention in trade by means of quantitative restrictions and subsidies may shift the balance of profits and other external benefits between countries. Economic leverage could open foreign markets simply by threatening to raise new barriers to trade. Rhodes (1989) argues that such a reciprocal strategy can affect another nation's calculation of self-interest and force other countries to co-operate. This kind of managed trade may consist of measures that are implied by formal trade policy (for example, section 301 of the American trade law) or camouflaged with political sentiments. As Bhagwati points out, 'The profit-shifting argument has a predatory flavour. It can therefore lead to retaliation. Once that happens everyone can be a loser' (Bhagwati 1991, p. 44).

Strategic trade policy may increase foreign trade frictions as well as the demand for trade sanctions in pursuit of foreign policy goals. Levine (1988) analyses the actual use that was made of Section 232 of the US Trade Expansion Act of 1962, that provides for import relief when the national security is at potential risk. He warns that Section 232 should not become a refuge for uncompetitive industries seeking trade relief. Carter (1988, p. 3) wonders whether the steel industry would discover human rights violations in South Korea or Taiwan and seek a ban on steel imports from these countries if the government's authority to impose import sanctions against these countries were expanded unconditionally. These are not merely theoretical possibilities as shown by the long tradition of policy makers opting for trade distorting measures even though such second-best 'solutions' can be shown (and have been shown) to be patently inefficient. For example, money clearly goes down the drain when bureaucracies succeed in reducing possibilities to trade and at the same time provide aid to the victims of their trade regulation. The EC's trade policy towards the Third World and central Europe are cases in point (see, for example, Page 1991 and Van Bergeijk and Lensink 1993). In addition Kaempfer and Lowenberg (1992, pp. 43—5) argue that many sanctions are designed to benefit interest groups in the sender country. All OECD countries, for example, boycotted South African exports of textiles, steel and iron, where protectionism is already the tune of the day.

Strategic behaviour, however, is a general problem if policy-making has global dimensions. The relatively small number of governments induces strategic behaviour. Being endowed with market power, governments can often effectively achieve an outcome that is superior for their own country, although it is (Pareto-)inferior for the world as a whole (Hahn 1990, p. 159).

International environmental policy
Fourth, trade sanctions are increasingly being proposed to enforce environmental policies in other countries. Folmer et al. (1993) suggest that a country that suffers from transboundary pollution may threaten to limit economic relations if the polluting source country refuses to co-operate and change its environmental policy. Sorsa (1992) points to the growing need to prevent a rise in the environment related trade frictions, especially with respect to the unilateral use of trade sanctions.

Environmentalists have expressed concerns that the effect of trade liberalization would be to increase demand which could exert exploitative pressures on natural resources and the environment in general. Some argue that the effect of trade liberalization would be to reduce prices and, consequently, increase demand which could then increase exploitative pressures on natural resources and the environment in general. Economic efficiency in their view equals larger transaction volumes and, consequently, more degradation of the environment. Some have argued that free trade is essentially incompatible with resource conservation and general environmental protection, thus undermining the case against trade measures for environmental policy making. The Brundtland report (WCED 1987) explicitly links Third World environmental destruction due to forced development to the production of agricultural and mining products that are exported to the OECD. In view of the foregoing, GATT was increasingly criticized during the Uruguay Round for lack of concern for environmental matters. Guided by popular sentiment and frightened by huge abatement costs, policy makers seem increasingly willing to opt for trade regulation and trade impediments as instruments to protect the environment, thus spoiling the potential contribution of trade to sustainable development (see Petersman 1991, Van Bergeijk 1991 and Anderson and Blackhurst 1992).

On several occasions measures have been taken that are at odds with GATT. International agreements that deal with specific global environmental problems often contain trade-related measures aimed against free rider behaviour from non-parties. The 1988 Montreal Protocol on the reduction of ozone-threatening chlorofluorocarbons, for example, embodies discriminatory treatment which is meant to exclude imports and exports of controlled substances, products containing controlled substances, and — if feasible — imports of products produced with but not containing controlled substances to states that are not part to the Protocol. Finally, the Protocol aims at discouraging the export of technologies for utilizing and producing such substances to non-parties. Hence the practice of international environmental policy-making so far points in the direction of an increase in the use of both multilateral and unilateral economic sanctions.

Proliferation has to be stopped
Finally, the proliferation of both nuclear, chemical and biological weapon production technologies, as well as of delivery systems for weapons of mass destruction, are decisive factors behind the spread and increase of regional conflicts. So while the end of the Cold War would seem to reduce demand for export control in general, specific cases, for example the Iraqi and Libyan military build-ups, have shown that global arms trade and the international flow of arms-related technology should be intensively monitored and if necessary redirected and/or restricted. Indeed, as argued by Roodbeen (1992), *détente* in the Gorbachev era at first sight appeared to have reduced the necessity for the embargo on technology in the context of the East—West conflict, which was administered by the Co-ordinating Committee for Multilateral Export Controls (CoCom). The

(intra)regional instabilities, however, that surfaced since the Soviet Union collapsed, vividly illustrate the inappropriateness of the case for a free and unrestricted flow of sensitive and strategic goods, services and knowledge. This, in a nutshell, is the practical rationale for export control in the 1990s and beyond. New institutional and diplomatic arrangements, however, will be needed for effective export control, as pointed out by, for example, the recent report of the US Committee on Science, Engineering, and Public Policy (1991). The Committee argues that the United States should opt for fully multilateral export controls, that the participation by China and the former Soviet Union is a prerequisite for viable export controls and, finally, that export controls should be tailor-made and reduced in number in order to address the enforcement issue.

1.4 Economics and Modern Diplomacy

Political instability, unbalanced capital flows, the reputation of unreliability as a trade partner or an active 'voluntary' export restraint policy may decrease the trust in free trade and reduce the potential for trade. Also on account of the advancement of peaceful international conflict resolution, the relative invisibility of diplomatic NTBs, the emergence of strategic trade policy theories, the practice of international environmental policy-making and the need to prevent proliferation of weapons of mass destruction, an increase in economic sanctions is to be expected.

Trade uncertainty arising from such political interactions may impose substantial costs on the world economic system, as this uncertainty reduces the extent of international specialization. If increased uncertainty reduces international trade, additional political costs will result since trade is an important incentive for international co-operation.

Politicians should take the real economic costs of these changes in the world economic system into account. Most importantly, enhanced reliance on economic sanctions and politically inspired increased trade frictions in general will increase the extent of uncertainty in the world trade system.

The problem is not so much that the probability of a specific country becoming a target of economic sanctions increases, since a potential target can influence this probability by behaving in accordance with the standards set by the international community (or specific sender countries). Rather the problem of (global) trade uncertainty derives from the fact that the overall probability increases that every country's trade partners will become the subject of economic sanctions. Moreover, in many cases the impact of boycotts and embargoes will spill over to the trade partners (and to each trade partner's trade partners and so on). So other, presumably innocent, countries will eventually suffer from the trade disruption that is aimed at specific 'ill-mannered' countries. Although gains from trade still exist in such a scenario, the welfare gains will decrease substantially below the level in a deterministic or simply a less uncertain trade setting. In this way the general (and possibly endogenous) trade uncertainty, that results if international politics resorts to economic warfare and economic surveillance more often, may change the global patterns of production and comparative advantage. The implied suboptimal allocation of the factors of production may be a substantial hidden cost that should be taken into account in any policy analysis or policy recommendation on the use of economic relationships as a source of international power. This is the task that I will try to perform in this book.

1.5 Plan of the Book

Part I (Chapters 2 to 4) will deal with the literature, the theory and the measurement of economic sanctions. Here the question will be how economic instruments should be used as a means of modern diplomacy. Part II (Chapters 5 to 7) focuses on the impact of diplomacy in general on international economic exchanges. It assesses some of the hidden, but real, costs and benefits of diplomatic activities and essentially deals with the question of why negative sanctions and other trade-related measures should be used with restraint only. Part III (Chapter 8) draws some conclusions with respect to the institutional settings of the world economic system.

Part I starts with a review of recent literature on the economic sanction instrument. A basic assumption is that sanctions should be considered as threats of economic damage to be inflicted if behaviour does not conform to certain standards set by the sender of the sanctions. Since enhanced reliance may impair the effectiveness of boycotts and embargoes as an instrument of foreign policy, we will first investigate the economic conditions that determine success and failure of economic sanctions. It will be useful to make a distinction between the conditions for, on the one hand, effective sanctions, that is boycotts and embargoes that cause economic damage (for negative sanctions or punishments) or do a lot of good in the target economy (for positive sanctions or rewards); and on the other hand, successful sanctions, the latter being economic measures that succeed in changing the behaviour of the target economy. Chapter 3 presents a model of economic sanctions. I will argue that both the concept of uncertainty and the role of expectations are very important for our understanding of the economic sanction phenomenon. Consequently, this chapter will develop the expected utility approach to economic sanctions that is especially relevant in the stochastic setting that provides the appropriate modelling structure to analyse the international system. We will be dealing with theories of both negative and positive economic sanctions. Chapter 4 will investigate empirically the determinants of success and failure of 103 cases of negative economic sanctions that took place since the Second World War. This investigation produces an equation that satisfactorily explains the success rate of the sanction cases on the basis of variables that are the determinants of potential effectiveness. The findings empirically support the threat concept and consequently show the appropriateness of the expected utility approach to economic sanctions.

Both empirical and theoretical work in international economics is hardly relevant if the politics of trade are not taken into account. Consequently, Part II concentrates on the impact of diplomacy on trade flows. The chapters follow the same line of discourse — literature, modelling, econometrics — as Part I. Chapter 5 reviews the literature on the impact of (expectations about) the diplomatic climate on trade and international specialization and starts with a review of economic theories that were developed in relation to the national defence argument for trade barriers. Chapter 6 will develop a theory of general (and possibly endogenous) trade uncertainty that will result if international politics resorts to economic warfare and economic surveillance more often. We will use essentially the same box of tools as in Part I. So while the analysis in Chapter 3 resulted in a new theory of negative and positive economic sanctions, Chapter 6 will derive a new approach to trade disruption on the basis of expected utility, a fresh and versatile use of an old and well-known method. If firms and consumers internalize the externality of political conflict and co-operation, that is to say if they take the impact of politics on uncertainty into account, the pattern of specialization will change. The implied suboptimal allocation of factors of production may be a substantial hidden cost next to the reduced effectiveness of the economic sanction instrument and its possibly inappropriate severeness. Next we will look into the empirical relevance of diplomatic trade uncertainty in the early 1980s. Deploying the so-called gravity model of international trade, Chapter 7 will estimate elasticities of exports and imports with respect to diplomatic behaviour. Diplomatic conflicts are shown to result in substantial trade reductions. Hence trade uncertainty that arises from political interactions imposes substantial costs on the global economic system. In contradistinction diplomatic co-operation may yield the economic benefits that are associated with the trade dividend and be a useful force enabling the peace dividend to materialize. The policy conclusion is not that the NWO is not economically feasible; the outcome of the analysis is that trade-and-investment-related measures have to be used carefully.

So in the final part of the book, Chapter 8, we will be dealing with the institutional changes that are necessary to create the economic background for the NWO against which the trade dividend and the peace dividend can be reconciled. More specifically, I will discuss the case for a World Trade and Investment Organization. In December 1993 an encouraging step has been made in the direction of such an organization when the Final Act of the Uruguay Round was adopted. However, much remains to be done in order to reduce political uncertainty and to provide a dispute settlement mechanism that can take care of political NTBs in an economic framework.

Notes

1. M. Camdessus, 'Transformation of former USSR is both challenge and opportunity' Georgetown University School of Foreign Service (15 April 1992), reprinted in: *IMF Survey* (27 April 1992) **21** (9), 129—34. Recent studies on the peace dividend include Fontanel (1994), Klein (1994) and Mintz and Stevenson (1992). Renner (1993) discusses institutional changes that are needed to build the international peace system that would seem to be a prerequisite for the peace dividend to exist.

2. For some recent assessments of the impact of trade liberalization on developing countries see, for example, IMF (1990), Table 18, IMF (1992a), 99—105, Jepma (1992), Table 6.5, Linnemann and Verbruggen (1991) and De Rosa (1992).

3. A good introduction into the theory and measurement of capital requirements is Lensink (1993).

4. Non-technical introductions into the strategic trade theory and into the practical policy implications of the new trade theories are Krugman (1986), Stegemann (1989), Baldwin (1992) and Van Bergeijk and Kabel (1993).

PART I
POSITIVE AND NEGATIVE ECONOMIC
SANCTIONS

2. Economic Sanctions: An Ineffective Instrument?

The increased use of economic sanctions that the end of the superpower rivalry presently seems to induce makes the question of the effectiveness of this economic instrument relevant and timely. This is especially so since mainstream economic analysis has not dealt in depth with boycotts and embargoes, although economists generally assume that economic sanctions are impotent diplomatic means at best. According to Leitzel (1987, p. 286), 'the gulf between policy significance and theoretical and empirical development is probably wider in the area of economic sanctions than in any other region at the confluence of economic and political streams of thought'. This part will be concerned with the efficacy of economic sanctions. This chapter introduces and discusses the main economic theories on this topic. Chapter 3 will develop an expected utility model of economic sanctions. Chapter 4 empirically investigates the determinants of success and failure of boycotts and embargoes. The study of economic sanctions essentially requires an introduction in what has been called the 'donkey psychology' of economic diplomacy. Just like a donkey, it is assumed, countries can be induced to move in the right direction by means of a stick and a carrot, that is to say, by negative and positive economic sanctions. The donkey psychology, however, also points out that sanctions can be counterproductive: if the donkey beater pulls a donkey by the tail, it will run away in an opposite direction. The donkey metaphor would be boring and cumbersome. So in the discussion the country or group of countries that imposes or threatens to impose the economic sanction is called the sender. The country (or group of countries) against which the sanction is imposed is called the target.

Negative sanctions are the best-known — and certainly the most spectacular — economic instruments of diplomacy. A negative sanction is a punishment or a disincentive. Generally speaking, three kinds of negative economic sanctions can be distinguished: boycotts, embargoes and capital sanctions. A boycott restricts the demand for certain products from the target country. A boycott can be administered by governments and international organizations, but some notable consumer boycotts have been effective as well. The 1991 oil boycott against Iraq and the consumer boycott of South African agricultural products are examples of both types. An embargo restricts the exports of certain products to the target economy. The oil embargo against Serbia is a recent example. Embargoes are enforced by a system of export licences and controls of destination, transit and transport. Capital (or financial) sanctions restrict or suspend lending (loans, credits, grants, etc.) to, and investment in, the target economy and often impose additional restrictions on international payments in order to hinder sanction-busting and trade diversion. In addition foreign assets of the target economy may be frozen. The sanctions by the United States against Iran in the wake of the 1979 hostage crisis are an example. This strict classification, however, may be blurred in actual sanction cases. Obviously, the combination of these three types may even be advisable in many cases. Neither is it necessary that sanctions are complete in the sense that all trade and investment is blocked. An embargo, for example, may be partial; that is, it may cover certain specific products and technologies only.

Positive sanctions are less spectacular, because these rewards or incentives to a large extent, although not exclusively, belong to the domain of silent diplomacy. Many kinds of positive sanctions, such as aid and technological and military co-operation, belong to day-to-day-practice and are hardly ever distinct enough from the constant flows of international interactions to stand out against this background as 'reportable'. Consequently, much is unknown about characteristics of successful positive economic sanctions and this is the reason to focus in this chapter on negative economic sanctions. Still situations do exist where only positive sanctions can succeed. Indeed the use of formal positive economic sanctions has increased recently, for example, in the lending conditions of the European Bank for Reconstruction and Development, which exclude non-democratic debtor countries.

This chapter will first deal with some methodological questions related to the definition of the success of economic sanctions and its proper measurement. The first section addresses the question of the inaccuracy of observations on the sanction phenomenon. The second distinguishes effectiveness and success: effective sanctions may fail although the economic hardship that they impose on the target is substantial. Likewise the threat of a sanction may be successful even when no economic damage is done. Section 2.3 deals with economic theories about factors that contribute to the effectiveness of economic sanctions. Neoclassical, Keynesian, residual demand, oligopoly and long-run growth theories are discussed. These five perspectives have several variables and processes in common and these common characteristics enable the development of a framework that can be deployed in further research. Section 2.4 analyses the success and failure of sanctions from several non-economic points of view, allowing for the political and psychological aspects of boycotts and embargoes. The final section takes a fresh look at some recent sanction cases in order to assess the practical utility of the theoretical approaches.

2.1 On the Inaccuracy of Our Empirical Knowledge

In this part we will be concerned with qualitative and quantitative characteristics of economic sanctions. So this first section is probably the right place for a dull warning on the reliability of data about economic sanctions. Obviously, observations about international economic warfare should not automatically be considered reliable.

First, there is the general problem that 'normal' errors of measurement, that cause concern to all researchers, are very significant in studies about international trade and investment flows. As early as 1950 the problem that generally accepted economic figures often have very large error components was put to the fore by Morgenstern. Many inconsistencies, however, still exist in generally accepted figures on international transactions that are supplied by the national Statistical Offices and the international organizations such as the OECD and the IMF.[1] In addition, inaccuracies resulting from differences in definitions are quite probable since this part studies a period of 45 years and countries with very different economic systems in various stages of development.

Second, in so far as the figures have been supplied by the sanctioning and the target governments, the reliability is questionable. Hayes, for example, points to the fact that even before the South African authorities suspended publication of detailed trade statistics in 1986 'considerable aggregation in the statistics of the figures for certain "sensitive" items and trading partners prevented detailed analysis of the effects of sanctions on the South African economy' (Hayes 1988, p. 271). The subject of this study being economic warfare, it is important to realize that both sides may have an interest in distorting and/or incompletely supplying data (Harris 1968, p.8). Indeed, according to Baldry and Dollery (1992, pp. 1—2),

> artificially-engineered data paucities have generated problems facing researchers. Quite apart from the suppression of disaggregated trade and investment statistics by the South African authorities, nations, firms and individuals engaging in economic relationships with South Africa tend to disguise or understate the extent of their transactions.

South Africa is not unique in distorting trade statistics for strategic reasons. Governments that are supposed to impose economic sanctions often dictate the official trade statistics. Saudi Arabia, for example, reported in April 1989 that it was fully complying with the UN oil embargo of South Africa and this official view was reflected in the Saudi trade figures. The Shipping Research Bureau (1989), however, established that 76 oil tankers sailed from Saudi Arabia to deliver oil to South Africa in the years 1979—1987.

With respect to the major data base on the efficacy of economic sanctions (Hufbauer and Schott 1985 and Hufbauer, Schott and Elliott 1990 — whenever possible I refer to the second edition) some methodological questions have been raised. Bull (1984, p. 221), for example, wonders whether the data are sufficiently comparable to lend themselves for useful generalizations. Moreover, the data base might be biased if only countries that have a comparative advantage in the implementation of sanctions use the economic instruments of foreign policy. Knowing they have little or no chance to succeed, specific countries might simply not use sanctions and hence be under-represented in the data base. Indeed large sender countries, most notably the United States, are over-represented in the Hufbauer, Schott and Elliott study. This may be especially relevant since the authors relate the declining success rate of the sanction instrument to the declining hegemony of the United States (Hufbauer, Schott and Elliott 1990, pp. 107—11). Finally, the answer of whether a specific sanction case is indeed a success or a failure has to be based on judgements of several authors.[2] Differences of opinion are very probable, as, for example, Hufbauer, Schott and Elliott (1990, p. 41) admit:

> since foreign objectives evolve over time, and since the contribution of sanctions to the policy outcomes is often murky, judgment plays an important role in assigning a single number to each element of the 'success equation'.

In addition, a number of methodological errors may hamper the proper interpretation of the major empirical findings on economic sanctions so far. This econometric aspect of the inaccuracy of our knowledge, however, will be dealt with in Chapter 4. All in all the student of economic sanctions definitely needs to take the unreliability of his empirical basis into account.

2.2. Effectiveness versus Success

The most striking characteristic of negative economic sanctions is the combination of their relative ineffectiveness and the economic profession's disbelief in the possible utility of boycotts and embargoes as instruments of foreign policy-making. According to Hufbauer, Schott and Elliott's (1990) *Economic Sanctions Reconsidered*, on average only about one out of three sanction cases since the Second World War succeeded in achieving their stated political goal.[3]

Table 2.1 on page 24 shows that about two out of three sanctions did not succeed in achieving their stated foreign policy goal in the period 1946—1989. The trackrecord deteriorated, as in the period 1976—1989 only a quarter of the sanction cases ended successfully. Moreover, only a rather limited number of cases appears to have induced substantial damage on the target economy. According to Hufbauer, Schott and Elliott (1990), only in a third of the 103 cases over the period 1946—1990 did sanction damage exceed the level of 1 per cent of the target's GDP.[4]

Table 2.1 The success rate of economic sanctions (1946—1989)

Period	Sanctions (1)	Successes (2)	Success rate (%) (2)/(1)
1946—1955	13	3	23
1956—1965	26	13	50
1966—1975	17	6	35
1976—1983	35	10	29
1983—1989	12	2	17
1946—1989	103	34	33

Source: Calculations based on Hufbauer, Schott and Elliott (1990)

Given this seeming ineffectiveness, it is not surprising that both popular and scientific interest in boycotts and embargoes as an instrument of foreign policy waned in the 1980s. Quite generally the usefulness of negative economic sanctions was considered to be rather low. Adler-Karlsson (1982, pp. 166—7) argued that it would hardly be possible to create the necessary political unity for forceful boycotts or embargoes and (if established at all) sanctions would be easy to circumvent. Lindsay (1986, p. 160), moreover, questioned the plausibility of a change in behaviour as a consequence of punitive economic damage: sanctions being public measures, compliance might damage the target leadership's world prestige or diminish its domestic support. He considered economic sanctions to be merely symbolic gestures. Seeler (1982, p. 616) pointed out that the lapse of time between the decision to use economic sanctions and their actual bureaucratic implementation offers the target country the possibility to adjust its economy, thus reducing the potential damage of the sanction. Some, for example, Reekie (1987) in the case of South Africa, went so far as to deny that sanctions could ever work. Indeed, according to Baldwin (1985, pp. 55—7), the tendency to denigrate the utility of economic sanctions has been a salient characteristic of the literature on economic statecraft.

   In sum, according to mainstream international economists five reasons pointed to the ineffectiveness of economic sanctions as an instrument of foreign policy. First, failure was considered to be evident in some widely publicized and discussed cases (South Africa, Israel). Second, the urge for free trade was considered to be too strong implying that sanction-busting and trade diversion were the most probable outcomes of economic sanctions. Third, the assumption that behaviour can be changed by means of economic damage was doubted on both political and psychological grounds. Fourth, a long-lasting complete embargo appeared hardly possible, either on economic grounds (for example, cartel theory) or on political arguments. Finally, the empirical evidence showed a rather low success rate.

Table 2.2 Success rate and proportional trade linkage (1946—1989)

Trade linkage (%)	Successes (1)	Failures (2)	Success rate (%) $(1)/\{(1)+(2)\}$
0 — 1	5	22	19
1 — 2	6	10	38
2 — 4	7	11	39
4 —10	6	8	43
> 10	8	9	47
Total	32	60	35

Note: Proportonal trade linkage is defined as the bilateral trade flow between sender and target as a percentage of the target's GDP and is measured in the year prior to the sanction.

Sources: See the Appendix to Chapter 4

The numerical predominance of failures *per se*, however, hardly provides any evidence for the ineffectiveness of the diplomatic use of economic relations. More specifically, a sanction should indeed fail if the — theoretical — conditions for a success are not being met. This caveat would seem to be fairly obvious. A sanction simply cannot be successful if, for example, no damage can be done. Table 2.2 relates the success rate to the proportional trade linkage, that is the share of bilateral trade with the sender as a percentage of the target's national income.[5] Table 2.2 illustrates that, as one would expect, a sanction fails if proportional trade linkage is not substantial. For example, the bilateral trade flows should exceed the threshold of 1 per cent of the target's national income. This point, however, was generally overlooked in the analysis.

Often sanctions fail because checks on the observance of the economic measures are simply impossible, as in the case of the sanctions against disintegrating Yugoslavia in the early 1990s. Moreover, many sanctions can only come about after long-lasting and laborious international consultation; a general characteristic of EC decision-making on international political activities. Sometimes the costs of effective sanctions are too large for the sender so that diplomacy never gets beyond the stage of angry words without decisiveness (that is to say that the necessary organizational conditions for a successful sanction are not being met; see Frey 1984, pp. 106—7). In all these circumstances sanctions should be expected to fail. Consequently, it is clear that not every failure is evidence for the inefficiency of the economic instruments of modern diplomacy.

Only from the comparison of sanction outcomes and the values of those determinants of failure and success can we possibly draw some valid conclusions about the potential utility of economic sanctions. A first step toward such an evaluation is to distinguish between success — that is the change in political behaviour — and effectiveness — that is the (potential) economic damage of an economic sanction (Losman 1972).[6]

The effectiveness of economic sanctions is probably the natural line of approach for economists. Their tool of analysis is the traditional trade model. Trade liberalization and the associated gains from trade are useful concepts because complete embargoes and boycotts are the mirror images of the movement from the no-trade situation of autarky to a state of the world in which free trade prevails and all countries benefit from international specialization according to their respective comparative advantage. Leaving the political aspects aside, this is the economist's realm *par excellence*, as Pen (1967, p. 37) once remarked: the comparative advantage of economists lies in analysing comparative advantage. Compelling evidence exists to support the basic findings of the 'gains from trade' that are suggested by the economic model of trade liberalization. Indeed, a good two centuries of economic analysis support the free trade recipe and hence the mirror images of these theories may provide insight into the mechanisms that determine whether sanctions are effective or not.

2.3 Competing Economic Theories on the Effectiveness of Sanctions

Economists are known to disagree, so it is a daunting task to try to develop a unifying framework for economic sanctions in this section. As will become clear, however, it is quite possible to find agreement on key-variables amidst the disagreement on the specific mechanisms that determine whether a sanction works or not. I argue that it is possible to identify a number of variables that play a part in different economic approaches to the sanction phenomenon. I discern five perspectives: neoclassical, Keynesian, residual demand, oligopoly and long-run growth. Variables that appear in these economic approaches would seem to be theoretically undisputed and this provides a framework for further analysis. Let us consider these five perspectives in turn and see both what these approaches have in common and what the specific facets are that these theories want to highlight.

Neoclassical approach
In the standard neoclassical trade model the imposition of a complete boycott or a complete embargo that halts all export and import of the target economy boils down to inverting the traditional theory that is often used to illustrate the gains from trade that a closed or autarkic economy can reap if it opens up to international trade. A substantial theoretical and empirical literature exists on these gains from international trade. Hence this well-established doctrine may be a useful point of departure for this discussion of the different economic approaches to the sanction phenomenon.

From the 'inverted trade liberalization model' of economic sanctions it follows that a sanction will produce more hardship on the target economy, the larger the pre-sanction target's dependence on trade with the sender and the more inflexible the target's consumption preferences and production structures.[7] Since both demand and supply rigidities basically are short term phenomena, it follows that the passage of time reduces the effectiveness of sanctions. Stockpiling may help in the short run, but as stockpiles run out, only increasing flexibility of markets and the internal mobility of the factors of production are viable options for the target in the long run.[8] Sanctions moreover may be partial: they need not prevent all imports or exports by the target. It can, however, be concluded that larger relative trade flows between sender and target and more universally applied economic measures constitute a larger relative loss of income for the target.

One way of measuring the gains from trade is to compare the income of a trading economy at international prices with the actual expenditure that would be necessary to obtain autarky comparable utility. An obvious problem is that autarky prices and consumption patterns in general are unknown since almost every economy trades at least a bit with other countries. Inverting the classical gains from trade argument in the cases of both a partial and a full boycott or embargo yields the conclusion that the sanction damage can be expressed as the difference between the target's income during the sanctions and the target's pre-sanction consumption and investment outlays valued at the prices that prevail during the sanction. In this case the variables can more readily be observed.

An important implication is that the neoclassical approach focuses on the market mechanism. It is often assumed that the free availability of goods that are covered by the sanctions on the target's markets indicates a lack of effectiveness and, consequently, a failure. The absence, however, of formal rationing activities can easily be explained if the market mechanism functions properly. A decrease in the supply of goods automatically feeds into higher prices, reducing the quantity demanded until a new equilibrium between demand and supply is reached. Accordingly, the market mechanism automatically distributes the goods among the population in the most efficient way and a formal rationing scheme will only be necessary if the rise in prices is deemed socially unacceptable. Anyhow, the absence of queuing or the free availability of specific goods does not provide evidence that the sanction is not working. Final conclusions can only be drawn from the simultaneous inspection of traded quantities and prices. In conclusion, the neoclassical analysis rightly deals with both prices and quantities that are measured before and after the sanction is imposed and so this approach is able to cover partial sanctions as well as complete sanctions.

Keynesian approach

The Keynesian analysis mainly deals with the short term since the production capacity of the economy is given. Investments and disinvestments may influence the aggregate or effective demand, but the resulting changes in the national capital stock do not influence the supply side of the economy that is summarized in the macro-economic supply function.

The impact of disturbances in the international economic relations in Keynesian-type models may be traced via two channels. First, export demand may decrease if the target economy is boycotted. Second, imports will have to adjust and this may pose an additional constraint on effective demand.

Consider a very simple Keynesian model for a small open economy in which government for convenience is not modelled explicitly. As is usually assumed in these models, consumption C and imports M depend positively on national income Y with marginal propensities c_Y and M_Y that are strictly positive and less than one. In contradistinction, investment I and exports X are assumed to be exogenous. The well-known national income identity for this economy is

$$Y = C + I + X - M \tag{2.1}$$

which can easily be rewritten so that the following reduced form equation of Y results:

$$Y = (I + X)/(1 + M_Y - C_Y) \tag{2.2}$$

where all variables (except Y of course) are exogenous. If export decreases, then the reduction in effective demand implies that national income directly decreases by the amount of the trade flow that is hit by the boycott. This first order effect, however, is aggravated by the foreign trade multiplier $1/(1+M_Y-C_Y)$ that for plausible values of the marginal propensities exceeds one. So the reduction in national income exceeds the decrease of the export turnover due to the boycott. For example, using the social accounting matrix for South Africa, Khan (1988, p. 136) calculates that if sanctions lead to a decline of exports by $1 million, then output will decline by $3 million.

Within the Keynesian framework it is, however, quite possible that the reduction in aggregate demand can be counteracted by the target government, for example, if it reduces taxes or increases government expenditures. The costs of such policies consist of an increase in the budget deficit and the stock of national debt. In the short run this may be considered responsible if future (post-sanction) policies counteract the deterioration of the fiscal stance.

An embargo is quite another matter in a Keynesian model. Now we have to add some supply side considerations. Imports are often demanded for the important role that raw materials and intermediate inputs play in the production process. A decrease of the availability of these goods can therefore constrain potential production. Since we have defined the import demand function as $M = M(Y)$, we may write the economic consequences of the externally imposed restriction on imports as

$$Y^* = M^{-1}(M_{max}) \qquad\qquad (2.3)$$

where M_{max} is the maximum amount of goods that can be imported by the target economy from other sources or by means of sanction-busting. So we have two relevant equations and the actual level of national income depends on the question of which equation is binding. The embargo bites only if the equilibrium income derived in equation 2.2 exceeds Y^*, otherwise equation 2.3 is a restriction that can only become of possible interest in the near future if the economy grows sufficiently.

This, however, is only one part of the story. Imports often consist of luxury goods. Moreover, many products that are imported from abroad can also be produced by domestic industries, especially if similar goods are being traded by comparable economies. Intra-industry trade is especially substantial for trade between OECD

countries. For example, in 1990 more than 80 per cent of the British
and the French trade in industrial products consisted of trade in the
same product group (at a level of aggregation of 100 different
product groups). For Germany, the United States and Japan, the
share of intra-industry trade in industrial products amounted to 69, 60
and 33 per cent, respectively.[9] A reduction of the consumption of
luxury non-essential goods and import substitution in sectors where
intra-industry trade is substantial are relevant policy options that will
not affect potential output negatively. On the contrary, the reduction
of M can now be modelled as a decrease of the marginal propensity
to import.[10] If M_Y decreases, then the denominator of the right-hand
side of equation 2.2 becomes smaller and, consequently, equilibrium
output increases due to import substitution and a reduction in import
leakage in terms of luxury goods.

Finally, both channels may be combined. A first-period slow
down could be followed by a substantial increase in national income,
when import substitution takes off. The UK-led UN sanctions against
former Rhodesia in 1966 may be a case in point, as the Rhodesian
annual growth rate was almost 6 per cent, thus illustrating that the
so-called infant-industry argument may be relevant in the context of
international sanctions (*cf.* Bornstein 1968, Losman 1972 and
Hermele and Odén 1988).

Residual demand approach
The more essential — or strategic — a good is for the target
economy, the more inelastic the target's demand for that commodity,
and hence the higher the welfare loss if the supply of such goods is
being decreased. One can, however, not confine the analysis to the
elasticity of the target's demand for the goods that are hit by the
sanction measures. Even if the target's demand is quite inelastic, one
needs to consider the possibilities of sanction-busting. If the sender so
to say artificially raises the price of the essential commodity, it faces
the possibility that other suppliers will not adhere to the sanctions and
supply the target economy with the much wanted goods. The
1980—1981 US grain embargo against the Soviet armed invasion of
Afghanistan was a failure in economic terms although Soviet demand
for grain was rightly considered to be quite inelastic. First, the
fungibility of grain implies almost infinite elasticity of substitution

between different suppliers. Second, the supply elasticity from non-US sources appeared to be rather large. The Argentine grain harvest, for example, was very good and Argentina redirected customary shipments to other markets, roughly doubling its sales to the Soviet Union that offered a premium price.[11] Indeed Argentina increased its share in Soviet grain imports from 2 to 10 per cent. In addition Argentina signed long-term agreements on the export of grain, soya beans and meat, thus reducing the Soviet Union's vulnerability even further (Ghoshal 1983; see also Paarlberg 1980 on some of the non-economic lessons from the grain embargo).

Since sanctions are essentially an exercise in the enforcement of market power, the sender may be considered as trading a homogenous output subject to non-disciplinable entry from a price-taking fringe. Consequently, the elasticity of the target's residual demand for the sender's product determines the potential sanction damage. On the assumption of perfect substitutability, the residual demand is the difference between the target's demand and the supply by countries that do not participate in the sanctions. Let Q_R be the residual demand for the sender's product, Q_F be the competitive fringe's supply and Q_T be the target's demand for the product. Hence

$$Q_R = Q_T - Q_F \tag{2.4}$$

so that

$$dQ_R/dP = dQ_T/dP - dQ_F/dP \tag{2.5}$$

By definition the elasticity of the target's demand η is

$$\eta = dQ_T/dP \times P/Q_T \tag{2.6}$$

Likewise, we have for the supply elasticity of the competitive fringe (ϵ) and the elasticity of residual demand (η_R)

$$\epsilon = dQ_F/dP \times P/Q_F \tag{2.7}$$

$$\eta_R = dQ_R/dP \times P/Q_R \tag{2.8}$$

Combining these equations and using the fact that the sender's share
in the target's imports f and the fringe's import share by definition
add to 1, equation 2.8 can be rewritten as

$$\eta_R = \{\eta + (1 - f)\epsilon\}/f \qquad\qquad (2.9)$$

So the elasticity of residual demand is smaller — and, consequently,
the sanction damage is larger — to the degree that the market share f
is larger, and the target's demand elasticity η and the fringe supply
elasticity ϵ are smaller. The sender's share in the target's imports in
particular is an essential parameter. For example, for $\epsilon = 0$, we find
$\eta_R = \eta/f$. Therefore if the sender controls 25 per cent of the target's
imports, the elasticity of residual demand will be four times the
elasticity of the target's demand. If the sender's share is 50 per cent,
the elasticity η_R will be two times η. Note that the influence of the
sender's share in the target's import will be even more important
because, in general, $\epsilon > 0$.

   A number of practical matters may complicate the residual
demand analysis. If some domestic production exists, so that
specialization is incomplete, residual demand must take not only
competitive fringe supply into account, but also that the target's firms
may produce the product that is boycotted or embargoed. In that case
we need to read f as the sender's share in the target's absorption of
the good. A second complicating factor is that the products produced
by the competitive fringe and the target's firms may not be perfect
substitutes. Taking into account the possibility of imperfect
substitutability reduces the transparency of the argument, but enforces
the qualitative results (see Van Duyne 1975 and Bayard, Pelzman and
Perez-Lopez 1983). Note, moreover, that in the long run
substitutability increases so that equation 2.9 in any case provides a
relevant framework for longlasting sanction episodes.

Oligopoly approach
So far the discussion has considered more or less homogeneous goods
only and assumed that producers and consumers take prices as given.
Recent trade theories, however, increasingly stress that most markets
are characterized by imperfect competition, for example due to
product differentiation, a limited number of competitors, scale

effects, etc. Table 2.3 summarizes the theoretically expected potential
effectiveness of multilateral and bilateral economic sanctions for
different world market structures. Interestingly, modern trade theory
suggests that bilateral economic sanctions will only have an economic
impact if competition is imperfect, which requires that products are
heterogeneous to some extent. Otherwise other suppliers will simply
enter the market and supply the target with the wanted goods and act
as new outlets for the target's products as well.

*Table 2.3 International market structure, co-operation and economic
impact of sanctions (complete embargo and boycott)*

Type	Perfect competition (Price takers in world trade)		Imperfect competition (Country specific prices in world trade)	
	Sender	Target	Sender	Target
Multilateral sanctions	Nil	Autarky	Some trade diversion if target is dominant supplier	Autarky
Bilateral sanctions	No effects		Depends on specific market conditions	

Source: Based on Schultz (1989)

Schultz (1989) analyses a Cournot duopoly in which the two firms
(one in the sender country and one in the target country) maximize
their profits while they assume that their rival will not change its
output decisions. In addition to the usual economic motives, the
sender country derives utility from its ability to influence the target
economy (and possibly its behaviour) as well as from its ability to
strongly express its disapproval of the target's behaviour and policies.
In this setting the sender country reduces the target's exports by
subsidizing its own industry. This creates a threat because the
sender's products become cheaper and this credibly limits the extent
of the target's foreign market. Given that the target's export volume

enters the sender's social welfare function with a negative sign, the 'sanction subsidy' exceeds 'optimal' subsidies that are suggested in strategic trade models, so that strategic warfare might result in a subsidy war. Indeed if markets are imperfect, such externalities may become important instruments for the target to counteract the economic effects of the sanctions as part of the sanction costs can be shifted to the sender.

One important implication of Table 2.3 is that, in terms of the impact on the target, sanctions appear much more likely to be effective if they are multilateral. The outcome of sanctions under imperfect competition is not a priori clear and can be shown to depend on specific market conditions, such as the number of foreign competitors, the timing of the policy measures and their duration, etc. Indeed, as this approach is inspired by the 'new' trade theories it suffers from the same defects, namely that the results are not robust and that small changes in the model's parameters can yield contradicting outcomes (compare Eaton and Grossman 1986 and Fisher 1989). For example, since the subsidy game is less visible these sanctions may on the one hand have the advantage that they do not call forth countervailing forces. On the other hand their invisibility may make them less potent, as they are easily overlooked and will have little if any expressive value. Consequently, no clear-cut policy advice emerges. The approach, however, points out some interesting mechanisms through which the target's behaviour can be influenced.

Long-run growth perspective
In addition to the direct costs entailing additional financial and real outlays immediately related to the imposition of sanctions (such as rising transport cost and risk premiums) the target's long-run development potential may be hurt. Since the growth of the capital stock (both quantitatively and qualitatively) is a very important determinant of economic growth the focus in the discussion is on this variable. In addition potential industries may simply not come into being (entrepôt functions, tourist accommodations, etc.), but theory has little specific to say about these forgone potentials.

Depending on the target's current account position essentially three macro-economically relevant situations can be distinguished.

First, assume that the target is highly dependent on foreign lending, investment or aid so that it runs a current account deficit. In this case sanctions by definition force a reduction of either consumption or investment on this economy. Most developing countries probably do not have an option: they will be unable to reduce consumption which is already near the subsistence level so that investment has to give in. Second, the capital account may balance implying that domestic savings equal domestic investment. Now the current account constraint may act as a restriction that bites directly into the target's growth. This is especially so since a sanction that reduces the target's income also shifts the consumption, investment and saving schedules with an increase of the average propensity to consume and a reduction of both the savings rate and the investment level as the most likely outcomes. If this happens the current account constraint immediately becomes binding. Third, the target's long run growth potential is obviously hurt the least if it ran a current account surplus prior to the economic sanctions. In this case the target population saves more than it needs to keep domestic investment going at the present level of consumption. So the target economy's domestic savings can be redirected to finance investment in import substituting production facilities. This does not preclude the possibility that the availability of capital in the near future will become a bottleneck. The analysis only points out that for a target with a current account surplus, shortage of capital from a macro-economic point of view is not a short-term problem.

It is, however, not just a question of foreign capital flows. The import of specific capital goods and specific services matters as well. So even if the target ran a current account surplus prior to the sanctions, boycotts and embargoes may constitute important threats to the target's capital stock and consequently the long-run growth potential may be hurt.

First, modern production processes often depend on foreign suppliers and sub-contractors as they use both product and process specific raw materials, spare parts, intermediate inputs and related services from abroad. Hence a lack of such products interrupts and may even end production. Unless exports and imports can be completely substituted, a substantial obsolescence of (part of) the economy's capital stock will result. This implies that an equilibrium on the trade account both for the economy as a whole and at the level of specific industries is a necessary condition to keep firms operating at the usual capacity levels. Since this condition is very restrictive and will not be met in general, it is probable that a reduction of the growth rate of the capital stock is an inevitable outcome of effective sanctions.

Second, the target's growth will be hampered by the fact that no new technologies become available to the target during the sanctions.[12] Inferior technology and suboptimal investment decisions are incorporated in the capital stock thus reducing subsequent capital accumulation. An official South African report, for example, estimates that the budgets in the Mossgas synthetic oil substitution project were exceeded by more than 100 per cent, basically because neither the latest technology nor international expertise were available.[13]

Third, even small direct or static real income losses may show up in efficiency losses and suboptimal allocations of the factors of production reducing marginal productivities and consequently the rate of growth (Porter 1979).

Capital effects are less visible since they represent losses of potential economic benefits, but they can be substantial and will ultimately outweigh the direct costs. Losman (1972, pp. 33—4) estimates the reduction of Cuba's annual growth rate due to capital effects at 1—3 per cent. This means that the annual welfare loss due to capital effects alone of the sanctions that have been in effect since the early 1960s could presently be estimated as some 50 to 150 per cent of Cuba's actual gross domestic product.[14] Note that ending the sanctions will not enable the target to recapture such losses in the short term. Only if the target's *post*-sanction growth rate exceeds its 'normal' or 'natural' level over a long period can the loss ultimately be cancelled.

Common characteristics of the five economic approaches
With all their differences these economic approaches implicitly share a number of variables, mechanisms and outcomes. Given this implicit agreement in a wide variety of theories about the determinants of the effectiveness of economic sanctions it seems that the following assessment might go largely unchallenged from a theoretical point of

view. The potential damage of economic sanctions is in general larger:

- the greater the importance of the open or target sectors for the target economy;
- the fewer the possibilities that are available to the target economy for substituting the goods that are the subject of the sanction measures;
- the less import substituting production is possible;
- the shorter the sanction period;
- the shorter the period between the political decision to use economic sanctions and their actual bureaucratic implementation of the sanctions;
- the greater the target's dependence on foreign capital.

A number of possibly relevant economic mechanisms have not been considered in the five approaches. For example, the discussion abstracts from international flows of labour (migration). Neither does it deal with the costs that can be forced upon an economy by the mere threat of disruption of international economic relations. A final caveat is that the costs of the sanction that the sender has to bear have not explicitly been investigated. The gains from free undisrupted international trade are reaped by both trade partners, and international investment benefits both the investor and the recipient. So clearly, the sender also suffers a welfare loss if it imposes economic sanctions and this is a relevant fact that needs to be considered when discussing actual sanction measures.

2.4 Non-economic Theories of Economic Sanctions

The sanction phenomenon is not purely economic. The economic approach to the sanction phenomenon merely asserts that damage (or potential damage) influences the target's behaviour, assuming that the target's population is homogeneous, that decision-making is rational and fully informed, etc. In reality, however, different (interest) groups of the target's population will be hit differently — both in a relative and in an absolute sense — while decisions are often based on imperfect information and made under stress. Indeed many political, psychological and sociological aspects are extremely important in assessing the potential utility of the economic sanction instrument in specific cases and may be decisive (see Figure 2.1).

Figure 2.1 The sanction black box

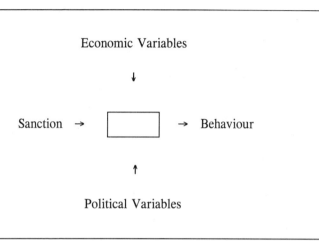

Some of these features of the sanction process have already been covered in, for example, the public choice approach to economic sanctions (Kaempfer and Lowenberg 1992) or in the related literature on the political economy of political pressure and lobbying (Potters 1992). Given the importance of politics and psychology in achieving success when applying economic sanctions, the present section will deal with these issues more specifically from the non-economist's point of view.

Essentially two questions should be addressed by the student of the utility of the economic sanction instrument. First, an assessment is needed of the potential damage that can be done with an economic sanction. This is the economic question that has been addressed in the preceding sections. Second, the question needs to be answered of how this disutility changes the target's behaviour. Here the interaction between economics and politics is the crucial element. In the next chapter a formal model will be developed. For now a more qualitative discussion of these points suffices.

Perceptions and political stability

Perceptions are very important in the analysis of the potential utility of economic sanctions. Targets will have an opinion about the likelihood that sanction measures will actually be imposed. This opinion depends partly on the reputation of the sender. The target's population will also balance the punishment against the misdemeanour in international politics and may consider the threat of punishment as too big in relation to their wrongdoing. Consequently, it may ignore the threat as either 'unrealistic' or 'unjust'. Moreover, it is not clear what exactly is disputable behaviour. Much depends on one's position. This ambiguity has been recognized by economists as well. Black and Cooper (1989, p. 192 *n*.), for example, argue that the analysis of the sender's motivations may be applicable for the target's behaviour as well. The dominant group in the target economy may obtain utility directly from taking a moral stance against some other nation's objectionable behaviour 'by *not* complying with the demands of the sanctioners'.

Economic sanctions ultimately aim at changing the target country's behaviour. The sender associates costs for the target with unwanted behaviour in order to reduce the attractiveness of this kind of behaviour for the target. Sanction damage negatively influences the (expected) economic yield of 'misconduct'. Consequently, the victim should be more willing to choose a different pattern of behaviour. Punishment, however, does not always call forth compliance. Take the case of an economic sanction that seeks to destabilize an undesirable regime. Criticism will only be directed against the domestic government if the targeted regime falters (Lindsay 1986, p. 162). If the regime has already stabilized its position, it may utilize the threat for its own purposes. According to Scolnick (1988) in addition to transference of intragroup hostility, increased public support may bolster the target state's government and may enhance both its short run and its long run material capacity to resist, thus deepening the enmities between target and sender, and economic sanctions will not call forth the desired result. Targets may even become senders themselves. A very strong example is the Indonesian decision in April 1992 to counteract the economic sanctions that the Dutch government threatened in reaction to human right violations in the former Dutch colony. The Indonesian government in an unexpected move actually rejected all development aid from the Netherlands thus gaining much popular support from its own population and creating a lot of fuss in the Netherlands.

Interactions between sender and target
The analysis in this chapter of the determinants of the effectiveness of the economic instruments of foreign diplomacy did not address the fact that economic sanctions are a game between several players. Hence the economic models that were discussed may suffer from the so-called Robinson Crusoe fallacy (Tsebelis 1989) since these models deal with the target economy only and ignore the interaction of players.[15]

Tsebelis (1990) develops a model in which these interactions are modelled explicitly. He shows that the target's equilibrium strategy only depends on the sender's payoff matrix. His model ably explains why small countries are not inclined to use economic sanctions as an instrument of their foreign policy, why so few sanctions succeed and why policy advice on the selection and application of sanctions is so poor. Tsebelis's model, however, requires a number of unrealistic assumptions. The payoff matrices of the players have to be known and are assumed to be independent (the latter is simply wrong in international economics). Much information is required about the valuation of uncertain outcomes and the sanction game is to be repeated many times. Finally, Tsebelis's model predicts that an increase in potential sanction damage does not influence the success rate, a proposition that will be refuted empirically in Chapter 4. Still Tsebelis's message is valid — especially in the long run — and the reactions of targets and senders will have to be considered in evaluation of specific sanction cases.

Other aims
Compliance is not the only objective of sanctions. Punishment may be an equally important aim (Nossal 1989). Research, however, almost exclusively focuses on the capacity of sanctions to change a country's behaviour. Lindsay (1986, p. 153) points out this 'naiveté of the research of sanctions' as the reason why most scientific studies find that sanctions do not work. He argues that in addition to compliance four major goals can be discerned: subversion,

deterrence, international symbolism and domestic symbolism. The conditions for successful sanctions that aim at subversion and deterrence are rather stringent so that it is likely that sanctions have limited value in achieving such aims. Sanctions, however, often succeed as international and domestic symbols. Indeed their use as diplomatic symbols may explain why sanctions are applied in cases where they are doomed to fail, for example because the level of trade linkage is negligible:

> Critics may deride the symbolic uses of trade sanctions as empty gestures, but symbols are important in politics. This is especially so when inaction can signal weakness and silence can mark complicity.[16]

2.5 Some Recent Experiences with Negative Sanctions

Recent experiences contradict the traditional economic arguments against economic sanctions as a potentially useful instrument in foreign policy.

First, in the early 1990s boycotts and embargoes have been shown to be effective both in terms of economic damage done and in terms of political impact. The US sanctions against Nicaragua clearly were effective, crippling the Sandinista economic policies.[17] Also the UN sanctions against the Iraqi occupation of Kuwait,[18] and the Soviet energy embargoes against Lithuanian anti-Soviet policies (and later in 1993 against anti-Russian policies) were very effective in delivering economic damage to the target country. Recent examples of successful sanctions comprise the sanctions by the United States against El Salvador and Poland, the Dutch—American sanctions against Surinam encouraging this former Dutch colony to improve on its human rights record and hold elections, the Indian sanctions against Nepal's intensified diplomatic relationship with China, and the UN and EC sanctions against South Africa. All these sanctions seem to have had a positive political pay-off for the sender countries.

Second, the UN sanctions against Iraq have shown that the achievement of the political unity that is considered to be a necessary condition for a forceful — and difficult to circumvent — embargo can be a matter of days (Smeets 1990). Indeed this is a unique case since the international community was able to impose severe and almost watertight sanction measures (Switzerland participated for the first time in history) and within an extremely short period of four days. It is thus likely that the end of the Cold War has made possible the grand coalitions that many consider a prerequisite for successful economic sanctions.

A case, however, in which the economic sanction instrument has been effective and/or successful cannot be used as proof for the potential utility of economic sanctions in general. Such an argument would suffer from the same logical error that hampers the traditional view that sanctions are ineffective. This is the more convincing since the very promising sanctions against Iraq did not succeed and eventually led to the military intervention of 'Desert Storm' (see Aspin, 1991). Also the utility of the EC and UN sanctions against Serbia in 1992—1993 seems to have been rather limited. Hence the fresh look at all theoretical and empirical aspects of economic sanctions in the next chapters.

Notes

1.   See for recent studies about the inaccuracy of international economic observations for example IMF (1983, 1987 and 1992b), World Bank (1991, p. 40), Yeats (1990 and 1992) and Van Bergeijk (1994).

2.   This is especially relevant since 21 of the 103 sanctions that were imposed since the Second World War are listed as on-going (and consequently, unresolved).

3.   One problem with the count of successes and failures is that the goals of a sanction may be multiple. In the study by Hufbauer, Schott and Elliott success is adjudged against the most ambitious announced objective. This implies that even evident successes with respect to minor policy goals will be considered as failures.

4.   The low level of sanction damage may be in part a consequence of the methodology that Hufbauer, Schott and Elliott use to estimate sanction damage. They deal essentially with the direct costs for a large target economy. This implies that sanctions influence the terms of trade positively and, consequently, shift part of the damage to the rest of the world (including the sender country). Moreover the long-run consequences of economic sanctions on economic growth are not taken into account.

5.   Table 2.2 is based on fewer observations (92) than Table 2.1 (103 sanction cases) because data on bilateral trade flows or national products are not available in 11 cases.

6. Other classifications such as the one proposed by Smeets (1992), who distinguishes between success and efficacy, essentially boil down to the same. One always has to distinguish the question of whether damage can be done from the question of whether potential disutility will influence behaviour.

7. Rigidity (unwillingness or inability to substitute) shows up in concavity of the production possibilities curve and convexity of the indifference curves.

8. See Van Bergeijk, Haffner and Waasdorp (1993) for an empirical investigation into the flexibility of macro economic markets and the costs of a market inertia.

9. Some figures on average intra-industry trade for 1985 at the 2 digit-Standard International Trade Classification (SITC) level are:

Intra-EC trade	85%
The Netherlands	79%
United Kingdom	78%
France	73%
Germany	65%
External EC trade	64%
United States	55%
Japan	28%

10. An alternative with comparable results would be to model an embargo as a decrease in the exogenous part of import demand, say M_0, that does not depend on income. In that case the nominator of the right-hand side of equation 2.2 increases as it can be easily seen that M_0 would enter this equation with a negative sign.

11. In addition Canada, Australia and the European Community more than doubled their grain sales using average sales over longer periods to 'lift' the agreed 'normal and traditional' level.

12. See, for example, Van Bergeijk and Lensink (1993), p. 895.

13. This *Special report of the auditor-general concerning the independent evaluation of the Mossgas project* was published by Pretoria in 1991.

14. Alternatively, a cumulative loss could be calculated as the aggregate of the differences for each year between potential (no-sanction) GDP and actual GDP. This aggregate loss amounts to 20 to 70 per cent of aggregate actual GDP.

15. The Robinson Crusoe Fallacy derives from applying decision theory in stead of game theory when more than one rational actor is involved (Tsebelis 1989).

16. Lindsay (1986), p. 171.

17. R. Graham, 'Economic War criples Nicaragua' *Financial Times*, 12 May 1987, p. 24.

18. See, for example, K. Elliott, G. Hufbauer and J. Schott, 'Judging From History, the Anti-Saddam Sanctions Can Work', *International Herald Tribune*, 11 December 1990.

3. The Expected Utility of Economic Sanctions

Sometimes sanctions actually work before they are even implemented. In 1921 the League of Nations was asked only to consider punitive economic measures against the Yugoslavian military incursions into Albania. The government of Yugoslavia, however, informed the Conference of Ambassadors within one week after this request that it would withdraw its troops from Albania. More recently, the United States and Canada threatened to bring South Korea's civilian nuclear programme to a halt by blocking the sale of reactors. This threat alone was effective in stopping the South Korean efforts to buy a nuclear reprocessing plant in 1975. In 1987 the United States threatened to reduce its aid of $185 million to El Salvador by 10 per cent only unless an amnesty ruling was reversed. The relatively small threat, however, led president Duarte to deny the amnesty.

In no case were the sanctions effective, as the economic sanctions did not go beyond the threat stage. So *ex post* there was no damage done. The cases, however, were highly successful and efficient as the targets changed their behaviour very quickly and the sender countries did not have to forego the welfare gains of international trade and investment. Admittedly, cases in which sanctions work *ex ante* are quite rare, but about 45 per cent of the successful sanctions require less than one year. At least 75 per cent of the successful sanctions achieve compliance within the relatively short period of two years. Economic theory that wants to deal with rather quick and sometimes even immediate successes should essentially be able to cope with an *ex ante* analysis of strategic economic threats. This means that our theory has to deal with key features of uncertainty, such as expectations and risk preference.

At the start of the 1980s, however, the economic theory of economic sanctions typically was of a (comparative) static macro economic nature (see for examples: Kemp 1964, Porter 1979 and Frey 1984), and where the time dimension was part of the analysis this was only in the sense that the target economy was allowed to react by stockpiling or by other policies aimed at reducing its vulnerability to foreign economic pressure. A new strand of literature, however, developed in the mid-1980s which recognized that not only the implementation of economic sanctions but also the mere threat to use boycotts and embargoes could be an adequate foreign policy instrument.[1]

Hughes Hallett and Brandsma (1983) use a macroeconometric model of the post-war Soviet economy in order to assess the optimality of strategies in a dynamic and unrestricted non-co-operative game between East and West in the early 1980s. They show that the main economic weapon of the West against the Soviet Union is not the actually implemented embargo on technology and defence-related exports, but the threat of a future embargo on other goods as well. This is so because the optimal Soviet reaction to this risk causes a very rapid deterioration of the Soviet's foreign trade balance. My 1987 article develops an expected utility model of economic—military deterrence. One of the findings is that the threat of the 'stick' may lead to perverse results as an increase of the threat of disutility may actually induce non-compliance. Kaempfer and Lowenberg (1988) show within a public choice setting that sanctions that create little or no economic hardship can still generate political change, pointing out, for example, that a sanction with little economic impact on South Africa might be conductive to ending apartheid. Using an equilibrium model of interest group competition within the target country Kaempfer and Lowenberg argue that 'sanctions can communicate signals or threats, not necessarily entailing severe economic damage, which in turn produce policy changes' (Kaempfer and Lowenberg 1988, p. 768). Eaton and Engers (1992) consider a sender that periodically specifies conditions that the target must meet to avoid sanctions. They consider the possibility that sanctions have an overkill capacity and show that the deterrence effect of the threat of sanctions can be enough to let a target comply in order to avoid sanctions even if they are not currently in place. Indeed Eaton and Engers (1992, p. 919) argue that the threat of sanctions probably plays a much greater role in the arena of international politics than their actual use in diplomatic relations seems to suggest.

3.1 The Settings: Threats, Promises and Rationality under Uncertainty

The common characteristic of these 'new' models is that the sender countries utter a strategic threat consisting of the announcement that economic sanction measures will (possibly) be applied. If behaviour is altered the game ends and the sender attains its objective in the most efficient way, since it does not have to bear the costs that result from the loss of some of the gains from international trade and investment.

Actually, this fits in the economic theory of strategic threats and reputation pioneered by Schelling ([1960]1980) and Boulding (1962). They pointed out that if a threat is not sufficiently credible to change behaviour, punitive action has to be carried out. This is painful and costly for both the sender and the target since both parties will be unable to reap the full benefits of free and undisturbed trade and investment relations. Consequently, a sanction might be too costly to be carried out and the threat may appear false.

The question of whether the potential sanction damage will be administered or not cannot a priori be answered with certainty. More specifically, a sanction threat could best be defined as a statement creating an expectation that is conditional on the performance (or perhaps non-performance) of some activity (Boulding 1962, p. 253). The key word here is 'expectation': the value of a sanction threat that enters the target's utility function as an argument must be the result of the confrontation of potential damage and the subjective probability of this potential actually being administered upon misconduct. In addition uncertainty with respect to the goals of opposing countries is a major feature of the international threat system (Tinbergen 1985, p. 175). Indeed, as Schelling ([1960]1980, p. 39) notes:

> In threat situations ... commitments are not altogether clear; each party cannot exactly estimate the costs and values to the other side of the two related actions involved in the threat.

This is why any theory of economic sanctions should not start from a deterministic setting; it has to deal with the stochastic outcome of situations in which economic sanctions have been applied. Since probabilities will be introduced one may prefer to speak about risk rather than uncertainty (Knight 1921). Throughout this analysis, however, I will consider uncertainty as a state of absent certainty.

The well-known Von Neumann—Morgenstern assumptions about expected utility can be used to construct indifference curves. By making different assumptions about the shape of the utility function it is possible to model distinct attitudes toward the risk that is typical of international threat situations and consequently of economic sanctions. The expected utility approach allows us to make a clear distinction between the *ex ante* expectations that guide decision-making, and the outcomes *ex post* that are the results of those decisions. Presented with the choice between the mathematically expected payoff of a gamble in international politics and undergoing that particular gamble, the target might prefer the gamble. If the game is 'lost', the outcome *ex post* may seem irrational indeed. The decision, however, to get involved in a very risky gamble showing a very low or even negative expected outcome should not be considered irrational unless the highest possible outcome is less than the outcome that results if the gambler does not play.

This distinction between *ex ante* and *ex post* utilities may provide an answer to the critique of amongst others Hout (1985, p. 401) who argues that the rational choice paradigm is hardly useful for the positive analysis of relationships between countries, essentially because the outcomes of many policy decisions suggest that the statesman's rationality often needs to be questioned and because his judgements are subjective. This is not to deny that purely political ends sometimes dictate the outcome of *ex ante* cost-benefit analysis (see Waltzer 1977, pp. 263—8). It all boils down to this: that the recognition of the inherent political boundaries of the problem does not impair positive economic analysis.

The rational choice paradigm has also been questioned by Schrödt (1985, pp. 379—87). He sees only very limited scope for the concept of *homo economicus* in the analysis of international relations. Schrödt offers four arguments against (expected) utility maximization:

- the relative absence of testable propositions;
- the lack of practical relevance for policy makers of the main theoretical findings;
- the fact that decision-making in internal politics is often a group process so that the unitary actor hypothesis is violated;
- the special characteristics of decision-making in international politics (slow speed of reaction, inefficient information structures, etc.) which may preclude maximizing behaviour.

While many of these points a priori would seem to be relevant to economic analysis in general, it is ultimately only the empirical testing of a theory that can shed light on the possible utility of a specific theory or analytic framework. The operationalization of the model is the subject of the next chapter.[2]

Many economic sanction theories do not distinguish between incentives and disincentives, because it is assumed that the target's opportunity costs of a penalty are equal to a reward of the same magnitude. That is to say, it is assumed that the opportunity costs of non-compliance coincide when a reward of X is offered or a penalty of $-X$ is threatened. The symmetry of incentives and disincentives, however, breaks down both in a stochastic setting and for non-neutral attitudes toward risk.[3] Moreover, as argued by Baldwin (1971), perceptions, time and conditionality influence positive and negative sanctions differently. In particular, the costs of implementation in combination with the prospects for success (and possibly side effects, after-effects and efficacy) may influence the extent and use of positive and negative sanctions differently. Reward and punishment are not merely two sides of the same coin (Lawson 1983, pp. 311—3).

From a policy perspective this analytical distinction has the additional advantage that it enables us to give a better, more comprehensive analysis of the full range of policy options, which may also take the question of legitimation into account. Consequently, it seems worthwhile to make the distinction and analyse both negative and positive economic sanctions.

In sum, the theory that will be developed in this chapter departs from the standard (or 'traditional') theory of economic sanctions in three respects. First, the decision process and the policy options of the target will be analysed. Second, this will be done within a utility setting that acknowledges the uncertainty that is inherent in situations in which economic sanctions are being used. Third, we will analyse the possibility of rewarding behaviour that apparently conforms to the standards of the international community. So contrary to common practice, the discussion will incorporate both economic incentives and economic disincentives that are conditional on whether misconduct ceases or persists. Earlier studies analyse either the threat of trade disruption or situations in which the exact timing of the trade disruption is uncertain. Hence these theories are either about the influence exerted by the target's awareness of the possibility of a boycott or an embargo and how this menace influences its behaviour, or about the target's behaviour given the certainty that economic measures will be deployed in the near future. The present analysis studies the possibility to omit misconduct and takes into account that even explicit threats need not be executed.

3.2 An Expected Utility Model of Economic Sanctions

This section will introduce and discuss the structure of the expected utility model of economic sanctions and investigate the outcome space. In section 3.3 the comparative statics of the respective policy instruments will be analysed in a formal model. Section 3.4. summarizes the main findings of the model exercises in a non-technical manner.

We will consider an international decision unit — the potential target of economic sanctions — that faces the possibility of a profitable act of misconduct. This act of misconduct, however, is heavily resented by the outside world. The target has the opportunity to be exclusively involved in neutral activities, which the outside world does not disapprove of or may even appreciate. The behaviour of the target is influenced, among other things, by the yields y_N (of neutral activities; one may think of it as GDP) and y_M (of misconduct; for example the occupation of foreign territory).

Misconduct carries a premium M so that the yield of neutral activities $y_N = N$ is less than the yield of misconduct $y_M = y_N + M$. The yield of misconduct often cannot be quantified unambiguously. What are the benefits to the target country; what for example is the 'value' of acquiring a nuclear bomb? Some sorts of misconduct, such as expropriation of foreign assets, nationalization, illegitimate extensions of the territory and repudiation of foreign debt, have a clear economic dimension. In contradistinction, measurement of the premium of misconduct is very difficult if sanctions are aimed at the target's social structures. Perhaps the benefits to the elite of a specific power structure can be expressed in money, but clearly in other cases such as adherence to human rights the measuring rod of money loses its utility. Moreover, the yield of misconduct essentially amounts to the benefits of a particular policy as seen by those in power at a given moment. So the yield of apartheid seems to have been valued very differently by Botha than by his successor De Klerck.

Anyhow, even if the yield of misconduct is essentially intangible, administering sanction damage can influence the target's decision. In most cases the yield of misconduct lies outside the influence of the outside world. Hence M is considered to be an exogenous variable that cannot be influenced by the sanction sender.[4] The variables M and N are supposed to be independent of one another and a common denominator (for example money) is assumed, that allows aggregation of the dissimilar components that play a part in the choice situation.

The outside world in this model has two sanction instruments to influence the target's behaviour. The international community may threaten to use a negative sanction (with potential damage D) and may deploy a positive sanction (with a potential gain of S). It follows that the yield of misconduct is either

$y_R = y_N + M — D$ if the threat is real or
$y_F = y_N + M$ if the threat is false.

In the case of a positive sanction the yield of neutral activities increases from N to $N + S$. Figure 3.1 on page 52 summarizes the target's choice set.

Figure 3.1 Choice set

Target's choice	Sender's options	
	No sanction	*Sanction*
Neutral activities	$y_N = N$	Positive sanction $y_N = N + S$
Misconduct	False threat $y_F = N + M$	Real threat $y_R = N + M - D$

The model offers a simplified representation of the international arena of politics only, as it relates to a two-country model in which the passive sender—target relationship does not leave much room for dynamic interaction. The impact of the sanction is studied with the pay-off matrix of Figure 3.1 that summarizes the possible outcomes for the target, given its own choice and the sender's decisions.

Moreover, the parameters are exogenous to the target and we will not study the problem from the perspective of a dominant economic power. This assumption, a version of the small country assumption, is generally made in the analysis of economic sanctions (see for examples Dekker 1973, Arad and Hillman 1979, Porter 1979 and Bergström, Loury and Persson 1985). It is clear that the transparency of the analysis that thus results carries a cost as the theory is less general and less fit for the interpretation of the real world. Reality, however, is not bent too much since less than 10 per cent of the cases in the Hufbauer, Schott and Elliott (1990) sanctions data base pertain to situations where the target's GDP exceeds that of the sender. Indeed in at least 80 per cent of the cases the sender's GDP was at least ten times larger than the target's GDP, giving credence to the small country assumption.

Now it is assumed that the target derives utility u from the resulting yield, so that $u = u(y)$, where $u' > 0$. The value to the target of a certain amount of y_i is known as the *ex post* utility of outcome y_i. Since the yield of neutral activities is independent of the threat, it is implied that the utility generated by the conduct of neutral activities is known with certainty so that the *ex post* and the *ex ante* utility of neutral activities correspond.

$$u\{E(y_N)\} = E\{u(y_N)\} = u(y_N) = u(N) \tag{3.1}$$

In order to model the target's decision whether or not to engage in misconduct, we need to assess the target's *ex ante* utility or the expected utility of the outcomes y_i and their associated probabilities of occurrence. So a function v is postulated which describes the *ex ante* utility that the target attaches to the uncertain outcome of misconduct. Let π denote the target's subjective probability ($0 < \pi < 1$) that the threat is real.

$$v = v[y_R, y_F; \pi, (1 - \pi)] \tag{3.2}$$

It is now possible to weigh the certain utility of neutral activities against the expected *ex ante* utility of the uncertain yield of misconduct. More specifically, if $v > u(y_N)$ the target will opt for misconduct. The function v will be based on the expected utility hypothesis that was originally developed by Von Neumann and Morgenstern (1944). The axioms that are the basic prerequisites for the construction of a Von Neumann—Morgenstern utility index seem rather reasonable within the context of economic sanctions. Essentially this approach requires continuity, transitivity and strong independence of preferences over outcomes as well as a desire for a high probability of success. Moreover it requires that the evaluation of a probability is based on the actual probability and not on the way the probability has been determined (i.e. it should not make a difference if π is a composite probability).[5] This is what we have first:

$$v = \pi.u(y_R) + (1 - \pi).u(y_F) \tag{3.3}$$

For a given value of the subjective probability, π, an indifference curve $v = u(y_N)$ can be drawn in outcome space, as illustrated in Figure 3.2 on page 55. This curve represents the boundary line between those combinations (y_R, y_F) that lead to the misconduct option (above and to the right of the curve) and the area that represents the combinations of possible outcomes for which misconduct does not come off. Note that by definition $y_F > y_R$ and that the range of y_F is positive. It can easily be checked that, regardless of the shape of the indifference curve, a point N^* on v exists where $M = D = S = 0$ and consequently $y_R = y_F = y_N = N$. The utility of the combination represented by N^* will be used as a yardstick to compare combinations of uncertain outcomes and for obvious reasons it will be called the certainty equivalent. The marginal rate of substitution in point N always equals $-\pi/(1-\pi)$.

Differentiating $v = u(y_N)$ while π is kept constant yields:

$$\pi.u'(y_R).dy_R+(1-\pi)u'(y_F).dy_F = u'(y_N).dy_N \qquad (3.4)$$

As long as we move along a specific indifference curve, the right hand side of equation 3.4 equals zero, so that the following expression for the slope of an indifference curve results:

$$-dy_F/dy_R = \pi.u'(y_R)/\{(1-\pi).u'(y_F)\} \qquad (3.5)$$

Shone (1981, pp. 38—9) argues that a utility function which is concave in the resulting yield ($u'' < 0$), leads to convex indifference curves in outcome space and implies a risk adverse or cautious decision unit. In contradistinction a convex utility function ($u'' > 0$) and the associated concave-to-the-origin indifference curves portray the risk preferer or risk lover. On the boundary the linear curve ($u'' = 0$) is found that expresses that the risk neutral target is only concerned with the utility of the mathematically expected outcome.

Consider Figure 3.2 which shows three different indifference curves for the cases of risk preference (v_0), risk neutrality (v_1) and risk aversion (v_2). The linear indifference curve v_1 represents combinations (y_R, y_F) for which the weighted average (with π and $1-\pi$ as weights) equals N. It is quite intuitive that v_2 is the indifference curve for a risk averse target, because every point on v_2 is above and to the right of v_1, with the exception of the so-called certainty equivalent N^*. Since v_2 and v_1 represent equal levels of utility $u(N)$ for different risk preferences and since v_2 needs larger uncertain yields to arrive at this utility level, the target of indifference curve v_2 must attach negative utility to uncertainty. Consequently, it is to be considered risk averse. Likewise v_0 portrays the risk lover. Observe that the curve for risk aversion approaches $y_R = 0$ asymptotically since it follows from equation 3.5, $y_R > 0$ and $u'' < 0$ that the marginal rate of substitution becomes negatively infinite as y_R tends to zero, from above.

Figure 3.2 Indifference curves for risk aversion, risk neutrality and risk preference

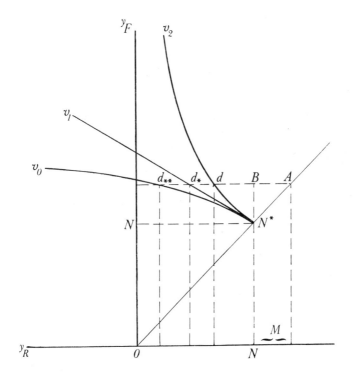

Figure 3.2 also clearly shows that the area above an indifference curve represents combinations (y_R, y_F) that lead to the choice for misconduct. Consider, for example, point A where by definition $v(N+M) > u(y_N) = u(N)$ or point B, which also results in misconduct because $v(B) = \pi.u(N) + (1-\pi).u(N+M) > u(N)$.

Taking limits for $u'' \to \infty$ and $u'' \to -\infty$, it follows that points to the right of $y_R = N$ will trigger misconduct irrespective of both the attitude toward risk and the subjective probability π (in the limit v can be represented by a vertical line through point N^*).

Finally, a well-behaved target will always show up if the condition $y_F < N$ applies. In this case the premium M would be negative; a situation ruled out by our assumptions. If misconduct occurs while this condition is being met, the target is not acting in a rational way. In that case we observe, as did Schelling (1960, p. 6) that

> the rationality of the adversary is pertinent to the efficacy of threat, and that madmen ... can often not be controlled by threats.

It is only in this sense that irrationality (or 'madness') of statesmen would support the dismissal of the utility approach to the subject of this book.

3.3 The Analysis of the Economic Instruments of Foreign Policy

The analysis concentrates on a utility maximizing actor that receives signals from the outside world that are aimed at influencing the target's behaviour. In order to keep the analysis as transparent as possible it is assumed that the target cannot utter meaningful (counter) threats. So the model deals with the typical case of a small (developing) country. In order to prevent misconduct the outside world may resort to a number of different instruments. In the first place the sanction threat can be enhanced. This can be achieved either by increasing potential sanction damage D or by enlarging the subjective probability π. The outside world may also try to influence the yield of neutral activities N. Finally, the possibility exists to reward or invite 'good behaviour' by means of a positive sanction S.

It should at this point perhaps be clarified that the concepts of both positive and negative sanctions are relative concepts, as the question of what constitutes a sanction to a large extent depends on the target's perception of the situation (Baldwin 1971). A promise not to kill if one behaves as requested may not be considered a positive sanction as it is a clear threat in the case of a hold-up. This implies that in practical policy-making the sender should first establish the target's baseline in terms of its expected future value position. For example, reducing or ending a negative sanction that is actually being implemented may be considered as a reward. In this sense negative sanctions can be used to lay the groundwork for the subsequent use of positive sanctions:

> What (the sender) is doing in such situations is using the stick to shift (the target's) baseline so as to make the subsequent promise of a carrot more attractive.[6]

The formal model that was developed and discussed in the previous section is designed to investigate the impact of the respective policy instruments. The positive analysis of these instrumental variables will focus on their contribution to the prevention or remedy of international misconduct.

Sanction damage
The capacity to force economic costs upon an adversary by means of economic sanctions was first analysed by Hirschman (1945). He labelled this effect the 'influence effect'. In general the influence effect will depend on the target's problems if the sanctioning economy is no longer available as a market or a supplier. Hirschman (1945, pp. 17—40) and Wolf (1983, pp. 404—5) give a prescription of how to achieve a large influence effect. The sender can increase the effectiveness of the sanction instrument (and simultaneously reduce its own vulnerability to foreign treats) by diversifying its exports both with respect to markets and with respect to goods. The sender should increase the number of trade partners on the import side as well and preferably import goods that are still in an early phase of production. Finally, trade partners with a low per capita income should be preferred and participation in transit trade should be stimulated. Next to this general prescription of how a country should shape its trade policy in order to get more influence and become less dependent, an important role is being played by the disutility which in an actual case can be brought to the fore in a relatively short period of time. The amount of disutility increases if more countries join the economic sanction measures, if a boycott complements an embargo (and vice versa) and if sanction measures for specific commodities and services are extended to include total

bilateral trade and capital flows (lending, aid, etc.). In addition the threat of sanction damage can also be increased by non-economic measures such as intensified surveillance and military blockades of physical trade flows.

The imposition or enlargement of a sanction threat is for given N, M and π associated with a lower value of y_R and, consequently, with a decrease of the expected utility of misconduct. By attaching (additional) costs to misconduct, the sender tries to lower the economic attractiveness of misconduct. Negative economic sanctions decrease the expected utility of misconduct, inducing the target to another — more acceptable — mode of behaviour. In the outcome space of Figure 3.2 on page 55 this shows up as a shift of all points (y_R, y_F) to the left, while the locus of the curve $v = u(y_N)$ remains unchanged. Any point in y_R, y_F —space located at the right of this indifference curve prior to the expansion of D and shifting to the left of that indifference curve due to enlargement of D shows that the behaviour of the decision unit is effectively influenced and that misconduct is prevented. Irrespective of the attitude towards risk an increase in D dissuades from misconduct.

The qualitative result of a higher D leading for given N, M and π to a lower y_R does not change when different attitudes toward risk are assumed. There will, however, be different conclusions with respect to the efficient amount of potential disutility D. In the case of risk-aversion, represented by curve v_2 in Figure 3.2, a sanction threat that is associated with the length of dA will do. To a risk-neutral decision unit the condition $D > M/\pi$ will prevent misconduct. It follows *a fortiori* that to contain a risk-loving daredevil just by increasing the potential sanction damage is an even more difficult task.

In Figure 3.2 this is illustrated by the minimum value of D that prevents misconduct. The necessary threat increases from $d*A$ in the case of risk-neutrality (represented by curve v_1) to $d**A$ for risk-loving behaviour (curve v_0), as compared to dA for risk aversion. The model, however, suggests that these observations are relevant only from the perspective that the threat may be too small. If a sanction threat is not credible enough to influence behaviour, the imposed sanction measures will also impose costs on the sender's economy. Superfluous threats in general would seem to achieve absolute deterrence and therefore need not be carried out. For some problems, however, economic sanctions simply are to be considered overkill. The United Nations air embargo (UN resolution 748, 31 March 1992) which was imposed against Libya on 16 April 1992 is an example. Indeed one wonders whether the diplomatic effort needed to create and co-ordinate a common UN position could have succeeded and could have been worth the trouble, given that the goal of the sanction was to achieve extradition of two Libyans who had not even been proved guilty beyond reasonable doubt of the PanAm bombing. The argument, however, that sanctions may be too large has a more general bearing. It is straightforward to show that any implementation beyond the minimally required level leads to the desired co-operation but at the same time involves unnecessary costs for the sender. Just as too small a sanction will not lead to the desired result, too large a sanction leads to unnecessary (potential) welfare losses both for the sender and the target (Van Bergeijk and Van Marrewijk 1994).

The credibility of the sanction threat
The subjective probability $\pi = \pi(E|I)$ depends on the event E of which the probability is to be estimated (will the sanction actually be implemented?) and on I, the given information (also called the weight of evidence). The target may thus be influenced by information about the sender's intentions. This information may be imparted explicitly as in the case of a diplomatic message, but it can also be communicated implicitly, for example, because similar kinds of misconduct have also been punished with negative economic sanctions in the past or because very strong verbal condemnations are issued suggesting that action may be taken upon misconduct. Graphically, an increase of π rotates the indifference curve $v=u(y_N)$ clockwise with point N^* serving as a hinge. This implies that increasing π reduces the willingness of the decision unit to antagonize the outside world.

Sometimes, however, the size of the threat may affect its credibility. This is not merely a theoretical possibility as the literature often suggests that superfluous sanctions are superior to limited threats (see, for example, Kaplow 1990). If such policy prescriptions are taken at face value, sanctions will exceed 'reasonable' levels and the target may not believe that the threat will be executed at all. Whenever the potential disutility becomes too large in relation to the kind of misconduct concerned, the subjective probability π may actually diminish if the threat is enlarged. Now let $\pi = \pi(D)$ describe the relation between the subjective probability π and potential disutility D and assume the possibility of a range for $\pi = \pi(D)$ where $\pi'(D) < 0$. The effect of this hypothesis can best be studied with the following expression of v for given N, M and, consequently, $y_{F,0}$:

$$v = \pi(D).u(y_{F,0}-D)+\{1-\pi(D)\}.u(y_{F,0}) \qquad (3.6)$$

Differentiate v with respect to D. The resulting relation is definitely negative — implying that a larger sanction threat dissuades from misconduct — as long as $\pi'(D) \geq 0$. However, for $\pi'(D) < 0$ a perverse reaction might result if

$$\pi'\{u(y_{F,0}-D)-y_{F,0}\} > \pi.\partial(y_{F,0}-D)/\partial(y_{F,0}-D) \qquad (3.7)$$

in which case the enlargement of the sanction threat — contrary to a priori expectations — triggers misconduct. Note that this possibility of a counter productive negative sanction is only relevant for the enlargement of existing sanction threats because the condition of equation 3.7 will in general not be met if initially no sanction threat was uttered ($D = 0$).

Neutral activities
The yield of neutral activities in many instances cannot be influenced by the sender. Economic growth, for example, depends to a large extent on the target's domestic economic policies, on exogenous movements in the terms of trade, on developments in world trade and on capital market conditions. Such factors in general cannot be influenced by another country. Instances, however, do exist where the sender willingly facilitates economic activity in the target economy or — for example by means of (military) action and sabotage — reduces the target's economic base. If this happens without any conditionality attached to it, the sender influences the yield of neutral activities, which have been defined as those activities of which the sender does not disapprove. Also where the sender does not consider the target's yield of neutral activities as an appropriate instrument for its foreign policy, it will be instructive to study both

this specific country attribute and how changes in N influence the target's decision whether or not to comply.

Figure 3.3 Unconditional increase in the yield of neutral activities for the case of risk aversion

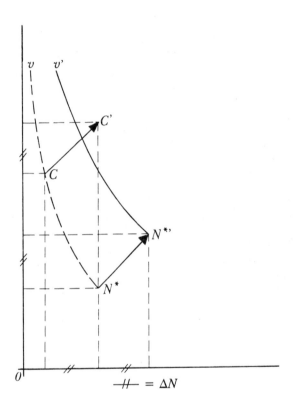

In contradistinction to the results that have been derived so far, the impact of unconditional changes in the yield of neutral activities N depends on the target's attitude toward risk. Figure 3.3 shows the consequences of an increase of y_N by $\Delta N > 0$ for the case of a risk averse target. As both y_F and y_R increase by ΔN, all points shift in outcome space parallel to the line $y_F = y_R$ with a vector of length $\Delta N.\sqrt{2}$. At the same time, however, the curve $v = u(y_N)$ is shifting outwards. The flattened shape on the new indifference curve $v' = u(N + \Delta N)$ ensues from the diminishing marginal utility

(u'' < 0), that is associated with risk aversion.[7] It follows that all points that were originally on $v = u(N)$, with the exception of point N^*, will emerge above and to the right of the new indifference curve, such as point C' in Figure 3.3. Therefore a reduction of the yield of neutral activities stops misconduct of a risk-averse target, while an increase in y_N calls forth undesirable behaviour from such an agent. This finding for the commonly considered case of risk aversion conforms to Marshall's (1923, pp. 168—70) observation that the cessation of trade often implies a larger real loss to a poor than to a rich country. For a given premium M a rich risk averse country (with large y_N) will be more inclined to opt for misconduct than a poor risk averse country (small y_N). Indeed the utility approach may offer an explanation for the intensified use of economic sanctions since the Second World War, as for given sanction damage D risk-averse opponents which experience substantial economic growth (represented by increasing N) will be more inclined to misconduct.

The same type of analysis shows opposite results for risk loving targets. Conforming more with common sense is the finding that a higher value of y_N promotes neutral activities and that a reduction of this yield acts as an incentive to misconduct. Finally, as can easily be seen from equation 3.2, manipulation of N does not influence risk-neutral behaviour.

Positive economic sanctions

Finally a positive sanction S is introduced. Positive sanctions often entail international transfers of purchasing power. Allies are often bought, negative side effects of compliance can be compensated and misconduct is often commutable. Some very visible examples of such financial transfers are the $10—$25 billion 'reparation payments' that the Gulf Co-operation Council offered in 1982 to persuade Iran to end its war against Iraq, the Dutch development aid programme to its former colony Surinam in the 1980s (aimed at restoring and stabilizing — democratic — government rule), the $1 billion aid programme that international donors in 1993 pledged to make available to Haiti in 1993 once its political crisis was solved and President Aristide was reinstated, and the Western aid to the restructuring economies in central and Eastern Europe in the early 1990s. The case of Western aid to cental and Eastern Europe is particularly illuminating. Article 1 of the Agreement establishing the European Bank for Reconstruction and Development (EBRD) limits eligibility for loans to those countries that are committed to and are applying the principles of multiparty democracy, pluralism and market economics. The political requirements are remarkable for an international bank.[8] Positive sanctions may include flows of goods. American food aid, for example, often has a political character, as discussed by Eggleston (1987) and Thompson (1992). In many cases positive sanctions pertain to intangible exchange such as technology.

Figure 3.4 The impact of a positive sanction

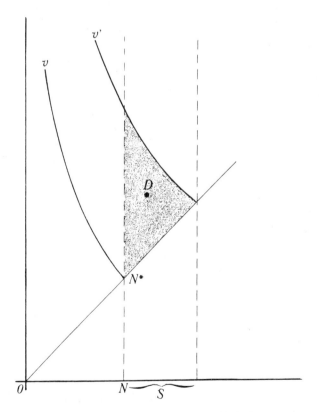

Analogous with the analysis of neutral activities it is assumed that the utility of a positive sanction is known with certainty:

$$u\{E(y_N)\} = E\{u(y_N)\} = u(y_N) = u(N+S) \qquad (3.8)$$

This assumption is satisfied whenever a set exists of economic activities that will automatically cease in the event of misconduct. This seems reasonable enough. Take, for instance military misconduct. Obviously in that case the use of civilian flight paths and harbour facilities as well as the transfer of technology will certainly cease. Note that the yields of these activities are a priori known with certainty, as is the fact that they will be cancelled if misconduct occurs. As a logical consequence positive sanctions are certain to make neutral activities more attractive.

The indifference curve $v = u(y_N)$ in Figure 3.4 on page 63 shifts outwards when a positive sanction is applied or increased, while the combinations (y_R, y_F) pertaining to misconduct remain in place. This result is independent of the target's attitude towards risk. Note that combinations (y_R, y_F) exist that cannot be influenced even if $\pi \rightarrow 1$ and $u'' \rightarrow \infty$ or $u'' \rightarrow -\infty$, as is for example the case with point D in Figure 3.4. This is so because points to the right of y_R will always call forth misconduct. If the sanction damage cannot be enlarged no other means but positive sanctions exist. A positive sanction of S will shift the indifference curve outward from v to v' so that the behaviour is influenced in those cases that are represented by combinations in the shaded area in Figure 3.4.

3.4 Some Lessons for Economic Statecraft

Baldwin (1985) introduced the term 'economic statecraft' to indicate the use that could be made of the economic instruments of foreign policy. In line with his assertion (1985, p. 4) that the utility of economic techniques has been systematically underestimated since 1945, the analysis in the preceding sections suggests that economic instruments can play a role in modern diplomacy. As Table 3.1 shows, the positive analysis of sanctions in an expected utility setting relates to three distinct attitudes toward the risk that is inherent in situations in which international influence attempts are being made. The different approaches to risk — as moulded by different shapes of the target's utility function — cover a wide range of decision entities varying from cautious to risk-loving ones. The utility of the uncertain yield of misconduct is weighed against the certain but presumably lower yield of neutral activities and if the former exceeds the latter the decision to engage in misconduct is rational. In order to establish how the choice between misconduct and neutral activities can be influenced by diplomatic economic instruments, four instruments were distinguished and analysed. First, we investigated negative economic sanctions. The threat of economic punishment consists of two elements: the potential sanction damage D and the target's subjective probability π of this potential being actually used upon misconduct. A second category of variables consists of the yield of misconduct M and the yield of neutral activities N. Finally, the analysis focused on positive sanctions S.

Table 3.1 Impact of the economic instruments on the relative attractiveness of misconduct

	Risk aversion $u''<0$	Risk neutrality $u''=0$	Risk preference $u''>0$
Neutral activities N	+	0	—
Sanction damage D	—/+	—/+	—/+
imposition (no prior threat)	—	—	—
Credibility π	—	—	—
Positive sanction S	—	—	—

Conclusions and caveats

Our conclusion is that the willingness of the target to antagonize the international community can only be unambiguously reduced by increasing the probability π, by the imposition of negative sanctions and by the imposition and enlargement of positive sanctions. This does not mean that misconduct is effectively prevented if these instruments are deployed, but that misconduct is made less attractive. The impact of both changes in the yield of neutral activities and of the increase of existing negative sanctions cannot be established a priori with certainty, as this impact depends on the attitude towards risk and the target's expectations formation process which in general cannot be observed before the sanction is actually imposed. So the use of these instruments may be counter-productive and induce misconduct rather than correcting or preventing it. The analysis clarifies that positive and negative sanctions are not two sides of the same coin. Indeed, even if the target is completely convinced that negative sanctions will be imposed it may still be impossible for the sender to impose sufficiently large negative sanctions while positive sanctions at the same time may be able to accomplish compliance.

It is true that the model does not include reactions to threats and, consequently, the target economy is perhaps modelled too passively. A more active attitude, however, may very well lead to paradoxical results. Smith (1986), for example, develops a formal model of a multinational that has to decide whether and how to enter new markets. Should the firm export or should it invest in productive capital? Clearly this long-term decision is influenced by the multinational's expectations about the sender's trade policy, that is to say by this nation's reputation for the political use of restrictions on international trade and foreign direct investment. This implies that the maximum economic impact of negative economic sanctions (the *ex post* damage) can only be produced by a country that has a reputation for not deploying sanctions. Such a country would by definition be unable to influence a target since for this country $\pi = 0$. On the other hand, a country which is capable of expressing very credible threats because of a long history of imposed and executed sanctions will usually find it difficult to inflict damage on an adversary that in the same historical record finds an important incentive to invest in either countervailing power or reductions in its economic exposure. Another caveat concerns the fact that the analysis in this chapter has been *ex ante* so that it does not answer the question of whether a threat will be carried out or not. To answer this particular question one would have to model the sender's trade-off between both the direct and future costs and the direct and future benefits of its (in)activity. As these complex processes have not been included in the analysis one might want to dismiss the model as being too simple.

It should be granted however, that despite its simplicity this model fits some of the main features of the international system very well, as it clarifies the distinction between the outcome of an *ex ante* expected utility calculation and the *ex post* outcome. Moreover, the theory offers a clear prescription of how the yield of neutral activities should be manipulated in order to prevent misconduct. The attitude of the target country towards risk not being known for certain, it follows that rewards in international politics will only be effective if they are conditional. Hence the analysis within a stochastic utility setting also offers an explanation for the failure of those international policies that offer profitable possibilities unconditionally.

The political economy of economic diplomacy
It is tempting to end with some comments on the contemporary relevance of what may otherwise seem to be mainly broad and largely inconclusive abstractions. Many proposals have come to the fore that in one way or another relate to the theoretical analysis in this chapter. With respect to the potential utility of the economic instruments of modern diplomacy for some of the 'grand schemes' of a New World Order (NWO) two findings in this chapter seem to be most relevant.

First, as the marginal impact of the manipulation of the unconditional yield of neutral activities depends on the a priori unknown attitude of the threatened decision unit towards risk, it follows that changes in unconditionally offered yields associated with unobjectionable behaviour cannot deliver the target's change of behaviour with certainty. Ungar and Vale (1985/86, p. 236), for example, cite the fact that no conditions had been imposed on South Africa in exchange for US favours as the main reasons for the failure of President Reagan's 'constructive engagement' policy *vis-à-vis* the apartheid regime. An efficient deployment of positive sanctions requires that the desired change in the target's behaviour is anatomized in subsets of attainable changes. In the case of the South African movement toward a non-racial society the necessity emerged to reward Pretoria by rolling back cultural, economic and political sanctions in order to keep the reforms acceptable for the white population. Such incentives may help to keep a country on the right track, because once accepted they provide a potential means for negative sanctions once more. The implication is that the order in which negative sanction measures are rolled back depends on the extent of reversal. So negative cultural and political sanctions should be ended first as they can be easily re-imposed. Trade sanctions are less appropriate as positive sanctions, but still more appropriate than capital sanctions since the conditionality of investment, credit and aid is negligible as reversal of such transactions is hardly possible. Likewise sanctions on (nuclear) technology and arms should be ended only in the final stage of the 'sanction game'.

Second, the phenomenon of an increase in conditional stochastic disutility (threat of punishment) possibly leading to a perverse result (a larger extent of misconduct) is important for policy makers. It is essentially this possibility of both a negative and a positive marginal impact of the deterrent concerned that impairs the suitability of negative economic sanctions, unless initially no threat was uttered. Indeed, Fischer (1984, p. 84) rightly stresses that in keeping peace with a potential adversary one should avoid subjecting this adversary to economic pressures, humiliation or threats as long as he keeps peace. Obviously, if a military strategy is complemented with economic warfare during peace time, the value of peace for the other side is reduced. More importantly, however, prior threats introduce uncertainty with respect to the impact of the economic instruments of modern diplomacy, implying a reduction of the effective availability of policy instruments for peaceful conflict resolution.[9]

On both counts it would seem that in the international system, conditional threats and unconditional rewards are inferior to both conditional rewards and unconditional decreases of the yield of misconduct. The failure of unconditional exchanges focuses attention on the need to design mutually beneficial economic relations that emphasize conditionality. In general this means that exchanges should be reversible or mutually beneficial. Trade in this respect may be superior to aid and direct investment, since capital flows are most often one-way traffic and, moreover, the availability of money that crossed the target's border is by definition no longer conditional upon the target's behaviour. Hirsch (1981, p. 49), for example, argues that economic instruments, economic policies and economic transactions should be directed at stabilizing and safeguarding peace between recent and potential belligerents. To achieve such a 'balance of prosperity' requires that the benefits of bilateral co-operation are substantial and that the realization of these benefits is conditional on continued co-operation. Welfens (1989, pp. 383—5) proposes an International Co-operation Initiative in order to strengthen global disarmament and co-operation. Mutual interests between East and West in the fields of trade, technology, transport, environmental co-operation, etc., should form the basis for this package bargaining deal. Welfens stresses the importance of *two-way* foreign direct investment as a means to increase mutual interests in the other's well-being. Following Frey (1974), Welfens proposes an important role for positive sanctions by the World Bank as this institution might be able to support conversion processes financially, for example, with an international 'Subscribe to peace' disarmament loan.

Positive sanctions may thus help to sustain a New World Order. Their role may be particulary important since the instrumental requirements of the NWO have to be met in the short run and in the long run. Recent game theoretic analyses suggest that negative sanctions may not be able to sustain an international system in the long run. Tsebelis (1990) shows that modification of the target's pay-offs by means of negative sanctions does not influence the level or the frequency of violations of (international) standards in so-called super games. This conclusion is valid under a wide range of assumptions about the available information, the continuity of choices and the rules of the game. Bonetti (1993) analyses negative sanctions as an iterated discrete time war of attrition in which sunk cost accounting explains the persistence and frequency of sanction episodes. He points out that rational nations may be reticent to engage in economic warfare because they tend to fight for too long. Bonetti argues that 'positive sanctions and diplomacy may provide the only viable and robust substitutes to the traditional policy techniques of warfare or armed deterrence.' However, as pointed out by Bornstein (1968), positive economic sanctions definitely are not a *panacea* and may, for example, not be fit for military situations, especially if states are to be convinced that they have to sacrifice what they consider to be the requirements of both their national security and their sovereignty.

Notes

1.   With respect to the impact on the target economy this 'new' approach to economic sanctions to a large extent follows the economic analysis that underpins the economic argument for national defence tariffs with which we shall deal in Part II. Indeed

Srinivasan (1987, p. 347) in his extensive review of this literature stresses that the threat of sanctions is more often used than the actual imposition of economic hardship.

2. See Isard (1988), especially pp. 121—75, on the cognitive framework for individual and group behaviour and decision-making under psychological stress and crisis conditions. See, moreover, Haney, Hertzberg and Wilson (1992) for a laboratory experimental test of the differences between unitary actors and advisory models. They conclude (p. 632) that 'the unitary actor model is on the right track. Such a model does not do great harm to model the larger questions'. Compare also Sandler (1992) on collective action theory which is grounded in maximizing models and pursues the problems of decision-making by group processes.

3. In controlling stochastic accidents in the profit maximizing firm, Just and Zilberman (1979, pp. 142—3) found that taxes (penalties) and rewards (subsidies) are asymmetrical. Indeed, subsidies may be superior to taxes, because an increase in punishment may lead to a reduction in safety (compliance).

4. The yield of misconduct can of course change in time. See, for example, Simon (1989) for an analysis that shows that land and other productive resources in general are no longer worth acquiring at the cost of war. Obviously, a smaller M will always reduce the incentives for misconduct.

5. The five basic axioms can be summarized as follows. Let $X > Y$ denote that X is preferred to Y, π_i be the probability of receiving i and $L(X;\pi)$ a lottery of receiving X with probability π. Then we may write the requirements as:
    *   Transitivity: $A > B$ and $B > C$, then $A > C$.
    *   Continuity: a π exists such that $B = (A,C;\pi,1—\pi)$
    *   Strong independence: if $B > A$ and C is any other prospect, then $(B,C;\pi,1—\pi) > (A,C;\pi,1—\pi)$
    *   Preference for high probability of success: if $A = B$ and $\pi_A > \pi_B$ then $L(A,\pi_A) > L(B,\pi_B)$.
    *   Compound probabilities: $L(L(B,\pi_1),\pi_2) = L(L(B,\pi_2),\pi_1)$.
    See for useful introductions into and discussions of the economic theory of expected utility Henderson and Quandt 1971, especially pp. 42—9, and McKenna 1986, especially pp. 21—5.

6. Baldwin (1971), p. 25.

7. As $\lim\limits_{\Delta N \to \infty} = \dfrac{u'(y_R)}{u'(y_F)} = 1$, it follows that $\lim\limits_{\Delta N \to \infty} \dfrac{dy_F}{dy_R} = \dfrac{\pi}{\pi-1}$.

8. See Menkveld (1991, pp. 52—5 and 70—2) on the multiparty democracy part of the EBRD's orientation.

9. See Hower (1988) on the utility of extra instruments in containing international conflict.

4. Failure and ... Success of Economic Sanctions

Economic sanctions are not generally considered to be an efficient instrument of foreign policy, at least within the economic profession. As discussed in Chapter 2, many economists believe that sanctions are ineffective in practice. At the same time, however, the theoretical foundations of this instrument appear rather strong. The two basic premisses belong to the core of economic science. First, boycotts and embargoes deprive the sanctioned economy from some of the gains from international trade and investment, and consequently sanctions reduce welfare. Second, the idea that (the mere threat of) this disutility influences the victim's behaviour can also be traced to the tenets of economic catechism. Still most economists point out the ineffectiveness of boycotts and embargoes. In this chapter we will empirically investigate the economist's disbelief in the potential utility of negative economic sanctions.

Economic research on embargoes and boycotts traditionally focuses on the effectiveness of economic sanctions, as it deals with the (potential) damage that is to be inflicted on the target economy. Empirical analyses have yielded significant insights into the potential damages of sanctions that were considered at the time of the research. Most economic historical research concerns realized *ex post* damage. In contradistinction the present chapter deals with success and failure, that is, with the question of whether the target's behaviour changed as a consequence of diplomatic economic measures. The analysis will be based on a recent study by Hufbauer, Schott and Elliott (1990), that for better or worse has become the established source on this topic. Section 4.1 describes and discusses the ins and outs of this source. Methodological errors hamper the proper interpretation of their findings and this is the *raison d'être* for the econometric investigation in the next sections. Section 4.2 sets out

71

the methodology of the present investigation and section 4.3 introduces the explanatory variables. Section 4.4 presents the empirical results. A small model predicts success and failure correctly in 83 per cent of the cases. The final section draws some conclusions with respect to economic diplomacy and the perspective of an increasing use of boycotts and embargoes.

4.1 Explaining Success

Although the debate on the effectiveness of the sanctions instrument runs since the early applications of sanctions by the League of Nations (see Daoudi and Dajani, 1983 for a review) and at least hundred sanctions have been imposed since the Second World War, systematic empirical research into the determinants of the success and failure of economic sanctions is scarce. Until recently a lack of sufficiently comparable observations prohibited empirical research on the subject. The publication of *Economic Sanctions Reconsidered* by Hufbauer and Schott (1985) offers a comprehensive and systematic treatment of 103 cases in which economic sanctions have been applied and a unique opportunity to put the sanction theory on an empirical footing. An update which appears as Hufbauer, Schott and Elliott (1990) contains twelve additional cases and a critical re-evaluation of the cases that were discussed in the 1985 edition. In two cases the authors changed their assessment of the sanction outcome in a significant way. The 1975 sanctions that the United States imposed in order to achieve more liberal emigration practices in Eastern Europe are now considered to have been a failure, while the US sanctions against martial law in Poland in 1981 is coded as a success in the 1990 edition. The 103 post-1945 cases in the update of *Economic Sanctions Reconsidered* are the observations that will be econometrically investigated in the present chapter.

The dependent variable in the Hufbauer, Schott and Elliott study is the success score of a sanction which is defined (Hufbauer, Schott and Elliott 1990, pp. 41—2) as the product of the assessments of the policy result (the extent to which the policy outcome sought by the sender country was in fact achieved) and of the sanction contribution to this result (the contribution made by sanctions to a positive outcome).

So we may write the success score as:

$$\text{Success score} = \text{policy result} \times \text{sanction contribution} \quad (4.1)$$

Since both these assessments are each an integer from the interval 1 ('none') to 4 ('important') the success score adopts the values 1, 2, 3, 4, 6, 8, 9, 12 and 16 only. The value of the success score is the subject of empirical investigations by Hufbauer et al. in which average scores are tabulated for potentially explanatory variables. Averages, however, are simply insufficient statistical means to describe the distribution of the subsets of sanction attributes; one would at least want to know the standard errors before any valid conclusions can be drawn. Such simple counts, moreover, lead to wrong conclusions, because this approach fails to hold other potentially relevant variables constant. This implies the need to investigate the success score by means of multiple regression techniques.

Hufbauer and Schott, (1985, pp. 99—102) accordingly seek to explain the success score using Ordinary Least Squares (OLS). Their regression model, however, is not appropriate. OLS cannot comply with the numerical restriction placed on the dependent variable. Moreover, the question whether a sanction is a success or a failure essentially concerns a binary dependent variable ('yes' or 'no'; 1 or 0) implying an analysis on the basis of some kind of probability mechanism. OLS-estimates will be biased when the dependent variable is a probability. According to Leitzel (1987, p. 287), the statistical evidence in support of the policy prescriptions that are formulated by Hufbauer et al. is 'scanty at best'. Bonetti (1991) discusses three additional objections to the multiple regression methodology in *Economic Sanctions Reconsidered*: *(i)* there is no certainty that the relationships are linear additive as is assumed throughout, *(ii)* the definition of success is biased in favour of finding failure[1] and *(iii)* the predictive and explanatory power measured by significance tests and the standard error of the estimated equation is extremely poor. All in all, their econometrics are not rightly applied and as a consequence not very instructive.[2] This is especially disappointing since the Hufbauer, Schott and Elliott study has become the major reference work on the subject of economic sanctions.

Hence the present attempt to create an empirical basis for discussion of the efficacy of the economic instruments of diplomacy.

4.2 Methodology

I will use a particular method to analyse the sanction mechanism. The black box approach is used to investigate how an economic sanction leads to a reaction by the target country. In the next sections a number of variables assumed to be of importance for the failure and success of economic sanctions will be inserted into a postulated quasi-reduced form equation. The more ambitious approach of fitting a regression on the basis of a detailed set of structural equations will not be followed, because opinions differ about the precise mechanism that inflicts damage on the adversary (Cooper 1986). Doxey (1982, p. 155), for example, states that 'even in embryonic form, no general pattern of international enforcement is discernible'. So the mechanism cannot be specified unambiguously on a priori grounds. In Chapter 2, however, it appeared possible to identify a number of common variables that play a part in several approaches to the sanction phenomenon. Since these variables seem to be theoretically undisputed a black box analysis becomes possible which may yield sound pronouncements about the direction and the extent of the influence of the explanatory variables. Note, however, that if relevant variables are omitted, then the estimated coefficients may just be attributing things to the included variables that should be attributed to excluded variables.

In the black box analysis the unknown system is defined in terms of its external characteristics. The choice of the relevant external characteristics (or sanction attributes) has been based on theoretical considerations. It is assumed that relations between observable inputs and outputs offer an indication about the process inside the black box (Klir, 1969, p. 243). In case no statistically satisfactory relationship between inputs and outputs is established it can be concluded that economic sanctions do not call forth a change in behaviour. If, on the other hand, economic and non-economic variables play a significant role in the black box process, it can be concluded that sanctions are effective instruments in international politics, because they result in a change of behaviour provided the economic and political conditions are being met. This is to say, that the successes that have appeared (33 per cent of the 103 cases over the period 1946—1989) should not be considered as mere coincidences in case a statistically and theoretically satisfactory relationship is found. In that case the successful sanctions are theoretically explicable and consequently, such outcomes may offer empirical support for the model that was developed in Chapter 3.

In this econometrical investigation the binary variable y_i serves as the dependent variable.

$y_i = 1$, if the i-th sanction is a success
$y_i = 0$, if not

A sanction is successful if behaviour satisfactorily changes and the sanction significantly contributes to this outcome. The success score in this case equals or exceeds 9 (Hufbauer, Schott and Elliott, 1990, p. 42). The outcome of a sanction case as given in the Hufbauer, Schott and Elliott (1990) study is adopted as the final decision about the value of y_i. As each outcome is the result of an evaluation of the literature on a specific case, it seems probable that differences of opinion exist about the value of the dependent variable in certain cases. Hufbauer, Schott and Elliott, for example, code the British sanctions against Argentina in 1982 as relatively successful in getting Argentina off the Falklands, whereas the Royal Marines would seem more deserving of the credit. In this study I will not discuss the Hufbauer, Schott and Elliott judgements about the outcome of sanctions in individual cases and simply accept their findings.

Hufbauer, Schott and Elliott divide the sanction episodes into five categories, classified according to the major foreign policy objective sought by the sender country (Hufbauer, Schott and Elliott, 1990, pp. 38—9): (*i*) change the target's policies in a relatively modest way; (*ii*) destabilize the target government; (*iii*) disrupt a minor military adventure; (*iv*) impair the military potential of the target country and (*v*) change the target country's policies in a major way. In the econometric investigation, however, I will make no distinction as to the sender country's objectives. First, an episode may have more than one objective. Destabilization presupposes a 'lesser' goal, and attempts to impair the military power of an adversary usually encompass an explicit or implicit goal of destabilizing the target country's government. Second, there are just not enough observations. There would only be some 15—25 cases per category and this impedes useful generalization in case the objectives are taken into account. The relation between the dependent and the explanatory variables will be estimated with LOGIT.

LOGIT-analysis makes it possible to calculate the probability π that a specified sanction case ends successfully. If this probability exceeds 0.5, a success is predicted; if not, a failure. This approach may seem to suffer from the drawback that the equation cannot distinguish between marginal and total successes (or failures), while this distinction is extremely relevant for policy purposes (Bonetti 1991, pp. 15—6). The LOGIT-specification, however, has the attractive feature that the probability π for a given case can be calculated a priori on the basis of the set of observable inputs for the black box system.

4.3 The Explanatory Variables

The literature that was discussed in Chapter 2 and the expected utility model that was developed in Chapter 3 guide my choice of the explanatory variables. The *ex post* damage that appears as the costs of the imposition of sanctions in the Hufbauer, Schott and Elliott study may not always be the most appropriate explanatory variable. It is not the actual *ex post* damage done but rather the *ex ante* threat of disutility that influences behaviour. The most efficient sanction immediately changes behaviour, implying that punishment is not necessary. As a consequence no externally imposed economic costs for the target economy might be measured.[3]

Moreover, it is difficult to estimate the total costs that result from a sanction. In addition to the direct costs entailing financial and real outlays immediately related to the imposition of sanctions (such as rising transport costs), Losman (1972, pp. 28—30) identifies indirect costs due to dislocation and forced underutilization of factors of production, and forgone potential. The latter relates to certain expected future economies of production and revenues that will no longer be realizable. The indirect costs and the loss of economic potential may exceed the direct costs significantly. To estimate these costs, however, one has to have either a complete macroeconomic model of the economy concerned or an applied trade model of its detailed export and import relationships.[4] Indeed, it is no surprise that Hufbauer, Schott and Elliott restrict their analysis to the direct costs. This yields a very rough underestimate of the potential welfare loss. Finally, it is also less appropriate to include the costs of the sanction together with other variables that are supposed to explain the extent of the sanction damage, as multicollinearity can be expected. So the research strategy will be to include variables that proxy both potential and actual damage, so as to capture both the comparative static and dynamic losses of economic sanctions.[5]

a) Trade linkage (ATL, PTL)
The inclusion of some measure of trade linkage is straightforward: (potential) sanction damage increases as trade linkage increases. No distinction is being made between boycotts and embargoes. A sanction that curtails the target's imports only does not exclude the possibility of an additional boycott. A sanction on specific transactions may foreshadow general measures. Hence it is the total bilateral trade flow that constitutes the basis of the sanction threat.

Wolf (1983) distinguishes absolute trade linkage and proportional trade linkage (incidentally both measures are shares). Absolute trade linkage *(ATL)* relates the bilateral trade flow between sender and target to the target's total trade flow, where both the nominator and the denominator are measured in the year prior to the sanction. High absolute trade linkage indicates dominance of the sender in the external economic relations of the target. The target's valuation of the potential sanction loss, however, depends on the importance of the bilateral trade flow in relation to other (domestic) economic activities. Low absolute trade linkage may imply a bigger loss for an open economy than high absolute trade linkage may imply for a closed, almost autarkic economy. Hence the proportional trade linkage variable *(PTL)* is defined as the sender's trade flows to the target, as a percentage of the target's GNP in the year prior to the sanction. A priori a positive relationship between π and both *ATL* and *PTL* is expected: the probability that an economic sanction succeeds is higher, the greater is pre-sanction trade linkage.

b) Sanction period (LSE, D73, ONG)

Many authors have argued that duration of economic warfare is essentially positively related to the probability of its success. Daoudi and Dajani expect that sanctions increasingly hurt when they last longer. Sanctions resemble slow poison. The consequences are revealed only in the course of time as 'the ability of the sanctioned nation to meet its domestic daily demands (is corrupted) weakening its integrity and eventually causing its collapse' (Daoudi and Dajani 1983, p. 168). Brady (1987, p. 299) claims that sanctions with time become effective because agreement on the international unacceptability of the target's conduct causes more and more countries to join the embargo. Hanlon and Omond (1987, p.12) argue that even tight sanctions will require several years to have an impact.

The textbook treatment of economic sanctions, however, suggests a negative relationship between success and duration. The question of how much damage can be inflicted on the target depends to a large degree on the target's (in)flexibility as it reacts to the sanction. Rigidity of economic structures being basically a short-term phenomenon, it appears probable that the passage of time erodes the economic impact of sanctions (Kemp 1964, pp. 208—17, Frey 1984, pp. 103—21 and Carbaugh 1989, pp. 144—7). Indeed, the common economic understanding of the influence of the time variable, maintains that a negative relationship exists between effectiveness and duration and many authors have on other non-economic grounds suggested that success and duration are negatively correlated as well. According to Dekker (1973, p. 396), the welfare loss should be sudden in order to prevent the target population from becoming, as it were, conditioned to make ever-increasing sacrifices. Moreover, as it is difficult to end an unsuccessful sanction without an awkward loss of face (Leyton-Brown, 1987, p. 308), and ineffective sanctions thus have a tendency to last, a negative influence of *LSE* on π seems more probable. *LSE* is measured as the natural logarithm of the number of years.

The relationship between the sanction period and π may be influenced by the fact that the data set consists of both resolved and on-going cases, while systemic shift, such as the declining hegemony of the United States since 1973, may lead to declining success rates (Hufbauer, Schott and Elliott 1990, pp. 107—11). On-going sanctions may be a special case, since sanctions that were still in effect in 1990 when the data were collected have by definition not been successful. The question is whether such cases will be considered successful in the near future, especially since, for example, very long-lived sanctions such as the Cocom sanctions against the former Eastern Block (42 years) and the United Nations sanctions against South Africa (28 years) are considered as on-going in the data set. Hence a dummy variable *ONG* will be included to test for differences in both slope and intercept in the relationship between π and *LSE*. In order to take the possibility of an impact from systemic shifts into account, a dummy variable *D73* is included that distinguishes the pre-1973 and post-1973 periods.

c) Political instability (INS)

In order to analyse the influence of the target's political and socio-economic condition a dummy variable is used. *INS* assumes the value 1 in case the target is confronted with a combination of critical economic problems, such as high inflation and unemployment, and political unrest, verging on chaos. Examples are Chile under Allende and Uganda in Amin's later years. This socio-economic situation corresponds with the most severe judgement of Hufbauer, Schott and Elliott concerning 'Economic Health and Political Stability' (Hufbauer and Schott, 1985 pp. 36—7). Since instability might be both a means and a goal of the sanction, the socio-economic and political condition has been defined as the target country's health and stability in the — hypothetical — absence of sanctions and over a period of time.

As sanctions have a better chance of succeeding against weak regimes it is assumed that *INS* influences π positively: the probability that a sanction succeeds is higher the more unstable the target's political situation at the beginning of the sanction period.

d) The sender's reputation (REP)

Since reputation is not an observable input, a proxy has been constructed. *REP* is defined as the sender's sanctions in the post Second World War period. It is not possible to give a decisive answer concerning the influence of this variable on a priori grounds. A long history of executed threats influences π positively as it increases the credibility of threat. Potential victims will, however, be induced by the same historical record to arm themselves against future punitive measures. Smith (1986), for example, points out that the activities of foreign subsidiaries often cannot be controlled by a multinational's home country and that this provides an important channel through which expectations decrease the effectiveness of sanctions. Sanctions seem unlikely to succeed in cases where technology and production capabilities are diffused through the actions of multinational firms in response to perceived embargo threats. Smith (1986, p. 12) concludes that 'for the embargo weapon to be most effective, it should be deployed by a country with a reputation for not deploying it.' All in all it seems reasonable to assume that the number of prior threats promotes effectiveness to some extent, while at the same time there may be a danger in excess.

The relationship between π and the sender's reputation will thus have to be established empirically. Inclusion of the reputation variable both linear and in squared form allows for the possibility of an initially positive (negative) influence that turns negative (positive) after a certain number of prior sanctions is exceeded.

e) Third parties (COO, HIN, AREA, NP)

Sanction-busting is a well-known phenomenon. Therefore attention has to be given to the target country's likelihood of finding alternative supplies and new outlets for its exports. Two proxies have been used to represent the possibilities for sanction-busting. If cooperation by other countries with the sender is significant according to Hufbauer, Schott and Elliott (1990, pp. 44—5), then *COO* assumes the value 1. If international assistance for the target country (overt military or economic aid) is observed *HIN* assumes the value 1 (Hufbauer, Schott and Elliott 1990, pp. 45—6). A negative relationship between π and *HIN* is assumed and a positive relationship between π and *COO*.

Two variables will be added to shed some light on the possible impact of sanction-busting, trade diversion and alternative sources. In the case of sanctions aimed at non-proliferation of nuclear arms and technology the number of alternative suppliers is rather limited and, moreover, intensive checks on trade and technology flows are common practice. Hence it is difficult to circumvent these particular sanctions. The dummy variable *NP* is 1 if the sanction aims at non-proliferation. A positive relation between π and *NP* is assumed. A second variable that highlights the possibilities for substitution is *AREA*, that is, the natural logarithm of the surface of the target's territory. *AREA* proxies the target's border length and this offers an indication for the opportunities for smuggling.[6] The larger the border length the better the opportunities for smuggling so that a negative relationship between π and *AREA* is expected.

f) Capital flows (FIN, AID)

In addition to the international exchange of goods, capital flows are important in our discussion of the efficacy of economic sanctions. Olson (1979, pp. 477—93) compares the effectiveness of government intervention in trade flows and the effectiveness of manipulation of foreign lending, development aid and foreign investment. His conclusion is that (official) capital flows often provide a better channel to influence other governments that boycotts and embargoes. The target is in a relatively dependent position *vis-à-vis* the sender and consequently the target is rather vulnerable. Moreover, Olson points out, financial sanctions can often be imposed more covertly, thus reducing the probability that the sanction induces increased public support that may bolster the target state's government and may enhance both its short run and its long run material capacity to resist. Kaempfer and Lowenberg (1992, pp. 111—2), however, argue that the impact of capital sanctions on the target's politics is tenuous. Unanticipated consequences of such sanctions may produce windfall gains for the target's population. Indeed it is not 'particularly likely that disinvestment will drive (the target) to abandon its politics'.

Since the available figures on international capital flows are characterized by even larger measurement errors than the trade flows, and data on bilateral capital flows are often unavailable, a dummy variable *FIN* will be introduced that assumes the value 1 if the sanctions pertain to private and/or official capital transactions. Analogous to trade linkage the implicit threat of the existing aid relationships is investigated by the variable *AID* that relates the aid flow from sender to target in the year before the sanction, to the target's national income. A positive relationship between π and both *FIN* and *AID* is expected a priori.

The relation between the dependent variable and the explanatory variables will be estimated with the LOGIT-technique. The probability of success (π) is written as (i denotes the observation, j denotes the specification of the quasi-reduced form equation):

$$\pi_i = 1/(1+e^{-\theta i,j}) \tag{4.2}$$

where $\theta_{i,j} = \alpha_{0,j} + \Sigma^N_{k=1}\alpha_{i,j,k} \times x_{i,k}$

That is the probability π_i that $y_i = 1$ is a function of the observed inputs and the coefficients of the model. Note that if $\theta \to +\infty$ so $\pi \uparrow 1$ and if $\theta \to -\infty$ so $\pi \downarrow 0$. Hence the logical restrictions on the dependant variable ($0 \leq \pi \leq 1$) are never violated. Table 4.1 summarizes some key statistical characteristics of the explanatory variables.

Table 4.1 Summary of the explanatory variables (N=103)

	Average	Standard deviation	Lowest	Highest	Expected sign
Costs (COST)	0.004	0.0003	—0.06	0.15	+
Trade linkage					
Absolute (ATL)	0.20	0.19	0	1	+
Proportional* (PTL)	0.05	0.07	0	0.41	+
Sanction length (LSE)	6.3	9.2	1	44	—
Still in effect (ONG)	0.20	0.40	0	1	?
Post 1973 (D73)	0.56	0.50	0	1	—
Instability (INS)	0.22	0.42	0	1	+
Reputation (REP)	24.6	22.1	1	69	?
Co-operation (COO)	0.26	0.44	0	1	+
Hindrance (HIN)	0.24	0.43	0	1	—
Non-proliferation (NP)	0.09	0.30	0	1	+
Territory (AREA)	2.8	6.0	0	24	—
Capital sanction (FIN)	0.77	0.42	0	1	+
Aid linkage (AID)	0.02	0.05	—0.02	0.43	+

* $N = 92$

4.4   Empirical Results

Tables 4.2 to 4.5 summarize the empirical results. The columns of Tables 4.2, 4.4 and 4.5 report the coefficients and test statistics of specific specifications of θ. For example, $\theta(5)$ in Table 4.2 reads as $\theta(5) = 15PTL - 1.6LSE + 2.3INS + 0.1REP - 0.003REP^2 - 0.1$ with an adjusted-R^2 of 0.41, F-statistic of 13.9, etc. Table 4.2 concentrates on three possible indicators for the economic impact. The *ex post* costs are the loss that the target actually experienced as a result of the sanction. In addition two *ex ante* measures of the potential costs of the sanction are considered. The absolute trade linkage relates bilateral trade flows between sender and target to the target's total trade flows. The proportional trade linkage relates this bilateral trade flow to the target's gross domestic product. Table 4.3 presents the errors of prediction for the preferred specification of the LOGIT-model. In Table 4.4 third party reactions and the contribution of financial sanctions are investigated. Table 4.5 takes a closer look at the impact of time (the sanction period) and possibilities for sanction busting.

Evaluating the model
In order to assess the model's performance a number of scalar criteria can be used (Amemiya, 1981, pp. 1502—7). The interpretation of the adjusted-R^2 is not straightforward, since LOGIT is essentially a heteroscedastic regression model and the adjusted-R^2 has been derived from the standard homoscedastic linear model.[7] This means that relatively low values for the adjusted-R² do not necessarily imply a bad model. More important, the F-statistic and the t-values of the model imply significance at the usual confidence levels and better. Indeed in general the empirical results should be considered as quite good. Finally, the number of wrong predictions also serves as a criterion. A prediction is classified as a Type I Error if a successful sanction is predicted ($\pi_i < 0.5$) when the event y_i does *not* take place. A Type II Error occurs when $y_i = 1 \wedge \pi_i < 0.5$. It is assumed that lower errors of prediction imply a better model. The criterion, however, is appropriate only when one has an 'all-or-nothing' loss function, because no distinction is made between $y_i = 1 \wedge \pi_i = 0.01$ and $y_i = 1 \wedge \pi_i = 0.49$.

Table 4.2 LOGIT estimates of the determinants of success and failure of 103 sanction cases (1946—1989)

Specification	$\theta(1)$	$\theta(2)$	$\theta(3)$	$\theta(4)$	$\theta(5)$
Number of observations	103	92	103	92	92
Economic impact	COST	COST	ATL	ATL	PTL
	34.0	31.6	3.6	4.8	15.0
	(2.5)	(2.4)	(2.3)	(2.6)	(2.7)
	{0.01}	{0.02}	{0.03}	{0.01}	{0.01}
Length of sanction(LSE)	—1.4	—1.5	—1.4	—1.6	—1.6
	(—3.8)	(—3.6)	(—3.8)	(—3.9)	(—3.8)
	{0.00}	{0.01}	{0.00}	{0.00}	{0.00}
Political instability (INS)	2.3	2.1	2.7	2.3	2.3
	(2.8)	(2.4)	(3.2)	(2.6)	(2.6)
	{0.01}	{0.02}	{0.00}	{0.01}	{0.01}
Number of earlier sanctions	0.8	0.9	0.6	0.8	1.0
(REP $*10^{-1}$)	(1.5)	(1.6)	(1.3)	(1.4)	(1.6)
	{0.13}	{0.12}	{0.22}	{0.16}	{0.12}
Idem, squared (REP^2 $*10^{-2}$)	—0.2	—0.2	—0.2	—0.2	—0.3
	(—2.4)	(—2.5)	(—2.3)	(—2.4)	(—2.6)
	{0.02}	{0.02}	{0.02}	{0.02}	{0.01}
Constant term	—0.2	—0.1	—0.4	—0.3	—0.1
	(—0.4)	(—0.1)	(—0.7)	(—0.5)	(—0.2)
	{0.70}	{0.93}	{0.50}	{0.60}	{0.86}
Test statistics					
Adj—R^2	0.42	0.42	0.37	0.40	0.41
F-test	15.7	13.9	13.3	13.4	13.9
Loglikelihood	—39.5	—36.2	—40.9	—39.8	—35.6
Errors Type I (%)	12	12	16	13	12
Errors Type II (%)	26	27	27	23	24

Notes   (t-values in parentheses)
{two-tail significance test between brackets}
Adj—R^2 is Lave's R^2 corrected for degrees of freedom
Errors Type I and Type II are expressed as a percentage of the cases
$\pi < 0.5$ and $\pi > 0.5$, respectively.

Reliance on a single criterion is ill-advised. Both economic-theoretic and all statistical criteria have to be taken into consideration simultaneously. All in all, it appears that the empirical investigation produces an equation which explains adequately. Table 4.2 shows that the *ex ante* measures of the potential welfare loss of economic sanctions have almost as much explanatory power as the costs that are measured *ex post*. The findings support the hypothesis that potential welfare losses enforce compliance. Moreover, the empirical results suggest that it is possible to assess the probability of success, π, as a function of the length of the sanction based on observed variables, such as the political instability, the pre-sanction trade linkage between target and sender and the number of earlier sanctions. The findings support the notion that the reduction of the number of available observations from 103 to 92 in the case where we focus on proportional trade linkage carries some costs in terms of the test statistics (especially since the coefficients of the economic impact variables change if the data set is reduced to those cases where observations on proportional trade linkage are available).

The preferred specification
The overall performance of the equation is quite satisfactory. Specification $\theta(5)$, for example, is relatively small while the coefficients (with the exception of the constant term and the number of earlier sanctions) are significant at the 99 per cent confidence level and better. Given the inaccuracy and the unreliability of the available figures, the varying socio-economic and political characteristics and the rather long period (1946—1989) that is studied, the explanatory power of the model is striking. In 83 per cent of the cases the outcome is predicted correctly (88 per cent of the failures and 72 per cent of the successes are predicted correctly).

In the discussion of the results for the individual variables the focus is on specification $\theta(5)$ that pertains to the smaller data set ($N = 92$). The reduction of the number of available observations from 103 to 92 does not seem to influence the empirical results to a large extent, given the outcomes that have been summarized in Table 4.2. Hence the selection of the 92 observations appears valid from an econometric point of view as well.

Table 4.3 Errors of prediction for model $\theta(5)$

Errors Type I Case	Year	π	Errors Type II Case	Year	π
US—El Salvador	1977	0.78	US—Brazil	1966	0.03
US—India	1971	0.69	US—Poland	1981	0.13
EC—Turkey	1981	0.67	US—Ceylon	1961	0.22
China—Vietnam	1978	0.62	US—El Salvador	1987	0.28
US—Kampuchea	1975	0.58	US—India	1965	0.46
USSR—Australia	1954	0.56	UN—Rhodesia	1965	0.48
US,UK—Somalia	1988	0.51			

Table 4.3 summarizes the errors of prediction for model $\theta(5)$ giving the in-sample prediction for the probabilities π that the specific sanction case will succeed.[8] The number of serious wrong predictions is quite limited.

The reference case
In order to analyse the relative impact of the explanatory variables a reference case is defined. This reference case is a hypothetical sanction where all variables assume their averages and the political climate is stable by assumption. So in the reference case *PTL* = 5.2 per cent, *LSE* = 1.18 (the natural logarithm of 3.3 years), *INS* = 0 and *REP* = 24.6 sanctions in the period 1946—1989.

Substitute these values in equation 4.2 using the coefficients of $\theta(5)$. This yields θ_{ref} = —0.45. Substitution in equation 4.2 gives $\pi_{ref} = 1/(1 + e^{-0.45}) = 1/1.64 = 0.39$. This means that the model predicts that the reference case is a failure. It does not mean that sanctions on average fail, that sanctions are successful in 39 per cent of the cases or that the probability of a sanction being successful is 39 per cent. The reference case is just a yardstick used to measure and compare the influence of changes in the values of the explanatory variables. Note that the relationships are not linear: the effects of changes in the explanatory variables will be more marked for lower values of π_{ref}.

a) Trade linkage (ATL, PTL)

In all specifications both *ATL* and *PTL* meet the requirements concerning sign and significance level without any problem. Highly significant coefficients at the 99 per cent confidence level point out the importance of trade linkage and the length of the sanction episode, whereas Hufbauer and Schott's (1985, pp. 99—101) 'preferred equation' shows insignificant effects only. The signs of their estimated coefficients conform to the present finding. Hence the present investigation supports the hypothesis that potential welfare losses enforce compliance. On the basis of both the statistical criteria (compare $\theta(3)$ and $\theta(5)$) and theoretical consideration a light preference for $\theta(5)$ emerges, although the difference between the two specifications is less pronounced for the reduced data set (compare $\theta(4)$ and $\theta(5)$).[9] A one percentage point increase in proportional trade linkage increases π_{ref} with 3.7 percentage points.

b) Sanction period (LSE, D73, ONG)

The length of the sanction episode clearly influences π in a negative way. All specifications support the notion that the passage of time decreases the probability that a sanction will succeed at the 99 per cent confidence level. Hence the hypotheses of Daoudi and Dajani, Brady, and Hanlon and Omond should be rejected. Indeed the findings offer a rather definite invalidation of the assumption that success and duration are positively related: time erodes the economic impact of a sanction. An increase of the sanction episode by one year decreases π_{ref} by 9.6 per cent points.

It is important to note that these results are neither significantly influenced by the fact that the sanctions were still in effect in 1990 or the question of whether the sanction was implemented before or after 1973. It is surprising indeed that the dummy variable *ONG* neither influences the slope nor the intercept of the established relationship between π and *LSE* as shown by specification $\theta(9)$ in Table 4.4 on page 88. The impact of the historic systemic setting on the probability of success does not support the hypothesis in Hufbauer, Schott and Elliott that the declining hegemony of the United States since 1973 relates to a decrease in the success rate of economic sanctions over time. Although the coefficient of *D73* is negative it is not significantly different from zero at the usual confidence levels.[10]

Table 4.4 Third parties and period: LOGIT estimates of success
　　factors for 92 sanctions (1946—1989)

	$\theta(5)$	$\theta(6)$	$\theta(7)$	$\theta(8)$	$\theta(9)$
Added variables		Coo	Hin	D73	Ong
		0.9	—0.0	—1.1	0.7
		(1.1)	(—0.0)	(—1.4)	(0.0)
		{0.27}	{0.98}	{0.16}	{1.00}
					Ong*Lse
					—0.2
					(—0.0)
					{1.00}
Proportional trade linkage	15.0	15.8	14.9	13.3	18.5
	(2.7)	(2.0)	(2.7)	(2.5)	(2.7)
	{0.01}	{0.01}	{0.01}	{0.02}	{0.01}
Length of sanction	—1.6	—1.7	—1.6	—1.7	—1.5
	(—3.8)	(—3.9)	(—3.7)	(—3.9)	(—3.1)
	{0.00}	{0.00}	{0.00}	{0.00}	{0.00}
Political instability	2.3	2.3	2.3	2.4	2.4
	(2.6)	(2.4)	(2.6)	(2.6)	(2.6)
	{0.01}	{0.01}	{0.01}	{0.01}	{0.01}
Number of earlier sanctions	1.0	1.2	0.9	1.0	0.7
	(1.6)	(1.8)	(1.6)	(1.6)	(1.2)
	{0.12}	{0.07}	{0.13}	{0.11}	{0.22}
Squared	—0.3	—0.3	—0.3	—0.2	—0.2
	(—2.6)	(—2.7)	(—2.5)	(—2.4)	(—1.9)
	{0.01}	{0.01}	{0.01}	{0.02}	{0.08}
Constant term	—0.1	—0.4	—0.1	—0.7	—1.0
	(—0.2)	(—0.6)	(—0.2)	(—0.9)	(—0.9)
	{0.86}	{0.58}	{0.87}	{0.35}	{0.35}
Test statistics					
Adj—R^2	0.41	0.43	0.40	0.43	0.43
F-test	13.9	15.1	13.9	15.1	10.9
Loglikelihood	—35.6	—35.0	—35.6	—34.6	—33.7
Errors Type I (%)	12	12	12	17	14
Errors Type II (%)	24	22	24	30	24

c) Political instability (INS)

The dummy variable *INS* appears to contribute substantially to the explanation of the outcome of an economic sanction. The coefficient of the variable is significant at the 95 per cent confidence level and better and its sign conforms to theoretical expectations. The impact of this crude dummy variable is shown by the fact that π_{ref} increases by 48 percentage points when the political climate is to be considered as unstable (*INS* = 1).

d) The sender's reputation (REP)

The ambiguity of the theoretical assumptions concerning the impact of the sender's reputation on the sanction's probability of success is clearly reflected in the empirical results. Inclusion of reputation both linear and in squared form, although not fully justified by the linear term's confidence level that remains a little below 90 per cent, allows for the detection of an initially positive influence that turns negative after a certain number of economic sanctions is exceeded. For the coefficients of specification $\theta(5)$ this happens when the number of sanctions exceeds 18, with a rather large standard error of 13.[11] Hence it can only be concluded at the 95 per cent confidence level that the marginal impact of *REP* is negative for sender countries that had implemented 34 or more sanctions in the period under investigation.

For the reference case an increase of *REP* by one sanction implies that π_{ref} decreases by 0.8 percentage points.

e) Third parties (COO, HIN, NP, AREA)

Contrary to Hufbauer and Schott the regressions do not show a statistically significant influence for international hindrance. Indeed the hypothesis that the coefficient of *HIN* is negative can be rejected rather confidently, since the confidence level to accept this particular hypothesis would only be a meagre 2 per cent. The findings in Table 4.3 conform to the Hufbauer and Schott study with respect to the fact that co-operation with the sender does not seem to influence the outcome of sanctions. This empirical result may, however, be the result of the fact that co-operation and hindrance depend to a large extent on the economic and political condition of the target and the potential success rate of the sanction case (Martin 1992, pp. 63—7).

Table 4.5 Sanction-busting and capital flows: LOGIT estimates of success factors for 92 sanctions (1946—1989)

	$\theta(5)$	$\theta(10)$	$\theta(11)$	$\theta(12)$	$\theta(13)$
Added variables		NP	AREA	FIN	AID
		—0.7	0.0	0.8	—0.0
		(—1.0)	(0.2)	(0.9)	(—0.3)
		{0.49}	{0.86}	{0.37}	{0.74}
Proportional trade linkage	15.0	14.7	15.2	14.1	15.4
	(2.7)	(2.7)	(2.6)	(2.6)	(2.7)
	{0.01}	{0.01}	{0.01}	{0.01}	{0.01}
Length of sanction	—1.6	—1.6	—1.6	—1.7	—1.6
	(—3.8)	(—3.9)	(—3.8)	(—3.9)	(—3.8)
	{0.00}	{0.00}	{0.00}	{0.00}	{0.00}
Political instability	2.3	2.2	2.4	2.2	2.4
	(2.6)	(2.5)	(2.6)	(2.4)	(2.7)
	{0.01}	{0.01}	{0.01}	{0.02}	{0.01}
Number of earlier sanctions	1.0	0.9	0.9	0.9	1.0
	(1.6)	(1.6)	(1.5)	(1.5)	(1.6)
	{0.12}	{0.12}	{0.13}	{0.15}	{0.11}
Squared	—0.3	—0.3	—0.3	—0.2	—0.2
	(—2.6)	(—2.6)	(—2.5)	(—2.5)	(—2.6)
	{0.01}	{0.01}	{0.02}	{0.01}	{0.01}
Constant Term	—0.1	0.0	—0.3	0.5	—0.1
	(—0.2)	(0.1)	(—0.2)	0.7	(—0.6)
	{0.86}	{0.95}	{0.81}	{0.50}	{0.89}
Test statistics					
Adj—R^2	0.41	0.41	0.40	0.42	0.41
F-test	13.9	11.7	11.5	14.5	11.7
Loglikelihood	—35.6	—35.4	—35.6	—35.2	—35.6
Errors Type I (%)	12	14	12	13	11
Errors Type II (%)	24	27	26	23	28

It is, however, also possible that the dummy measures for third-party activities in the international diplomatic arena are simply too crude, although for example the inclusion of neither the non-proliferation dummy variable *NP* (that applies to cases where the opportunities for trade diversion are rather limited) nor other proxies for the possibilities for sanction-busting (*AREA*) appear to influence the probability of success significantly. According to Kaempfer and Lowenberg (1993) the negative sign of *NP* is to be expected because the target countries perceive such sanctions as threats to national security. Consequently, sanctions motivate rather than deter attempts to acquire nuclear capability.

All in all one should not conclude from the findings that are summarized in Tables 4.4 and 4.5 that sanction-busting does not reduce the effectiveness of economic sanctions. The only conclusion is that no satisfactory statistical relationship can be detected.[12]

f) Capital flows (FIN, AID)

The empirical results for the variables that measure the impact of capital transactions seem to support the notion that the 'trade, not aid' recipe also applies to the case of the economic instruments of diplomacy. The dummy variable *FIN* in specification $\theta(12)$ is insignificant although the sign of the coefficient conforms to the a priori expectation (Hufbauer and Schott (1985, p. 100 find an insignificant negative coefficient). The (insignificant) sign of *AID* in specification $\theta(13)$ is negative.

The insignificance of the coefficients should not come as a surprise, since a dummy is a very rough proxy for the manipulation of capital flows while measurement errors may account for the finding for *AID*. Moreover, since trade and capital flows are often highly correlated the impact of *FIN* and *AID* may have been captured by the trade linkage variables. Indeed a specification of θ in which *PTL* is replaced by *AID* shows the expected positive relationship although only at the 40 per cent level. All in all the results should be interpreted with caution. The findings, however, offer some support for the notion, developed in Chapter 3, that capital that has already crossed the target's border does not offer a threat, since the availability of this sum is no longer conditional upon the target's behaviour.

4.5 Some Implications for Policy

The empirical investigation identifies a number of explanatory variables as the determinants of success and failure for boycotts and embargoes in general. The model predicts success and failure correctly in 83 per cent of the cases. Indeed the model beats alternative forecasting techniques such as tossing a coin or always predicting a failure. So this investigation answers affirmative to the question of whether economic sanctions can be successful instruments in international politics, offering a rational basis to discuss the merits of using sanctions to achieve foreign policy goals.

The probability that an economic sanction succeeds in changing the target's behaviour is higher, the larger the pre-sanction trade linkage, the more unstable the target's political situation and the shorter the sanction period. The results support the idea that prolonged duration of a sanction decreases its efficacy. Concerning the sanctioner's reputation as an executioner of threats it was found that the positive marginal influence of the number of prior sanction threats diminishes and even turns negative after a certain number.

The empirical findings may guide policy in two respects. First, the estimated equations suggest which determinants of sanctions are important to investigate if the diplomatic use of sanctions is considered. Second, the findings give some food for rethinking the desirability of increasing the use of the sanction instrument in modern diplomacy.

Identification of potential successes
The empirical findings offer the possibility of identifying on an *ex ante* basis whether a specific sanction has a substantial chance to succeed. For example, Table 4.6 reports calculations based on specification $\theta(5)$ for the expected probability that the sanction will succeed for three recent cases. The table offers a numerical basis for the comparison of these three very different cases. From their start the sanctions against Libya seem to be doomed to failure, while the use of economic warfare against Panama's Noriega seems promising. The calculations also clearly show the impact of the sanction period. Initially the probability of success of sanctions against South Africa is slightly better than the average success rate for the whole population

of 103 sanctions. In the third year of the sanction the probability of success has decreased to 8 per cent only.

Table 4.6 Probability of success for three recent US sanctions

Target		Expected success rate (%) in year					
		(INS=0)			*(INS=1)*		
	Year	*1*	*2*	*3*	*1*	*2*	*3*
South Africa	1986	5	2	1	35	15	8
Libya	1986	2	1	0	17	6	3
Panama	1988	6	2	1	41	18	10

Although the discussion about the prospects of a specific sanction can be objectively evaluated in this way, it should be noted that the analysis starts from a very aggregated level. Often country-specific conditions such as the geographical location or the availability of raw materials and natural resources appear decisive. Hence additional analysis is needed of the specific characteristics of the target's decision process while its economic and political structures have to be taken into account as well.

Increasing the use of economic sanctions?
The New World Order both increases and decreases the effectiveness of economic sanctions. On the one hand the probability of political co-operation certainly has increased since the end of the superpower conflict. At the same time the extent of hindrance (that is third party support for the target) has decreased. While the empirical results suggest that both hindrance and co-operation do not significantly influence the success rate of economic sanctions, these changes in the international diplomatic arena may considerably enhance the success rate in specific cases. On the other hand the empirical results show that enhanced reliance on sanctions as an instrument in foreign policy will probably blunt negative sanctions as a diplomatic economic instrument. The findings suggest an initially positive influence from reputation on success, which turns negative after some threshold. This implies that a clear danger exists in excess, suggesting that using

sanctions too often may deprive the NWO of its ultimate non-violent instrument and, consequently, might trigger military interventionism. This clearly cannot be in support of international security. Consequently, economic diplomacy will have to be used with restraint. Only very serious infractions against international rules should be considered as a potential case for the use of sanctions. Most importantly, boycotts and embargoes should only be used when other non-military measures have failed or could be expected to fail, as enhanced reliance on economic sanctions entails some hidden costs too. Trade uncertainty arising from political interactions imposes substantial costs on the world economic system and reduces the extent of international specialization. Additional political costs will result since trade is an important incentive for international co-operation.

Notes

1. The success score's expected value for the case of randomly assigned scores for policy result and sanction contribution would be $(5/2)^2 = 6.25$. For a success score of 8, however, the sanction will be considered to have failed.
2. The authors seem to have realized the weaknesses in their regression techniques as the 'success equation' no longer appears in the second edition. This, however, does not solve the problem that partial regressions only give partial explanations and makes the present analysis the more necessary.
3. Of course there is always the loss of the economic yield of misconduct, but this cost in general can hardly be specified. In most cases the loss is completely immaterial (for example, loss of face).
4. Examples of this approach are Porter (1979) for South Africa and Bayard et al. (1983) for the East Block.
5. A formal model of dynamic expected utility of economic sanctions appears in Van Bergeijk and Van Marrewijk (1993).
6. In addition, *AREA* proxies the potential availability of (natural) resources and thus the target's dependence on external supply in general. This also points to a negative relationship between π and *AREA*.
7. The adjusted-R^2 is Lave's R^2 that corrects for degrees of freedom and is defined as

    $$\text{adjusted-}R^2 = 1 - N(1-R^2)/(N-K)$$

    where R^2 is Efron's R^2 that is defined as

$$R^2 = 1 - \{\Sigma(y_i - \pi_i)^2 / \Sigma(y_i - \mu)^2\}$$

Here K is the number of regressors, N is the number of observations and $\mu = \Sigma y_i / N$.

The F-statistic is

$$F = (N-K-1)R^2 / \{(K-1)(1-R^2).$$

8. In addition the 1968 US sanction case against Peru that Hufbauer, Schott and Elliott (1990) have coded as two separate cases (one a success, the other a failure) are wrongly predicted by the model. These errors, however, ultimately depend on the arbitrary classification in time and would disappear if the sequence were to be changed.

9. Another reason to opt for *PTL* in stead of *ATL* is that the results are comparable to an earlier investigation into the data set based on the first edition of *Economic Sanctions Reconsidered* (Van Bergeijk 1989a). The present empirical results are in agreement with these earlier findings for 1946—1983.

10. Martin (1992) has empirically investigated what factors determine international co-operation on economic sanctions using the Hufbauer, Schott and Elliott (1990) study. She presents empirical evidence that quite definitely refutes the hypothesis that declining hegemony affects the decision to co-operate with the sender.

11. Differentiate $\theta(5)$ with respect to *REP*. The first order condition can be rewritten as $\alpha - \beta REP = 0$. Assuming that the LOGIT estimates of $\theta(5)$ yield unbiased estimates of the coefficients α and $\beta/2$ and that the distribution is sufficiently normal, the variance of the ratio α/β can be approximated by:

$$\text{Var}(\alpha/\beta) = \text{Var}(\alpha)/\beta^2 + \alpha^2 \text{Var}(\beta)/\beta^4 - 2\alpha \text{Cov}(\alpha,\beta)/\beta^3$$

(see Kendall and Stuart 1977, pp. 246—7), so that the estimated variance of α/β can be used to determine a confidence interval.

12. Alternative indicators for the target's relative economic power, such as the target's GDP in constant purchasing power parity corrected dollars or the ratio of the sender's GNP over the target's GNP turned out insignificant as well.

Appendix: Data sources

As a general rule the data have been derived from the Hufbauer, Schott and Elliott (1990) study in order to prevent the number of sources from rising unacceptably. Additional sources, however, have been used as well and are listed below. Hufbauer, Schott and Elliott take economic data from well-know economic sources like the International Monetary Fund's *Direction of Trade* and *International Financial Statistics*. They derive other variables from contempory observations and historical reviews like *Keesing's Contempory Archives*.

Neither all observations nor all variables collected in the Hufbauer, Schott and Elliott study have been used. First, the analytical power decreases as the number of explanatory variables increases. Second, observations for both the First and Second World War and the *interbellum* seem less suitable because of both the special character of the period and the limited availability of data. The number of observations *N* further decreased from 103 to 92 because data on bilateral trade flows or national products were not available. For this reason, for example, the Chinese 1974 sanctions against Albania had to be excluded from the data set. In several additional calculations, the number of observations may reduce even further due to data deficiencies.

Sources

The Economist Books Ltd, 1990, *The Economist Book of Vital World Statistics: A Complete Guide to the World in Figures*, Hutchinson: London.

Eurostat, 1984, *Basisstatistieken*, Brussels.

   Hufbauer, G.C. and J.J. Schott, 1985, *Economic Sanctions Reconsidered: History and Current Policy*, Washington D.C., Appendix C, pp. 107—753.

Hufbauer, G.C., J.J. Schott and K.A. Elliott, 1990, *Economic Sanctions Reconsidered: History and Current Policy*, 2nd edition (2 volumes) Washington D.C., Appendix B and Supplemental Case Histories.

International Monetary Fund, 1977 and 1984, *Direction of Trade Statistics*, Washington D.C.

International Monetary Fund, 1950, 1960, 1961, 1971, 1980, 1982, 1986, 1992, *International Financial Statistics*, Washington. D.C.

Joint Economic Committee Congress of the United States, 1985, *East European Economies, Slow Growth in the 1980s* (Volume 1 Economic Performance and Policy: Selected Papers, Washington D.C., pp. 32, 33, 126, 144, 174.

Summers, R. and A. Heston, 1988, A new set of International Comparisons of Real Product and Prices: Estimates for 130 countries 1950—1985. *Review of Income and Wealth* 24 (1), pp.1—25.

United Nations Statistical Office, *Monthly Bulletin of Statistics*, 12/1956, 12/1960 and 5/1987.

United Nations Statistical Office, 1986, *National Account Statistics: Main Aggregates and Detailed Tables 1983*, New York.

World Bank, 1977, 1978, 1980 and 1981, *World Bank Atlas*, Washington D.C.

World Bank, 1976 and 1984, *World Tables*, Washington D.C.

PART II
DIPLOMATIC BARRIERS TO TRADE

5. Trade and Conflict

Economists often neglect the political dimension when they analyse the economic relations between countries. Their domain pre-eminently is international trade, capital flows, the transfer of technology and the co-ordination of macroeconomic policy, in sum the whole area where co-operation among countries yields higher welfare for all. One wonders whether this abstraction in the analysis is desirable. Relations between countries are just as unlikely to be permanently harmonious as personal relationships. Conflict seems to be a radical characteristic of human activity. Disregard of this dimension may yield deceptive results in the analysis of the international economic system. Still textbooks on international economics hardly deal with the impact of politics on international trade and investment patterns. Indeed it is difficult to find a textbook that warns the student of international economics that to 'attempt analysis of a *specific* international issue solely in economic terms is liable to result in some very silly conclusions' (the caveat is from Schiavo-Campo, 1978, pp. 7—8n).

The topic of Part I was the direct impact of the explicit diplomatic use of international economic relations through positive and negative sanctions. Part II will deal with the more subtle and indirect impact of variables that characterize the diplomatic climate in terms of co-operation and hostility. This chapter reviews earlier findings on the theoretical and empirical relationships between, on the one hand international trade and investment, and on the other hand international conflict and co-operation. The focus is on the influence exerted by the diplomatic climate on foreign trade, but we will also look into the twin question of the influence of trade on the diplomatic climate. Our knowledge about the trade—conflict relationship essentially derives from five sources. Since little is known, it pays to consider these sources in detail before developing a model in the next chapter and empirically investigating the trade—conflict relationship in Chapter 7.

The first source is the eighteenth and nineteenth century political economy literature in combination with some of the Marxist and development literature that remained outside the realm of mainstream neoclassical trade theory. The second source is the formal theoretical literature on the national defence tariff, that was essentially developed in the 1970s. The third source is the political science approach which deals with the impact of trade on political conflict and co-operation. The fourth source is a number of scattered empirical studies that follow up on Tinbergen's 1962 seminal analysis for the Twentieth Century Fund's study *Shaping the World Economy. Suggestions for an International Economic Policy*. Related to the fourth source is the empirical literature that deals with the impact of politics on international capital flows (lending and investment). Trade and capital are often related phenomena. Hence it may be useful to look into the relationship between, on the one hand international capital flows, and on the other hand co-operation and conflict as a fifth source on the trade—conflict relationship. The final section draws some conclusions and identifies a number of white spots in the literature.

5.1 The Political Dimension of International Trade Relations

It is often said that the theory of international economics on the whole tends to neglect the interactions between economic and political variables in the international sphere. Bailey and Lord (1988, p. 93), for example, state that 'no subject has been more unjustifiably ignored than the relationship of economics to national security.' According to Intrilligator (1987, p. 367), 'It is impossible to separate out and treat economic issues independently of political, military, and other issues. These concepts of global interdependence have yet to be analysed in a fundamental way...'. Frey (1984, p. 11) even asserts that 'the theory of international economics has as a whole refused to take into account the fact that political factors influence the international economy', while Spero (1977, p. 2) claims that 'politics and economics have been divorced from each other and isolated in analysis and theory'.

This is probably true for mainstream neoclassical ec/
exists, however, an old tradition of International Politic
the study of all conditions that affect the wealth and pov.
organized societies and the policy options of their governments
(Knorr 1975, p. *xi*). It is well beyond the scope of this chapter to
discuss the extensive literature on this subject, which has been
reviewed by Hirschman ([1945] 1980, esp. pp. 3—12), Kindleberger
(1970), Baldwin (1985, esp. pp. 70—95), Rosecrane (1986),
Hutchison (1988), Hont (1990), De Wilde (1991), etc. Neither is it
feasible to discuss the reasons for the trade economist's expulsion of
the political influence from his theory. Instead some highlights on the
topic will be discussed briefly.

For the founding fathers of international free trade theory,
political and economic relations were very much interrelated. The
domination of political considerations over free trade is already well-
established by Adam Smith. Smith ([1776] 1976, pp. 484—7) argues
for the necessity of trade regulation if national defence requires so:
defence is of much more importance than opulence. The influence of
political variables on international trade was recognized even by
Ricardo, who is sometimes seen as the archetype of the modern
neoclassical economist (Collini et al. 1983, pp. 56—7). Ricardo
([1820] 1962, p. 231) stressed the importance of political power for
the determination of the division of the gains from trade between the
motherland and her colonies. Indeed, Ricardo did pay a lot of
attention to the exogenous disturbances imposed by both war and
peace (Grampp 1987). Such alterations in the state of the
international system, Ricardo argued, cause considerable distress to
trade as this changes the optimal allocation of capital over sectors.
Essentially Ricardo was dealing with reallocation issues. He deemed
government intervention a prerequisite for this process since capital
would have been allocated in the previous period in directions 'from
which (one) is unable to withdraw without the sacrifice of a great part
of (one's) capital' (Ricardo [1871] 1962, p. 177). So Ricardo's
Principles of Political Economy and Taxation often deals with
political power and questions related to peace and war. The same is
true for John Stuart Mill. Mill ([1840] 1968, p. 594) believed in
contradistinction to Smith (who argued that foreign trade enriches a
country and that this helps its defence) that intensified international

economic relations would reduce the incentives for conflicts among nations:

> It is commerce which is rendering war obsolete, by strengthening and multiplying the personal interests which are in natural opposition to it.

Here we find a reason why trade economists might not be interested in problems related to war and peace. If commerce can supersede war, specialization probably pays. So analyse and stimulate free trade as pure economists and secure peace as a by-product. Schumpeter (1954, pp. 766—7) points out that around 1870 many observers implicitly and explicitly expected 'the victory of those principles and practices of foreign policy that are associated with free trade, such as the settlement of disputes by mutual concessions or arbitration, reduction of armaments ... and the like.'[1] Friedman and Friedman (1980, pp. 43—4) still hold this position. A less naive proposition is that the probability of conflict between countries, as opposed to co-operation, can be reduced by intensifying economic relations (see, for example the discussion on the work of Polachek in section 5.3). Anyhow, neoclassical theory which dominates mainstream economics, generally speaking, hardly ever reflects on the politics of trade.

The belief — shared by classical and neoclassical economists — that intensified economic ties could be the basis of peaceful relationships between countries at first sight makes economic analysis of co-operation and conflict unnecessary. It is almost as if economists should do their job and focus on ways to secure free trade and full employment. Not all economists, however, would agree although these topics never have become an issue in the general economic discourse. Although their example was hardly followed by the profession, individual economists have often been involved in economic analysis of questions related to conflict and co-operation.

Keynes, for example, took some risks, both financially and with regard to his career, in publishing his *Economic Consequences of the Peace* ([1919] 1984). He was well aware of the aridity of economic science with respect to his topic. Keynes ([1936] 1986, pp. 380—2) was especially concerned with finding solutions for the war problem in terms of demand management, pointing out the economic causes of war: pressure of population and the competitive struggle for markets.

But if nations can learn to provide themselves with full employment by
their domestic policy ..., there need be no important economic forces
calculated to set the interest of one country against that of its neighbours
(.. and) there would no longer be a pressing motive why one country need
force its wares on another ....

Marx introduced a new analytic framework subjecting historical
events, such as wars and social institutions, to the explanatory
process of economic analysis. Marxism treats these factors not as
exogenous variables or data (the usual approach in economics), but as
endogenous variables (Schumpeter [1943] 1966, p. 47). Although
Marx did not put a meaning to wars-between-states as a phase in the
development of capitalism, Marx and Engels ([1848] 1928, p. 14) did
recognize that modern industry needed more and larger markets
(especially in undeveloped countries) both as an outlet for its
production and to supply raw materials. They did not deal with the
struggle between nations in their major work (Maclean 1988), but
they were fascinated by military technology and tactics and Marx
dealt with the war topic in a lot of newspaper articles. Using Marx's
box of tools, others developed the theory of imperialism. The Marxist
point of view on international relations has to a large extent been
influenced by Hobson's *Imperialism* ([1902] 1988).

Imperialism seeks to explain war-like tendencies amongst the
major capitalist countries around the turn of the century on the basis
of the growing economic and political power of large private
companies, typically exercised over less developed countries. The
discovery of economies of scale caused a top-heavy production
apparatus in the industrialized world and lead to such a superfluous
supply of goods that the domestic market could no longer absorb
domestic production. Hence international markets had to be won in
order to create the necessary outlet. This meant colonization as a
defence against the competition from other capitalist countries that
have identical problems at home. The resulting clash of commercial
interests *notwendigerweise* results in a more or less permanent war
threat.

Schumpeter heavily criticized the theory of imperialism: 'the more
completely capitalist the structure and attitude of a Nation, the more
pacifist — and the more prone to count the costs of war — we
observe it to be' (Schumpeter [1943] 1966, pp. 128—9).

Interestingly, moreover, leading communists also pointed out the possibility that commercial relationships might help establish peaceful political relations among countries. Lenin ([1920] 1967, p. 90) stressed the benefits of attracting foreign direct investments from the West:

> We shall thus gain a lot and make it difficult for capitalist powers that enter into deals with us to take part in military action against us, because war cancels everything, and should one break out we shall get possession of all the buildings, installations and railways.

Bernstein, the father of Revisionism, was an outspoken supporter of free trade (see Hyrkkanen, 1987). He argued that the struggle against protectionism should be a socialist principle and that the international exchange of goods and services should be the basis for a network of mutual interests and interdependencies as an antidote against 'aggressive' imperialism.

The end of the Second World War started the era of decolonization. While political colonization visibly ended some authors contended that formal dependence was replaced by *de facto* economic colonization. The literature on this 'new' imperialism or neocolonialism is relevant because the politics are so obvious in this theory of the world economic system. Explaining the global pattern of international specialization is one of the main tasks of this so-called structuralist approach. In addition economically exploitative relations are seen to give rise to violence, military take-overs and political repression. As an outgrowth of Marxist thinking by amongst others Baran and Sweezy, *dependencia* or centre-periphery theories invaded economic thought via the work of Prebisch, the first Secretary-General of UNCTAD. The literature is vast; I will be brief and deal with the basic issue only.[2] *Dependencia* theory argues that fundamental structural disadvantages limit the scope for growth in the developing countries. Income elasticities, for example, in the rich 'centre' are low with respect to their export products, so that an increase in export volume will result in terms of trade losses. The upshot is that these structural impediments will continue unless appropriate policy measures are taken. This focuses attention on the international political power structure and on political efforts to change international institutions. *Dependencia* theory inspired the movement toward a New International Economic Order (NIEO) in 1974. The four main issues of that NIEO were renegotiation of debts, market access at favourable trade conditions, reform of the IMF and compliance with UN targets for development assistance. Ironically, neo-Marxists see aid as a means opening up a developing country so that 'exploitation' by the centre can begin. Radical Marxists contend that aid, like trade, is an instrument for the centre's control and profit only.

Anyhow, neo-Marxism remained quite peripherical in economics as the neoclassical paradigm prevailed. The lack of attention for political factors, however, has increasingly become a bottleneck for the creation of relevant economic knowledge. Weck-Hannemann and Frey (1992, p. 31) argue that political forces must be taken into account if one moves from the theoretical world of perfect competition and frictionless exchange to reality. This aspect however, has been neglected in the established international trade theory. Interestingly, Bhagwati (1991, p. *xvi*) in the introduction to the fifth volume of his collected writings complains:

> Economics and politics are natural bedfellows: How can we possibly explain what happens unless we bring in the political equations into our modelling at the same time.

Since the early 1990s the scientific community seems to have accepted the challenge with the revival of the international political economy approach and the start of scientific journals like *Economics and Politics* which provides an important outlet (and consequently a major stimulus) for analytic work and scientific progress.

5.2 National Defence Tariff Theories

The national defence argument is often classified as one of the so-called non-economic reasons for government intervention in foreign trade. In general economists accept the validity of such policies on national security grounds. GATT, for example, embodies this exception to the free trade principle in article XXI that explicitly allows countries to invoke security considerations to refuse disclosure of sensitive information, and to impose import and export controls. In addition article XXI allows GATT contracting parties to take appropriate (trade-related) actions in pursuance of their obligations under the UN Charter for the maintenance of international peace and security.[3] Adam Smith ([1776] 1976, p. 484) has already noted that a case would seem to exist in which

> it will generally be advantageous to lay some burden upon foreign (trade), for the encouragement of domestic industries (namely) when some particular sort of industry is necessary for the defence of the country.

Often trade-related measures are justified by pointing out that trade may improve on the adversary's military capabilities. This justification, however, as it is based on the strategic use of foreign trade, clearly belongs to the domain of negative economic sanctions which has already been discussed in Part I. The national defence considerations that will be considered in this section deem the free trade outcome suboptimal because specialization in the 'wrong' kind of good reduces the skills and goods that are considered vital for the nation's defence capability. What is at stake then is the need to secure a minimal level of economic activity in terms of either production in key industries (for example aerospace), consumption of dual-use goods (such as computers) or certain skills. Trade intervention, however, is in these cases clearly a second-best policy. Standard theory shows that it is most efficient to subsidize output, consumption and schooling in order to internalize the national defence externality (Srinivasan 1987). In addition the practical applicability of the national defence argument can be questioned because of the very substantial information requirement for knowing how to cure the market failure, identifying the precise source of the policy problem or to establish the probable length of an embargo (Helpman 1987).

Consequently theoretical (or formal) interest in political factors shaping trade relations has remained rather limited. An interesting literature, however, developed in the second half of the 1970s. This highly formalized literature deals with policy responses to the threat of market disruption and shows that the classification of the national defence tariff as a non-economic phenomenon is inappropriate since such a tariff can be justified on criteria that are related to economic efficiency. Essentially this new approach argues that the costs of an abrupt change in the production pattern that is forced upon an economy when trade is blocked suddenly, may be so high that it may be a wise policy to limit the international division of labour to some extent.

In their seminal 1976 article Bhagwati and Srinivasan examine the optimal policy intervention required in an exporting country when there is a possibility of a market-disruption-induced trade restriction being invoked by the importing country. They use a traditional general equilibrium model in the 2 goods × 2 countries × 2 periods setting. Bhagwati and Srinivasan investigate how first-period (free trade) actions may influence outcomes in the second period that is characterized by trade disruption. Such actions comprise of investment to create second-period production capacity and the first-period allocation of the factors of production over the various sectors if reallocation takes time and/or is costly. They also analyse the possibility of an endogenous probability of trade disruption, for example, if this probability depends on the volume of trade in the first period. Their subject is trade disruption in general so that this kind of endogeneity seems to be a reasonable assumption: so-called Voluntary Export Restraints, for example, are more likely to be imposed when import volumes are considerable. So some self-restraint may be useful in preventing trade disruption in the near future.

Mayer (1977) deals with a country's optimal trade policy when embargoes and other trade interruptions are threatening, while individual consumers and producers have imperfect foresight. Actually, Mayer assumes that economic subjects believe that the relative price structure will not change. Given the perceptions of the policy maker an optimal pre-embargo (second-best) tariff and a pre-embargo (first-best) subsidy can be calculated. Unfortunately, Mayer leaves the central question unanswered of why government officials in this setting provide better estimations of the probability of trade disruption *vis-à-vis* their private sector counterparts.

Optimal policy choices, moreover, depend on the behaviour of both individual consumers and individual producers. It seems reasonable to assume that the costs of trade disruptions will be internalized by economic units that trade with foreign economic units. Tolley and Wilman (1977) use a partial equilibrium framework to analyse the impact of an expectation of trade disruption which may be expressed in terms of both an embargo frequency and a probability distribution of embargo length. The expectation of trade disruption should lead to private adjustments to specialize to a lesser extent in accordance with comparative advantage and hence to restrict the potential for foreign trade. An embargo leads to unequal long-run marginal value responses in consumption and production. This is so because embargo losses result from individual behaviour along short-run curves. These short-run curves determine the scope for individual action at a given point in time. The position of the short-run curves, however, depends on the long-run equilibrium quantity. Hence a rationale for government intervention emerges if private decisions do not internalize the potential embargo losses. Unfortunately the analysis of Tolley and Wilman is restricted to the consequences of decreasing possibilities to import and neglects the effects in the exporting sector of the economy. Moreover, they do not make clear whether or not private decision-making is superior to collective action. I will return to these questions in the next chapter.

Several authors have investigated specific policy measures such as strategic stockpiles, which may be a viable option for non-perishable goods if these goods are both difficult to produce and essential for either the economy or the defence sector. The analysis boils down to a trade-off between the certain cost of the stockpile and the uncertain benefits if this stockpile is available during emergencies (Bergström et al., 1985). An additional gain may be that the stockpile counteracts market power or helps to prevent price hikes due to unexpected supply shocks. An example is the case of the strategic oil reserves that OECD-countries hold since the 1973 oil crisis. These strategic reserves proved to be very useful in 1990 in reducing the economic impact of the political supply shock during the Iraq crisis.

5.3 Conflict and Trade

In the early 1980s Solomon Polachek initiated a new research strategy on the topic of how the volume of bilateral trade and the extent of conflict between nations may be related. His approach starts from a different perspective — unlike the present chapter the title of Polachek's influential 1980 article puts the word 'conflict' first, hence inverting the suggested causality.[4] While the findings of this line of analysis may improve our understanding of the problems at hand, the causality is a matter of ongoing debate (see, for example Pollins 1989b and Sayrs 1988a and 1990). The main virtue of the new research agenda is its orientation from the start on vigorous empirical investigations.

Polachek's approach especially appealed to political scientists, probably because it fits in a tradition that goes back to Richardson's (1960) well-known analysis of the impact of trade on arms races. Polachek starts from the assumption that a rational utility maximizing government will take the potential impact of its diplomatic and military activities on its international trade and investment flows into account in the decisions that a country has to make about its foreign relations:

> Specifically, if conflict leads to a diminution of trade, then one implicit cost of conflict is the lost welfare gains associated with trade. Ceteris paribus, the rational actor would engage in smaller amounts of conflict the greater the associated potential welfare loss. In short, trade enhances co-operation and deters conflict.[5]

Polachek justifies his assertion with a standard neoclassical trade model in which maximizing material welfare is the nation's policy goal. From an economist's point of view the crucial assumption would seem to be that conflict leads to terms of trade losses.[6] At first sight this hypothesis seems reasonable: more conflict makes trade difficult because of retaliatory measures such as tariffs, quotas, embargoes and other prohibitions to trade and investment. Unfortunately, this link between the terms of trade and conflict is an assumption only that so far has not been tested. Indeed the fact that conflict influences potential trade in an *ex ante* sense may prohibit the proper identification of such a relationship from the actual *ex post* observations. Guided by his formal model, Polachek estimates reduced-form equations in which the dependent variable is the diplomatic climate and the explanatory variables are bilateral trade flows and country attributes such as population, schooling, economic activity and defence expenditures.

The main weakness of this approach lies in the assumption that politicians include in their decisions the implicit (and often invisible) costs and benefits of diplomatic activity in terms of both trade and investment opportunities, whereas these shadow costs of political behaviour appear in the real world to be hardly ever considered. Another weakness is that Polachek wants to consider 'net' conflict, although conflict and co-operation are not simply two sides of the same coin. This particular assumption that conflict and co-operation can be aggregated into one meaningful indicator was first made in Richardson's seminal 1960 study on arms race modelling. It leads Polachek to use an index measure for the overall conflict between any pair of trade partners. This index, the so-called net frequency of conflict, is defined as the frequency of conflictual events minus the frequency of co-operative events. According to Sayrs (1988a, p.5), the result of such linear blending has been to

> discern effects for trade which are based on an underlying false continuity. The net conflict measure (conflict minus co-operation) widely used in this literature not only obscures differences in the effect of trade on co-operation as distinct from conflict, but the measure disregards the actual relationship between conflict and co-operation, i.e., they are not reciprocal behaviors.

These critical remarks, however, should not deny the major strength of the conflict and trade approach, namely its consistent finding of a negative relationship between net conflict and trade, both across methodologies and for very different periods and countries. Moreover, the findings of the conflict—trade literature increase our awareness of the problems posed by causality: does trade influence diplomacy; or does the chain of causation run the other way around?

Several attempts have been made to redo the Polachek approach deploying other indicators, weighing schemes, etc. Table 5.1 summarizes the findings of these conflict and trade studies. The table reports the elasticities of net conflict between a pair of nations with respect to their bilateral trade flows.

Gasiorowski (1986) points out some methodological flaws in Polachek's empirical analysis, mainly about the definition and measurement of the variables. Polachek uses simple counts of hostile and friendly events for the construction of his net conflict measure and the dollar value of imports and exports for the trade variable. Both measures may introduce a bias in cross-sectional investigations creating a statistical artefact when events in important nations are deemed more newsworthy. This implies that the size of an economy may be positively correlated with both the volume of trade and the number of counted events. Gasiorowski's main point, however, is that theory is ambiguous about the impact of trade on the diplomatic climate.[7] Yes, the gains from trade may provide an important incentive to limit conflict. At the same time, however, trade may create diplomatic problems, for example, between the United States and Japan over Japanese cars or between the EC and the United States over agriculture. Correcting for the methodological problems by using relative instead of absolute values, Gasiorowski finds (p. 36) that 'trade interconnectedness is associated with a decline in conflict only when its costly effects have been controlled for'.

Table 5.1 Percentage reduction in net conflict due to a 1 per cent increase in trade

Source	Period	Number of coun-tries	Conflict elasticity with respect to		
			Trade	*Export*	*Import*
Polachek (1980)	1958-67	30		0.19	0.19
	1958-67[a]	30		0.15	0.15
	1958-67[b]	30		0.36	0.31
Gasiorowski (1986)	1960-77	44	0.33[c]		
Lundborg (1988)	1946-81	157	0.30		
Polachek (1992)	1958-67	105		0.19	0.19
	1948-78[a]	105		0.15	0.15
	1948-78[b]	105		0.36	0.31
Polachek *e.a.* (1992)	1973	14	0.47	0.28	0.50
	1973[d]	14		0.12	0.35

Notes [a] including country attributes
[b] two and three stages least squares
[c] standardized regression coefficient
[d] manufactured goods only.

Lundborg (1988) analyses 5,246 roll-casts in the United Nations General Assembly for the years 1946—1981.[8] He finds that the effects of both US and Soviet trade with single member countries yields significant results. More trade increases the probability of agreement on the issues that are brought to the fore in the General Assembly. Interestingly, the elasticities of trading with the Soviet Union are considerably higher than the corresponding elasticities of trading with the United States.

Both the conflict—trade approach and the trade—conflict analysis (that will be studied next) have found a place in the GLOBUS model (Bremer 1987, see also Isard 1988, pp. 322—6). This world simulation model deals with a subset of 25 large countries and was designed to analyse politico—economic problems such as East—West political relations, alternative economic orders, the North—South gap, domestic political stability, etc. Unfortunately, this comprehensive modelling effort appears to be rather insensitive with respect to the impact on trade of major changes in the global political context. Cohen et al. (1992), for example, use GLOBUS to investigate the consequences of *détente* and find that the political—economic developments in the exchanges between East and West do not lead to significant changes in economic variables. Indeed, according to Cohen et al. (1992, p. 160), this

> raises questions whether the original objectives of GLOBUS, in terms of modelling the interaction between economics and politics, were fully fulfilled.

5.4 Empirical Findings on the Trade—Politics Relationship

Although the research output on the topic of the impact of international politics on trade is probably best characterized as meagre, a number of investigators have dealt with the empirical question of the influence of politics on trade. Since we have very little systematic knowledge about this important question and because the available findings may serve as a basis of comparison when I present my own findings in Chapter 7, these studies will be dealt with in some detail.

Using dummy variables for preferential and semi-preferential trade relations in a so-called gravity model of international trade, Tinbergen (1962, p. 288) found substantial 'colonial or ex-colonial' trade multipliers. Tinbergen himself appears to have been a bit puzzled by the actual size of the political trade multiplier, that, however, is a consistent finding in alternative specifications and data sets. Tinbergen attempts different valuation methods for GNP and derives the value of bilateral export flows not only from the trade statistics of the exporting countries, but uses the import statistics of the countries of destination as well. His data set is for 1959 and covers about 70 per cent of world trade. It comprises 42 countries, which include developing nations and 16 major OECD countries. Tinbergen starts from a model in which only economic variables play a role. Noting that the correlation coefficient is not high — about 0.8, which leaves at least 35 per cent of the variance of exports essentially unexplained — Tinbergen sets out to identify deviations between the actual observed pattern of trade and the normal ('ideal' or 'theoretical') trade pattern that could be expected on the basis of economic variables such as GNP and distance. Tinbergen estimates the trade-increasing effects of adjacency at about 75 per cent of the normal trade volume. The trade-stimulating effect of preferential treatment is estimated to yield 'colonial or ex-colonial' trade multipliers of ten, indicating that colonial ties give rise to ten times the usual trade volume. The line of this research programme is a typical example of the 'overlapping generations approach' in which Ph.D. students become supervisors themselves, so that generations of academics can continue to work on the original problem. Tinbergen's associate and doctoral student Linnemann, for example, whose 1966 publication has become the standard reference on the gravity model in international trade, is the tutor of Bikker who wrote a thesis on the subject in 1982. The latter, incidentally, in a recent study asserts that the preferences based on colonial ties from the past have become weaker in the course of time (Bikker, 1987, p. 330).[9]

Roemer (1977) investigates trade patterns using area and sector intensities for 43 sectors of manufactured goods. The investigation focuses on the United States, Japan, the United Kingdom, Germany and Canada *vis-à-vis* fourteen areas of the world in the year 1971. A trade intensity relates the share of country A in country B's import market to country B's share in the imports of the rest of the world, and reveals, so to say, the relative preference of country B for the products of country A. Trade intensities are calculated for total (bilateral) trade flows, for manufactured goods only and for specific industries. What emerges from the calculations is a biased sectoral pattern of trade in manufacturing — the five countries typically tend to market their weak sectors disproportionately in their strong areas.

Roemer looks into two types of market imperfections that may explain the biased sectoral pattern, namely transportation costs (distance) and sphere of influence causes that reflect historical and political factors (for example, better communication channels, preferential tariffs, tied aid, tastes and the activities of multinational subsidiaries). Roemer finds that trade intensities in the Western world cannot be explained solely by economic factors, but must result in part from causes that are in the narrow sense not economic. Indeed, according to Roemer (1977, p. 327), trade intensity may be part of

> (an) imperial legacy, whereby former colonies remain bound to their mother countries through ties of culture, communications and influences of various sorts. In some cases these ties may be concretely observable in tariff structures or exchange controls (...or tied aid); in other cases the mechanism may be ... more subtle embodied in utility functions.

All in all, sphere of influence effects, in this study, appear important in explaining trade intensities and in the case of the United Kingdom they are even absolutely more important than transportation costs.

Pollins (1989b) sets out to test the empirical relevance of incorporating a measure of diplomatic relations into a 25-nation gravity model of international trade for 16 annual cross-sectional estimations for the years 1960—1975.[10] The investigation covers eighty per cent of world trade. In addition to traditional economic variables such as GDP, prices and distances, Pollins includes dummy variables for GATT-membership and for 'intra-trade' by members of regional trade organizations, such as the EC, Comecon and the Latin American Free Trade Association (LAFTA). His major innovation is the inclusion of a diplomatic climate indicator based on political events that have been collected in the COPDAB-data set. The theoretical justification for this assumption is meagre. According to Pollins (1989b, p. 741), political factors should be included in the utility function because of 'very traditional security concerns, the desire to reward friends, to punish adversaries, and to minimize risk'. Pollins decides to combine conflict and co-operation into one 'net' indicator, rather than to include these flows of diplomatic exchanges individually, because of strong covariation and since a net indicator represents the general tone or climate that he contends to be of importance for the development and direction of international trade flows. Pollins's weighed co-operation index W_{ij} represents the 'amount' of co-operation sent by county i to country j and is defined as $W_{ij} = C_{ij} \times C_{ij}/(C_{ij} + H_{ij})$, where C is the 'amount' of co-operation and H is the 'amount' of hostility. Pollins's indicator, however, is logically flawed as it is included in a multiplicative way, implying that trade is only possible if some sort of political co-operation takes place. Indeed in his model a positive trade flow formally requires $C > 0$, which may or may not be the case.

In his 1989a article, Pollins builds a traditional import demand equation of bilateral trade flows on the basis of a public choice approach. In this model the same summary indicator of international conflict and co-operation is included. The import demand equation is estimated for Egypt, India, the Soviet Union, East and West Germany and the United States *vis-à-vis* 24 trade partners for the years 1955—1978. Most interestingly, the investigation suggests the possibility of differences in the way countries manage their trade relations. The effect of diplomatic co-operation in East Germany and the Soviet Union, for example, is at least twice as large as it is in West Germany and the United States. Unfortunately, Pollins's econometrics are clouded by a desire to produce nation-specific equations that link levels of trade to levels of co-operation. This by-product of a related modelling effort for the GLOBUS world model unnecessarily introduces substantial problems related to heteroscedasticity and autocorrelations that could have easily been prevented if rates of change instead of levels had been used. Anyhow, in both studies Pollins finds that the relative co-operation and hostility of bilateral political ties does affect trade flows, that the importance of these ties is as large as economic variables such as prices and that the estimates are robust and warrant inclusion on both statistical and theoretical grounds.

Summary (1989) develops a gravity type model for the United States *vis-à-vis* 66 trading partners, including 40 developing countries, 15 OECD countries, five oil exporters and six Warsaw Pact countries. Semi-economic and international political factors, such as arms transfers from member countries of the North Atlantic Treaty Organization and the number of foreign agents registered in the United States, appear significant enhancement factors in export and import equations for the United States in the years 1978 and

1982. The estimated equations explain 80 per cent of US exports and 60 per cent of US imports. The elasticities for the significant semi-political determinants of exports and imports range between 0.2 for US arms transfers to 0.3 for the number of foreign agents. The number of US civilian government employees in the trade partner's country was significant only in the export equations with an elasticity of about 0.2. The political (or human) rights situation in the trade partner's country did not significantly influence the flow of trade. Although Summary's results are representative only for the United States and do not allow for the separation of semi-economic from political factors, the study shows that 'pure' economic factors are not the only determinants of US trade.

A substantial empirical literature recently developed on the policy relevant question of the impact of *détente* on the trade potential of Central Europe, giving credence to the assumption that the change of diplomatic climate between East and West will result in substantial improvements in trade orientation and performance in the formerly Centrally Planned Economies. Examples of these studies — that typically deploy gravity-type trade models with dummy variables that mimic political barriers in the bilateral trade flows between East and West — are Van Bergeijk and Oldersma (1990), Havrylyshyn and Pritchett (1991), Wang and Winters (1991), Döhrn and Milton (1992), Ezran *et al.* (1992) and Hamilton and Winters (1992). These studies show substantial improvements of the world trade potential and important shifts in global trade patterns. Havrylyshyn and Pritchett (1991), for example, establish that a revolution is also to be expected in the geographic pattern of trade by the mid-European countries. In the past 60 — 80 per cent of their activities focused on the Comecon partners and only about 20 — 30 per cent on Northern and Western Europe. According to this World Bank study, however, the natural trading pattern is exactly the reverse. The upshot of such studies is that the conflict-era of the Cold War imposed substantial costs on the economies both in the East and in the West, reducing trade well below 'normal' levels, so that the end of conflict may substantially enhance trade.

5.5 Capital, Conflict and Co-operation

Stability, both economic and political, is often a prerequisite for obtaining private foreign funds. Political factors have long been considered important by bankers and international investors. Bankers probably are most sensitive to political risks.[11] Indeed most banks have large departments that assess the extent of country risk (Cataquet 1985). Two econometric studies support the banks' sensitivity with respect to political factors in particular. Citron and Nickelsburg (1987) find that the number of changes of government, which proxies domestic political instability, significantly influences the probability that a debtor country defaults on its foreign loans. Balkan (1992) shows that the level of democracy reduces the probability of default. As in the case of trade and conflict, causality may be ambiguous with respect to capital flows as Balkan (1992, p. 1004) concludes that 'efforts to support democratic movements in (developing countries) would contribute to stability of the international financial system'.

Foreign direct investment is another area of decision-making in internationally operating firms that acknowledges the importance of political factors. Schneider and Frey (1985) give a review of two literatures: the 'much politics, little economics' approach to foreign direct investment and the 'much economics, little politics' school. No clear picture, however, emerges from their review of these early econometric investigations. So Schneider and Frey proceed to assess by means of a politico-economic model what role economic and political factors play for 31 countries in the years 1976, 1979 and 1980. Bilateral aid appears to provide strong political incentives and disincentives to invest. It stimulates the flow of foreign direct investments for Western aid, but the impact is negative if communist countries provide aid to the potential recipient country. Political instability is also a significant barrier to foreign direct investment. Maizels and Nissanke (1986) investigate military expenditures in 83 developing countries with cross-sections for the years 1978 and 1980. They find that whereas foreign exchange availability acts as a constraint to military expansion programmes, foreign capital penetration is negatively correlated to military expenditure. This, according to the authors, suggests that multinational corporations prefer to invest in countries with low levels of both instability and defence expenditures. Although they are careful not to draw any conclusion about the implied invalidity of the *dependencia* school argument, Maizels and Nissanke (1986, p. 1133) state that 'it would seem that the opposite view is more generally applicable'.

All in all private capital flows appear to be to a large extent correlated with international and domestic political variables. It is, however, not only private lending and investment that is influenced by political factors. The activities of the multilateral institutions appear to be governed by political considerations as well. Frey and Schneider (1986) test four competing models for the World Bank's lending behaviour. The models are informal and heuristic: they mainly describe assumptions about the relevance and assumed influence of subsets of possible explanatory variables. Their first model assumes that World Bank lending aims at those countries in greatest need of official foreign finance. This 'needs' model links World Bank credits to indicators for poverty, scarcity of real resources and the strain of demand on foreign resources. Their second model assumes that World Bank credits go to countries with large potential for development. This 'deserts' model takes credit-worthiness into account and focuses on indicators of economically and financially responsible behaviour.[12] Their next model (called the 'benevolence' model) starts from the official World Bank charter which states that the World Bank is a multilateral non-political organization. Hence the variables of the pure neoclassical model appear in the quasi-reduced form equations in combination with a dummy variable that captures the organization's hypothesized preference for a capitalistic climate. The fourth model is 'politico-economic' and deals with both internal and external political motives. With this model Frey and Schneider study the role of bureaucratic, possibly game-theoretic, motives. Next to these political considerations of top officials in the World Bank the model looks at variables that in a technical sense determine capital requirements and lending capacity. Frey and Schneider use the four models to explain the patterns of World Bank loans and International Development Assistance with combined cross sections/time series for 60 developing countries in the period 1972—1981. Although some important partial derivatives (for example, with respect to external debt) may convey mistaken information, the politico-economic model performs best in the econometric tests. The results suggest that decision-making in the World Bank is — often informally — influenced by political donor—recipient relationships, such as former colonial ties, economic dependence and trade linkage. The conclusion is that students of international capital flows will have to take international political variables into account if they want to produce a useful description of their topic.

5.6 White Spots

Perhaps the reader will be impressed by the amount of empirical and theoretical evidence that was presented for the existence of a relationship between international economics and international politics. In particular the rich literatures of the 'old' international political economy, the studies on the economic national defence tariff and the conflict and trade approach seem to provide an important underpinning for the empirical investigations that were discussed.

More probably, however, the reader will be amazed that it is indeed necessary to present such arguments to the scientific economic community. It is common-sense that economics and politics are inseparable in the real world. Reading one's newspaper or listening to international bankers, businessmen and investors would seem to provide ample evidence as well, and probably in less time and in a more accessible way.

Modesty, however, is more appropriate. First, most research is clearly on-going. Many questions remain unanswered, while at the same time discontinuity is an important characteristic of this subject, as research efforts appear to be rather scattered with respect to both time and place. Second, the theoretical underpinning of the trade—conflict relationship is not completely convincing (at least not to economists, especially if they are trained in the neoclassical tradition). Third, the relevance of the empirical findings may be questioned as most research is dated, deals with regularities that relate to the 1960s and 1970s, or focuses on a limited subset of (especially large) countries. Fourth, behaviourial differences between countries and different types of transactions are neglected.

Obviously it is impossible to fill all the blank spots, but it would seem worthwhile to explore these questions a little further in the rest of Part II, as the impact of politics on trade may be especially relevant for the economics of the New World Order. The next chapters will attempt to make some progress as they develop a formal model of uncertain trade and investigate empirically the impact of conflict and co-operation on the exports and imports of 40 countries in the year 1986.

Notes

1. See also Kennedy (1989, p. 158) on this particular view on the world economic and political systems.
2. The reader may wish to consult Griffin and Gurley (1985) or Södersten (1980) pp. 165—63 and 243—58 for a more critical review.
3. A rigorous discussion of the national security exceptions in GATT appears in Carter (1988, pp. 95—8 and 131—40).
4. See, for example, Erickson (1975) for an early study on the possible simultaneity of trade and diplomacy.
5. Polachek and McDonald (1992), p. 273.
6. See, however, Sayrs (1990) for a political scientist's perspective. She signals three assumptions that may be crucial as well. These assumptions are that the state is a unitary actor, that domestic policies can be treated as a constant and that conflict and co-operation can be derived from the same utility calculus.
7. Compare Keohane and Nye (1977).
8. See Richardson (1978) for an early study on the impact of dependence on UN voting behaviour.
9. See in this respect also Anderson and Norheim (1993) on the European switch from imperial to regional trade.
10. The order of publication would seem to contradict the order of origination. In this discussion I follow the order in which Pollins appears to have written the articles, rather than the order in which he got his research output published.
11. See, however, for a very instructive view on actual banking practices — and other forms of human ostrich attitudes: Guttentag and Herring (1986).
12. A comparable 'deserts' model for private bank lending is Lensink and Van Bergeijk (1991).

6. Trade Uncertainty, Specialization and Trade Volume

Foreign traders have to deal with uncertainty. Relative prices and exchange rates are characterized by high volatility. Government interventions in foreign trade are widespread. Clearly, this creates uncertainty concerning foreign trade conditions that must influence the desired amount of international trade and the extent and pattern of specialization among nations. This chapter investigates a particular kind of uncertainty, namely uncertainty about the trade regime for a small country, in order to formalize the trade—conflict relationship in the context of the neoclassical trade model. This uncertainty about the volume of trade is assumed to result from the diplomatic interactions between nation states. The analytic method, however, can be more generally applied to situations where uncertainty pertaining to a stochastic trade regime characterizes the course of international exchange.

Uncertainty has formally been introduced in economic trade models by assuming, amongst others, state dependence of endowments, preferences, technology and prices (see Pomery 1984 for an overview of modelling strategies). Most theoretical papers in international economics that deal with uncertainty follow the seminal article by Ruffin (1974) and focus on relative prices as the source of uncertainty in trade.

Uncertainty concerning the traded quantities, however, appears equally important. Tariffs, quotas, boycotts and embargoes may be imposed unexpectedly. Likewise, market shares can be lost in a short lapse of time. Indeed, as will become clear in due course, recognition of the fact that it is often quantity rather than price which is uncertain for a small open economy, allows for a versatile modelling strategy. The assumption of uncertain quantities answers the critique by Helpman and Razin (1978) concerning the difference between *ex ante* and *ex post* trading decisions. In the *ex ante* trading approach decisions about exports and/or imports are made before the resolution of uncertainty, which does not seem very logical. Admittedly, in the real world decisions on the domestic pattern of specialization usually have to be made before world market prices (and quantities) are known, but to fix international exchange in advance as well seems unnecessarily restrictive.

Since the international price level is given for the small economy the shortcoming of the traditional *ex ante* analysis, which assumes that trading decisions are made before prices are known can easily be avoided.[1] In the model the economy a priori decides on the pattern of specialization, but a trade commitment will only be made once the uncertainty concerning trading possibilities is resolved. As we deal with a small economy, the *ex ante* trade volume can always be realized at the prevailing world market price if the free trade regime is the actual state of the world. Obviously, in isolation the trade volume is zero. Hence, given either state of the world, there is no inconsistency between *ex ante* and *ex post* trade.

The investigation will also deal with different types of the decision-making spectrum and look at decisions made by 'omniscient central planners' in a command economy and by firms and consumers in liberal democratic market economies, thus illustrating that differences in trade—conflict patterns may be due to differences in economic policy making.

6.1 An Expected Utility Model of Uncertain Trade

This chapter studies a small open economy that produces, consumes and trades two goods, x and y. This economy derives utility, u, from the consumed quantities C_x of good x and C_y of good y. The utility of a specific combination (x, y) can be described by a utility function $u = u(C_x, C_y)$ which is strictly concave and has the usual properties $u_{C_x} > 0$ and $u_{C_y} > 0$ (subindices of functions refer to derivatives). The efficient production combinations (x, y) are described by a production possibilities frontier (or transformation curve) $y = \varphi(x)$ which is defined on the interval $[0, x_m]$, where x_m is the maximum attainable production of good x (that is in the case of full specialization in x and given the endowments of land, labour and capital and the available production technology). The production possibilities frontier has the usual property of diminishing opportunity costs so that $\varphi_x<0$ and $\varphi_{xx}<0$.

The assumption that the economy is small implies in this model that the international relative price p is exogenous and certain $(p=p_y/p_x)$. The economy, however, is confronted with uncertain trade possibilities, that is a stochastic volume of potential trade.[2] In order to keep the analysis as transparant as possible two extreme trade regimes will be discerned. This abstraction can, however, be interpreted as describing the economy's actual view on the future in terms of an average of these extreme states of the world. First, in the free-trade regime the economy can in principle trade any quantity at the prevailing international relative price. Second, in the no-trade situation the economy is isolated and international trade comes to a virtual halt.

The economy decides on the pattern of domestic production before it is known which state of the world prevails. Once the decision about the optimal pattern of domestic production has been made, the allocation of the factors of production cannot be changed. Hence the model essentially deals with the short-term consequences of trade uncertainty. If the planning horizon is to be increased, the costs of reallocation need to be taken into account, but this would complicate the analysis unnecessarily. For the present purposes reallocation costs are implicitly assumed to be infinite, which in the short term seems to be a reasonable assumption.

Figure 6.1 on page 126 illustrates the decision problem of the economy that is subjected to a stochastic trade regime. The figure portrays the familiar neoclassical graphical representation of the macroeconomic gains from trade that an economy can reap if it opens up to international trade. Figure 6.1 contains a production possibilities frontier, that is concave to the origin, a linear international relative price curve, that represents the trading opportunities, and three convex indifference curves that represent utility of specific sets of consumption combinations. The further a production possibilities frontier lies from the origin, the higher is the production level, and likewise the further the indifference curves are from the origin, the higher the level of utility. The steeper the international relative price curve, the more expensive good x is in terms of good y.

The gains from trade can easily be read off. A is the autarky point, that is the production and consumption combination that results if international trade is not possible at all, so that specialization is absent. International trade allows the economy to exchange its products and consume outside the boundaries of the production possibilities frontier. Point F is the consumption point which yields the highest level of utility in a situation of free trade and specialization, given the exogenous world price ratio. Point I is the concomitant free trade production point. The utility derived from consumption in the case of free trade U_F exceeds the utility of the autarky consumption combination U_A.

Figure 6.1 International trade and allocation

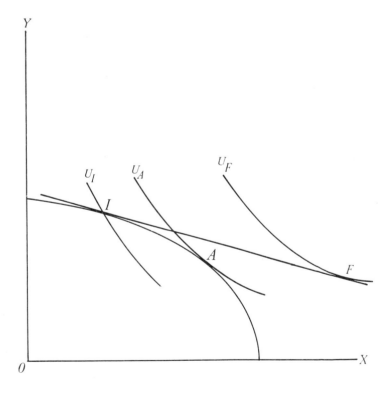

Figure 6.1, however, also allows for a different interpretation in the case of trade uncertainty. International specialization conform comparative advantage does not always yield a utility outcome that improves on welfare in the case of autarky. Whether this happens or not depends on the particular trade regime that occurs. In the free trade situation the economy consumes in point F and achieves utility U_F. If the no-trade situation, however, emerges while the economy is specialized, consumption drops to the production combination that is actually being produced. Since this production combination is the result of a decision that assumes that international trade is possible, the resulting consumption combination cannot be optimal if trade is impossible. Indeed in isolation, it is the allocation of the factors of production that determines utility. So consumption in isolation is at I and utility becomes $U_I < U_A$. In other words, the economy that is unexpectedly isolated is worse off than the autarkic economy that does not specialize according to comparative advantage and does not utilize the possibilities to trade.

It seems quite reasonable to assume that economic subjects will take into account that the possibility of some sort of trade disruption exists when they make their decisions about the extent of their specialization. In general economic subjects will consider the expected utility of certain production decisions and prefer a pattern of specialization that is associated with a point in between the autarky production point A and the free trade production point I. In order to model this decision process two functions need to be formulated that describe the indirect utility of the consumption that is realized in the case of free trade and no-trade, respectively.

Consider the free trade situation first. The usual small country assumptions apply, so that the international relative price p of good x in terms of good y is given and cannot be influenced by the choices of consumers and producers in this country. National income Y is measured in units of good x valued at international prices. So the national income $Y(x)$ of the production combination $(x, \varphi(x))$ is by definition:

$$Y(x) \equiv x + p(\varphi(x)) \tag{6.1}$$

Maximizing utility for each combination of p and $Y(x)$ with respect to C^*_x and C^*_y yields the 'free trade' indirect utility function $f(x) \equiv \vartheta(p, Y(x))$. This indirect utility function describes the maximum utility that can be reaped from the product combinations $(x, \varphi(x))$ in the case where free trade is the actual state of the world. A sufficient condition for strict concavity of the free-trade utility function $f(x)$ is that the marginal utility of income is non-increasing.[3] Note that this assumption of constant (decreasing) utility of income implies risk neutral (risk averse) behaviour. Figure 6.2 graphically illustrates the variables that have been introduced in this setting.

Figure 6.2 Variables and functions that play a role in the decision

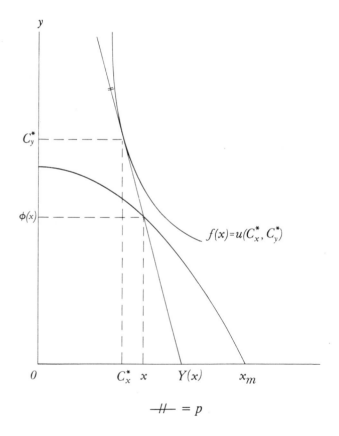

Remember that the model essentially pertains to a two-period framework as it is assumed that producers cannot reallocate once the decision on the optimal pattern of production has been made. If all trade halts and a combination $(x, \varphi(x))$ is produced, the maximum attainable utility can be described by the 'no-trade' utility function $g(x)$. In this case the direct and indirect utility functions coincide, because in the no-trade regime no international exchange takes place. Note that a no-trade production combination only equals the traditional autarky production combination (where the indifference curve is tangent to the production possibilities curve) if individual producers and consumers believe that the no-trade regime will prevail, and themselves decide on a production combination that does not allow for any trade.

Let π be the subjective probability that the free trade regime will occur.[4] This subjective probability is a function of the diplomatic climate. The state of the diplomatic climate will be described by a variable K, which may be a composite index of conflict and cooperation or an indicator of net conflict.[5] Obviously, long-lasting trade relationships will be influenced by other factors as well. One can easily think of other factors that explain the existence, quantity and direction of trade flows, such as the uncertainty that results of price fluctuations, technological developments, changing consumer preferences, bad harvests, exchange rate variability and transfer problems. Evidently in general more factors play a role, but as this book deals with the impact of diplomacy on trade, such factors are not explicitly considered in order to keep the analysis as transparant as possible.

An improvement in the diplomatic climate is associated with an increase in K and an increase in the subjective probability π that the free trade regime will prevail. Likewise, a deterioration is represented by a decrease in K and leads to lower π. So we have $\pi = \pi(K)$ and $\pi_K > 0$. Now the choice problem can be summarized in Table 6.1.

Table 6.1 Choice set

Produce $(x, \varphi(x))$		
Trade Regime	*Free trade*	*No trade*
Probability	$\pi(K)$	$1-\pi(K)$
Ex post utility	$f(x) = \vartheta(\pi, Y(x))$	$g(x) = u(x, \varphi(x))$

The empirical work by Pollins (1989a) and Polachek (1992) has already been discussed in Chapter 5. They found that the correlation between trade and conflict (and vice versa) is different for different groups of countries. One way to look into these differences is to see how decisions are being made. On one side of the spectrum we find the omniscient central planner: the benevolent bureaucrat who decides what is the best for all. On the other side we find the liberal democratic market economy where economic patterns emerge due to decentralized decision-making by households and firms. The next two sections study these archetypes of decision-making in the context of trade and diplomacy.

6.2 Collective Centralized Decision-making

Assume that Von Neumann—Morgenstern ([1944]1980) expected utility is being maximized by means of collective centralized decision-making, which takes the interests of both production and consumption simultaneously into account. One may imagine a centrally-planned economy or even a market in which some sort of institution, for example by means of tariffs and subsidies, gives incentives to market participants that induce the optimal production and consumption patterns.

Obviously this implies an enormous information requirement for the 'central planner' and it may not be reasonable to assume that the information is available at the detailed level and speed that the model requires. I will not dwell on this problem, but simply assume that the information requirement is being met, not so much because these are realistic assumptions, but simply because it does not really matter since the goal of the present chapter is quite modest. All I want to do is to sketch two extreme situations in order to clarify the mechanism by which different types of economic policy-making may yield differences in the empirically observed trade—conflict patterns.

The decision problem and process may now be formalized as a maximization of the expected utility with x (that is to say the pattern of specialization) as the instrument variable.

$$\max_{x} \pi f(x) + (1-\pi)g(x) \tag{6.2}$$

The first order condition of problem 6.2 is $\pi f_x(x) + (1-\pi)g_x(x) = 0$.

This problem has a unique solution for the production combination (x, y). The boundaries of the area of possible solutions are the autarky product combination x_{au} and the free trade product combination x_v, as illustrated in Figure 6.3 on page 132. The position of the free-trade function $f(x)$ *vis-à-vis* the no-trade function $g(x)$ results within the context of this traditional neoclassical trade model from the fact that international trade always offers opportunities to reach for a higher indifference curve (with the exception of the traditional autarky point where the international price ratio equals the marginal rate of substitution in the production point).

If $\pi = 0$, then x_{au} is the solution, since $\pi = 0$ by equation 6.2 implies that $g_x(x_{au}) = 0$. Likewise if $\pi = 1$, then the solution of problem 6.2 is $f_x(x_v) = 0$. So the no-trade function $g(x)$ has a global maximum for x_{au} and the free-trade function $f(x)$ is at its global maximum in x_v. Both functions are strictly concave, increasing to the left of x_v and decreasing to the right of x_{au}. Consequently, the expected utility of the chosen product combination $(x, \varphi(x))$ that is a weighted average of these functions (with the subjective probabilities as weights) must have a global maximum between x_{au} and x_v.[6]

For a country with a comparative advantage in the production of good y (implying $x_v < x_{au}$) the total differential of the first order condition of problem (6.2) becomes:[7]

$$\{\pi f_{xx} + (1-\pi)g_{xx}\}dx = \{g_x - f_x\}d\pi \tag{6.3}$$

Figure 6.3 The free-trade and no-trade utility functions

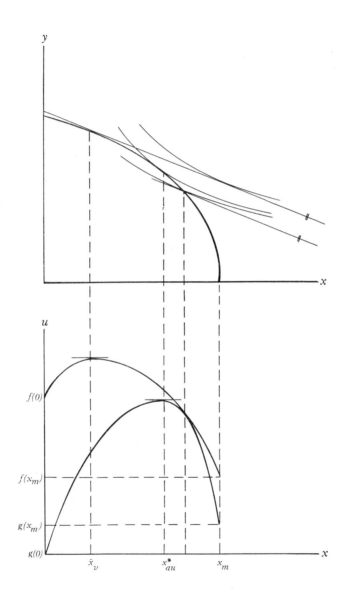

As the first order condition of problem 6.2 implies that $f_x = (\pi-1)g_x/\pi$, equation 6.3 can be rewritten as

$$\mathrm{d}x/\mathrm{d}\pi = g_x/\pi\{\pi f_{xx} + (1-\pi)g_{xx}\} < 0 \tag{6.4}$$

which implies that

$$\mathrm{d}x/\mathrm{d}K = \pi_K \mathrm{d}x/\mathrm{d}\pi < 0 \tag{6.5}$$

So in this collective decision process we have a strict one-to-one correspondence between, on the one hand, the subjective probability $\pi(K)$ that the free trade regime prevails, and on the other hand, the production combination $(x, \varphi(x))$. An improvement of the diplomatic climate (K increases) induces a shift of the production point in the direction of the free trade production point. Hence international specialization according to comparative advantage increases and so does the potential trade flow. If trade actually takes place (so the free-trade regime prevails) then one may observe that an improvement of the diplomatic climate as it reduces the probability of the no-trade situation enhances the volume of trade. Likewise, a deterioration of the diplomatic climate reduces the probability π that trade will take place and decreases the potential trade volume in the free trade regime.

6.3 Private Decentralized Decision-making

Will a decentralized market economy produce at the optimal point of production as well? This is a relevant question since producers and consumers face given prices if markets are characterized by perfect competition. If we ignore the limiting cases where either free trade or autarky is certain, then a private decentralized economy will not produce in the point that would be optimal given the concomitant probabilities. A second question pertains to the existence of a strict one-to-one relation between π and the chosen production point.

Figure 6.4 on page 134 illustrates the decisions facing households and firms. Both consumers and producers incorporate the possibility of a no-trade and a free-trade regime into their decisions.

*Figure 6.4 Prices and quantities that play a role in the consumers'
and producers' decisions*

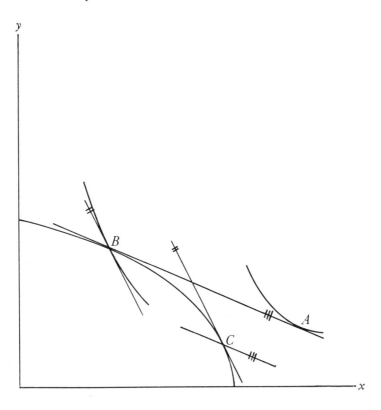

$$-\!\!/\!\!/\!\!- = p_d; \quad -\!\!/\!\!/\!\!/\!\!- = p$$

If the free trade regime prevails, consumers maximize utility in point
A where the price ratio equals the international terms of trade p. In
the no-trade regime, however, the consumption combination B
results, which given the indifference curves, yields the no-trade
domestic price ratio p_d. Rational risk-averse expected utility
maximizing households will prefer a price ratio between p and p_d,
that is a production combination between point C (where the
transformation curve is tangent to the no-trade domestic price ratio)
and the free-trade production point B. Producers on markets that are
characterized by free competition face the choice between production

point C which would maximize their profits if the domestic no-trade ratio equals p_d and point B which maximizes their profits in the free-trade regime. So like the consumers in this decentralized economy, expected profit-maximizing firms will also choose a production combination between points C and B. There is, however, no a priori reason why consumers and producers for given and identical subjective probabilities hold identical preferences about the optimal point of production.[8] Indeed they will have different preferences about the optimal production point as will become clear in due course.

If producers maximize expected profits, taking prices as given, then their problem may be summarized as:

$$\max_{x} \ \pi(x+p\varphi(x)) + (1-\pi)(x+p_d\varphi(x)) \qquad (6.6)$$

and the first order condition of 6.6 becomes $[\pi p + (1-\pi p_d]\varphi_x + 1 = 0$.

But if no trade occurs, domestic prices will have to adjust such that consumers want to consume at the chosen production point $(\varphi(x))$. This obviously requires that $p_d = U_2(x, \varphi(x))/U_1(x) \equiv p_d(x)$. Now this decentralized market economy reaches its equilibrium when producers want to produce at the point generated by domestic prices, implying that

$$[\pi p + (1-\pi)p_d(x)]\vartheta_x(x) + 1 = 0 \qquad (6.7)$$

Note that in determining the equilibrium outcome, one should no longer assume that the domestic price is to be considered exogenous. The proof of the existence of a strict one-to-one relationship between $\pi(K)$ and x is analogous to the case of centralized collective decision-making. The total differential of the first order condition of equation 6.5 can be written as:

$$dx/d\pi = \varphi_x\{p_d - p\}/[\varphi_{xx}\{\pi p + (1-\pi)p_d\} + (1-\pi)\varphi_x p_d\}] < 0 \qquad (6.8)$$

Also in this case the boundaries of the area of possible solutions are the autarky product combination x_{au} and the free trade product combination x_v.

As the question of the strict one-to-one relationship between the subjective probability $\pi(K)$ and the production combination $(x, \varphi(x))$ has also been answered affirmatively for the case of a decentralized market economy, attention will now be focused on the question of the trade conflict patterns in both types of economies.

From equation 6.2 it follows that in the case of collective decision-making the optimal point has to meet the requirement $\pi f_x(x) + (1-\pi)g_x(x) = 0$. Moreover $f_x = u^*_x(1 + p\varphi_x)$, where u^*_1 is evaluated in the consumption point that is optimal for given π and $Y(x)$. Note that $\vartheta_y = u_1$ since good x is the numéraire good. Now the derivation of the difference between private and central planning is straightforward. Divide equation 6.2 by u_1 and rearrange so that the first order condition for collective centralized decision-making becomes

$$(\pi p + (1-\pi)p_d)\varphi_x + 1 \quad + \quad \pi\{(u^*-1)/u_1\}(1+\pi\varphi_x) = 0 \qquad (6.9)$$

Here, obviously, the first term is the first order condition of the producer problem of equation 6.2. Hence private decentralized decision-making and collective centralized decision-making will only yield the same outcomes if the second term equals zero. This is only the case if either π equals zero, the economy is isolated with certainty, or if $\varphi_x = -1/p$, the free-trade case. In all other situations the chosen product combination in the market economy differs from the collective or social solution. Consequently, production in the decentralized market economy is suboptimal.

Indeed, since the economy by assumption has a comparative advantage in y and due to international specialization is able to consume outside the production possibilities frontier (to the right and above the production point), it follows that both $u^*_1 < u_1$ and $-1/p > \varphi_x$. Consequently, the second term in equation 6.9 is strictly positive. Now remember that the first term is the first order condition of the collective centralized economy which depicts as shown before a global maximum for this particular type of decision-making. Hence the first term is the derivative of a function that achieves its global maximum at the optimal collective decision. Now, since the second term is strictly positive, the first term of equation 6.8 must be negative. This, however, can only be the case if the private decentralized equilibrium is to the left of the collective centralized equilibrium (the derivative of the expected utility equation has to be negative for the case of collective decision-making). So the private economy will produce less *x* in which it has a comparative disadvantage and, consequently, produce too much of the good in which it has a comparative advantage *vis-à-vis* the plan economy. All in all, a strict one-to-one correspondence has been established between on the one hand, the probability of free trade *versus* trade disruption and on the other hand, the extent of international specialization and hence the potential for international trade. The lesser extent of specialization in centrally-planned economies *vis-à-vis* market economies conforms to Marer's (1985, pp. 98—9) observation that

> the consensus of experts is that trade participation ratio's of the centrally planned economies are certainly not higher and are almost probably significantly lower, than those of market economies of approximately the same size and development level.

6.4 Extensions: More Goods, Numéraire and Endogeneity

The model in this chapter has been extended along several lines. It was made truly general in the sense that it covers an arbitrary number of goods. Moreover, the analysis has been improved so as to cope with the numéraire problem (*cf.* Schweinberger 1993). Finally, trade uncertainty has been endogenized. This section discusses the main results while trying to prevent the argument being swamped by the mathematical abstraction that is often unavoidable if one wants to prove the points formally.

More goods
The first extension of the model has been to generalize the results for an arbitrary, but finite, number of goods, as was done in the Appendix to Van Marrewijk and Van Bergeijk (1990). This generalization is important since in reality many kinds of goods are being traded. Hence it is relevant to know whether the two-goods assumption is crucial for the existence of a one-to-one relationship between diplomacy and trade.

Fortunately it can be shown for this general many-goods-case that the necessary conditions for a one-to-one correspondence are met as the no-trade and free-trade utility functions and the income function are strictly concave. Consequently, the point of production is unique and there is a one-to-one relationship between the probability of trade disruption and the set of optimal production points, provided some gains of trade exist. Finally, it appears also that in the case of an arbitrary number of goods it is 'extremely unlikely' that private production coincides with the optimal production point, unless autarky or completely free trade prevail.

Numéraire

Van Marrewijk (1992) clarifies why private production diverges from the social optimum in this setting. Under certainty the standard neo-classical model formally optimizes production and consumption in two steps. That is to say, production is first chosen so as to maximize national income for given technologies and given world prices. Next consumption is determined given domestic production, world prices and consumer preferences. Once uncertainty is introduced, the optimality of this procedure may break down, as production decisions need no longer be consistent with consumption decisions. Van Marrewijk shows that this suboptimality is neither caused by the absence of a stock market — as suggested by Diamond (1967) and Helpman and Razin (1978) — nor by different attitudes toward risk of firms and consumers. Instead this suboptimality directly results from the choice of numéraire: a small 'two-step' market economy that maximizes expected revenue over-produces the non-numéraire good. Van Marrewijk's solution is to deflate prices in this economy by a perfect 'overall' price index. Now the result of different patterns of specialization in centrally planned economies *vis-à-vis* market economies would seem to vanish. Indeed, Van Marrewijk (1992, p. 368) argues:

> In reality, however, firms do not use a specific good as numéraire. Instead, they are confronted with a monetary world and nominal prices. Being trained economists, not blinded by money illusion, they realize that these nominal prices will have to be deflated by a price index (and...) if producers maximize national output taking nominal prices deflated by the exact price index as given, then private production takes place at the social optimum.

Calculation, however, of the 'exact price index' requires extensive and very recent knowledge, at a very detailed level, not only of the prices, but also of the quantities and technologies of all traded goods and services. Such detailed knowledge may be available (although unmanageable) in centrally-planned economies, but in decentralized market economies a deviation between optimal and private specialization is by definition a fact of life. Anyhow, Van Marrewijk's findings still agree with the strict one-to-one correspondence between the extent of uncertainty about the trade regime and the extent of international specialization.

Endogenous trade uncertainty

The third extension is the endogenization of the probability of trade disruption (Van Marrewijk and Van Bergeijk 1993), which shows that endogenous trade uncertainty may force an economy to specialize in the production of the 'wrong' good (that is, the good with comparative *dis*advantage), although this reversal in the pattern of incomplete specialization in production is not reflected in the trade pattern. The probability of trade may be influenced through a country's level of exports although this country does not have monopoly power, so that it cannot influence its terms of trade. This is so because an embargo, even against a small country, will not be effective unless the level of its foreign trade exceeds a certain threshold level, so that low levels of trade are associated with low probabilities of trade disruption (see, however, Helpman 1987 for a contrary opinion).

The relationship between the volume of trade and its uncertainty can be expressed as an elasticity, the so-called 'responsiveness of trade' parameter, which is positive by assumption (if it were zero the model reduces to the case of exogenous trade uncertainty studied in the previous sections). An increase in the elasticity, for example, in the wake of increasing trade frictions, *ceteris paribus* decreases the probability of trade and reduces the extent of specialization. If the elasticity becomes too large the probability of trade becomes negligible and the optimal production point is at autarky. If, however, the probability of trade disruption is endogenous and comparable to that in the exogenous case we should expect a lower optimal level of trade in the endogenous case. The more an economy trades the more likely trade disruption becomes. Indeed it can be shown that an economy may increase the probability of free trade by specializing against its comparative advantage. Consequently, endogenous trade uncertainty can make it optimal for a country with a comparative advantage in the production of good y to specialize in the production of good x.

Changes in the 'trade inclination' parameter reflect shifts in exogenous uncertainty that were studied in the previous sections. Political instability, unbalanced capital flows, the reputation of the trading partners or an active 'voluntary' export restraint policy may decrease the trust in free trade and reduce the potential for trade. In case the New World Order implies that the international community resorts more often to an active boycott policy π will be reduced and thereby the NWO imposes a real cost on the economy.

Two important facts should, however, be stressed. First of all, gains from trade do still exist if endogeneity of trade disruption forces an economy to specialize against its comparative advantage, even though the gains from trade may substantially decrease below the level in a deterministic trade setting. Second, it can be optimal for an economy with a comparative advantage in the production of good y to specialize in the production of good x, but if trade takes place the economy still exports the good in which it has a comparative advantage, so that our model does not affect the analytic use one can make of comparative advantage to explain the direction of trade flows. Endogenous trade uncertainty, however, makes the traditional tool of comparative advantage less able to explain the existence of international trade. Comparative advantage *per se* is not sufficient to explain trade. In other words, trade uncertainty destroys potential international exchanges that would be mutually advantageous.

6.5 Uncertain Trade

Introducing uncertainty with respect to the trade volume in a traditional neoclassical trade model for a small open economy yields less specialization in accordance with comparative advantage and hence to a reduction of international trading opportunities. This result is independent of both the number of goods, the extent to which economic decision-making has been decentralized and the question of whether this uncertainty is exogenous (that is 'systemic') or endogenous ('trade-related'). Hence the analysis improves on a number of theories that were discussed in Chapter 5.

The present approach avoids several inconsistencies as it focuses on uncertainty with respect to quantity. It is more general than the economic theories of the national defence argument, since it provides a general equilibrium framework for large numbers of goods, that allows for different types of decision-making and covers both risk-neutral and risk-averse behaviour. The assumptions of the model are, moreover, much more general than both Polachek's deterministic relationship between the terms of trade and the level of conflict and Pollins's inclusion of national defence considerations as an argument in the utility functions of consumers and producers. These novelties, however, are mainly relevant to theoretical economists, since the results of the analysis are not spectacular — in general this chapter shows that findings that so far have been based on partial analyses have a more general validity than could be assumed on the basis of the existing literature.

Two general conclusions with respect to policy emerge from the analysis. First, in the decentralized private market economy government intervention could improve on welfare by co-ordinating economic decisions whenever uncertainty exists with respect to the future trading climate. If one, however, wants to reduce government intervention, then the second conclusion becomes especially relevant, namely that it is desirable to create clarity concerning the future trading policy, for example, by strict adherence to GATT principles and conflict settlement procedures. Reducing the influence of politics on international trade by means of the rules and procedures of the open multilateral trading system tackles the uncertainty externality at its very source. Hence strengthening GATT is the first-best policy advice that can be derived from the analysis in this chapter.

Notes

1.   More specifically, the model abstracts from price uncertainty as it is designed to highlight the impact of uncertainty about the traded quantity. In addition the small country assumption assures that the economy is too small to be able to influence the world price level.

2. It does not really matter whether the analysis pertains to a uniform distribution or a binominal distribution between free trade and no trade.

3. Van Marrewijk and Van Bergeijk (1990, pp. 17—8) proves this proposition for an arbitrary, but finite, number of goods.

4. See the discussion on subjective probabilities in Chapter 3.

5. See Chapter 5 for a discussion of quantitative indicators for the diplomatic climate, that have been used in empirical analysis of the trade—conflict and the conflict—trade relationships.

6. Actually, all we need is strict concavity of the (indirect) utility functions since the equilibrium points x_{au} and x_v are globally stable.

7. The assumption $x_v < x_{au}$ does not affect the generality of the analysis. For $x_v < x_{au}$, $dx/d\pi$ becomes positive, but since x is now the good with comparative advantage, a positive sign for the total differential is in accordance with the results that are to be obtained below.

8. Note that the assumption of identical subjective probabilities for households and firms can easily be relaxed. I use this particular assumption only to show that the differences in the outcomes are due to differences in the decision process and not to different attitudes to risk in the sectors of the economy.

7. The Weight of Diplomacy: Its Impact on Trade

At first sight the tough dynamic world of commercial exchange and the subtle glamour of diplomacy do not seem to have much in common. Still, as every newspaper reader knows, international economic relations are an important factor in the diplomatic sphere of influence and vice versa. No matter who reigns, the merchant reigns, and trade follows the flag. This chapter investigates the relationship between trade and diplomacy econometrically, not to discover the obvious, but to see whether an empirical basis exists to either confirm or refute common sense: does the diplomatic climate have a measurable impact on international trade flows? In the investigation diplomacy has not been restricted to the activities of diplomats only; it is a broad concept that covers all kinds of international co-operation and international conflict. The focus in this chapter is on the influence that is exerted by the diplomatic climate on international trade flows. The twin question of the influence of trade on the diplomatic climate is not dealt with.

In order to investigate the influence of political relations on trade flows, the diplomatic climate will be added to the so-called gravity model of international trade. Indicators for co-operation and hostility in bilateral diplomatic exchanges are added to this model in an attempt to explain more fully the global pattern of bilateral trade flows. The reason for including these political variables in an empirical investigation of global trade patterns is that (expectations about) non-economic ends, such as political and military security, or non-economic events, such as recalling of ambassadors or strategic political support, may influence (expectations about) the course of trade. Spero (1977, p. 9), for example, argues that 'economic policy is frequently either shaped by political concerns or becomes an explicit tool of national strategic and diplomatic concern'.

The first section introduces the gravity analysis. In this chapter the usual practice of using dummy variables in a trade model to represent the diplomatic climate will not be followed. Instead I will use so-called events data to construct political indicators, as will be discussed in section 7.2. This allows differentiation and shows more nuance than the crude dummy measures deployed in some of the earlier studies on trade and diplomacy. Individual indicators will be constructed for, on the one hand the 'amount' of conflict between a pair of nations, and on the other hand the amount of co-operation between these nations. Section 7.3 presents the empirical results of a cross-section gravity model that deals with the bilateral trade flows of 40 countries in the year 1986. In order both to avoid reverse causation and to reduce the possible problem of simultaneity, the explanatory politico-economic variables are measured in 1982—1985. The investigation shows that the diplomatic climate significantly influences the pattern of international trade flows and, consequently, suggests that international trade theory should reflect on both economic and political factors. Section 7.4 concentrates on differences by country. A clear boundary between those countries for which the diplomatic climate does seem to influence the trade flows and those countries for which it does not, cannot be drawn on the basis of the empirical results. A distinction, however, with respect to instruments (export versus import controls) can be made. Changes in the diplomatic climate appear to affect the export flow in a market economy and the import flow in a centrally-planned economy. The final section explicitly considers costs and benefits of diplomacy.

The study in this chapter should be seen as an extension of the earlier empirical studies on this topic that have been discussed in Chapter 5. First, the sample of countries has been increased in order to become more diversified with respect to both the size of the trade partners and the economic systems covered. Second, different reaction patterns for (groups of) countries will be investigated. As was argued in Chapter 6, it does not seem far-fetched to assume that the expectations about the future trading climate to a large extent depend on the bilateral political climate. Consequently, a testable proposition results from the expected utility model that was developed in that chapter: an improving (a deteriorating) bilateral diplomatic climate *ceteris paribus* increases (decreases) the bilateral trade flows.

7.1   The Gravity Model

A lot of models have been used to describe international trade flows. Models do not only differ with respect to the degree of detail but also with respect to the specific theoretical interest of the investigator.[1] For the present study I use probably the most simple empirical model. The basic idea of this model was first set out by Isard (1954). Tinbergen (1962, pp. 262—93) developed the gravity model as it is known today. Linnemann (1966) has become the traditional reference on the gravity model.[2] As the review of empirical findings in Chapter 5 suggests, the gravity model provides a versatile approach to analysing the relationship between trade, co-operation and conflict.

Pros and cons of the gravity approach
In assessing the potential utility of the gravity approach for the present empirical investigation one has to consider both the strengths and the weaknesses of the method. On the one hand, the critics of the gravity model are right in many respects. For example, the analysis is essentially of a comparative static nature and the model reads in wrong units, which causes problems if the analysis is applied to pooled cross-section data for several years (Bikker, 1987, pp. 316—7). Only one equation is used to explain the value of total exports to another country. So basically, we have a turnover relation in which prices are not specified. Moreover, no attention is being paid to the development of exports over time. The traditional formulation of the gravity model is not cogently derived on the basis of economic theory and substitution between flows is absent. Also the loglinearity of the gravity equation has been questioned (Sanso et al., 1993). Finally, the model's assumption of constant parameters across countries may not be entirely appropriate.[3]

On the other hand the model's simplicity constitutes its strength, because the model deploys only a limited number of variables and this facilitates computation and keeps the data problem manageable. Moreover, many of the theoretical problems have been solved. Bergstrand (1985) relates the gravity equation to its microeconomic foundations and Bergstrand (1989) gives a formal derivation of the gravity equation within the context of a general equilibrium model of world trade with imperfect competition and product differentiation.

Bikker (1987 and 1992) provides a method of analysing substitution between trade flows in the context of a gravity model. Noteworthy is the gravity equation's ability to incorporate 'empirical regularities', such as intra-industry trade, the impact of transport costs and the influence of differences in per capita income on trade flows.[4] According to Isard (1988, p. 311), the appeal of the gravity approach is that it lays bare the two key system variables in operation (mass and resistance to movement) without confusion with the many microeconomic forces that are at play.

More important, however, is the fact that the problem that is addressed in this chapter concerns the question of increased explanation when the diplomatic climate is included in a traditional trade model. As this investigation deals with the actual impact of bilateral diplomatic activity on the level and pattern of bilateral trade flows, the choice of the gravity model is almost unavoidable. Both Ricardo and Heckscher Ohlin type analyses are only able to explain the composition by type of good of a country's trade flows. The gravity model provides an empirical explanation for the pattern and the level of bilateral trade flows. In addition, robustness and general acceptance of the method are essential for the analysis in this chapter. So although the gravity model could be extended considerably and although the method has some imperfections, for the present study it suffices. This is especially true as the empirical results obtained with the gravity model have always been judged to be very good (see, for example, Deardorff 1984, pp. 503—4). In general the gravity model offers a good approximation of (the world pattern of) bilateral trade flows.

The gravity equation
In the basic model three explanatory variables appear: *(i)* the exporting country's Gross Domestic Product (Y_i), *(ii)* the importing country's GDP (Y_j) and *(iii)* the distance D_{ij} between the two countries. The basic model is known in international trade theory as the gravity equation, because of its similarity to the Newtonian law of gravity: the bilateral trade flow is supposed to be a function of the economic masses of the two trade partners and the inverted distance between the countries. The rationale for this formulation is that:

- the supply of exports depends positively on the exporting country's economic size which is represented by its GDP;
- the demand for these exports depends positively on the importing country's market which is also represented by its GDP;
- transportation costs, transportation time and the 'economic horizon' of the exporter (assumed to correspond roughly with the geographic distance between the exporting and importing country) have a negative impact on trade.

Usually the populations N_i and N_j of the trade partners are added as explanatory variables in order to take into account the influences which are exerted by economies of scale, indivisibilities in production, as well as the influence of income per capita on the diversification of demand.[5]

In its basic form the trade flow equation is:

$$E_{ij} = Y_i^{\alpha 1} Y_j^{\alpha 2} D_{ij}^{\alpha 3} N_i^{\alpha 4} N_j^{\alpha 5} \tag{7.1}$$

with $\alpha_1 > 0$, $\alpha_2 > 0$, $\alpha_3 < 0$, $\alpha_4 < 0$ and $\alpha_5 < 0$ and

E_{ij} = exports of country i to country j
Y_i = GDP of the exporting country i
Y_j = GDP of the importing country j
D_{ij} = geographic distance between i and j
N_i = population of the exporting country i
N_j = population of the exporting country j

The trade flow equation is estimated cross-country for 40 countries for the year 1986. So we have $40 \times 39 = 1{,}560$ possible observations. The data sources are described in the Appendix (see pages 168—75). In order to estimate the coefficients of the model with the Ordinary Least Squares (OLS) method, equation (7.1) is rewritten as:

$$\ln E_{ij} = \alpha_0' + \alpha_1 \ln Y_i + \alpha_2 \ln Y_j + \alpha_3 \ln D_{ij} + \alpha_4 \ln N_i + \alpha_5 \ln N_j \tag{7.1'}$$

Some estimation issues

For practical estimation purposes 251 zero-flow observations (16 per cent) were left out. The most obvious practical problem is that ln(0) is not defined. Note, moreover, that a zero trade flow according to equation (7.1) would seem to require that at least one of the explanatory variables is zero. The gravity model predicts zero flows only when at least one explanatory variable is zero and for the explanatory variables in the present model this is unlikely to be the case. Hence for (approximately) zero trade flows, the model may not give an appropriate description of the relationship between trade flows and its explanatory variables.

Trade data sources, however, generally only report annual bilateral trade flows that exceed some threshold, for example, $ 500,000 (as is the case for the trade data base that is used in the present investigation). Consequently, relatively small transactions may occur when the data source reports a (rounded off) zero. The combination of actual trade and officially reported zero flows may also occur in the case of smuggling or politically sensitive goods such as military procurements. So the trade registration system obviously generates zero or near-zero flows that do not require one of the explanatory variables to be zero.

Several methods may be used to deal with the problem of zero observations. A first option would be to substitute an arbitrary value (for example, the threshold of the trade data source) for the observed trade flows in order to take account of this feature of the data. A second option is to use a censored-sample regression model such as the Tobit procedure (see, for example, Balassa and Bauwens 1988, pp. 180—3 and Biessen 1991). A third option would be to estimate the relationship on the basis of the non-zero flows only. From an econometric point of view neglecting zero observations means that one is losing information (for example that trade becomes negligible when hostility becomes larger than some empirically estimated threshold or that some level of co-operation is needed for strictly positive trade), while substituting small values for the zero observations may bias the estimated coefficients of the gravity equation. From a statistician's point of view, however, it must be doubted whether the zero-flows actually contain relevant information. Much depends on the cause of the zero flow. If the cause is, for example, rounding-off in the trade statistics or deliberate misreporting, then alternative censored-sample methods will also produce biased coefficients (Linnemann and Verbruggen 1991, p. 549). Finally, it should be noted that the findings that are reported in this Part suggest that a number of zero-flows can be explained, both theoretically and empirically, with reference to the diplomatic climate.

The third option reduces the number of observations available for the estimation procedure to 1,309, but leaving out the zero-flow observations allows for an additional check for the model: one may make out-of-sample predictions for the cases where a zero trade flow is reported on the basis of the estimated model and the exogenous variables. These strictly positive predictions may serve as a standard to judge the model's performance and explanatory powers concerning relatively small trade flows. All in all a combination of the first method and the third method will be used as this seems the best way to present the inherent uncertainty and ambiguity in the estimates in the most transparent way.

7.2 The Diplomatic Climate

In order to construct indicators for the diplomatic climate Azar's (1980) classification of international political activities is used. Azar (1980, p. 146) focuses on so-called 'events'. These are occurrences between nations which are distinct enough from the constant flow of transactions (trade, mail flow, travel, etc.) to stand out against this background as 'reportable' or 'newsworthy'. Azar classifies these events into fifteen categories which vary in intensity from (1) 'unification' to (15) 'complete war' (see Figure 7.1 on page 150). As the most recent observations in Azar's data base pertain to 1978, data on actions, reactions and interactions of nation-states have been derived from *Keesings Historische Archief*, 1982, 1983, 1984, 1985 and 1986 (the 1986 volume describes some events that took place at the end of 1985).[6] A major difference with Azar's Conflict and Peace Data Bank (COPDAB) is that daily events reported in journals are recorded in COPDAB, while *Keesings Historische Archief* summarizes the main 'newsworthy' items. COPDAB thus covers the events more fully than the source used in the present study.

Figure 7.1 Classification scheme

High intensity of co-operation {weight 3}
  (1) Complete unification
  (2) Creation of strategic alliance or common market.

Medium intensity of co-operation {weight 2}
  (3) Military, strategic or economic support
  (4) Non-military economic agreements
  (5) Beginning of official diplomatic relations. Technical and
    scientific co-operation

Low intensity of co-operation {weight 1}
  (6) Verbal support
  (7) Minor official exchanges

Neutral activities {weight 0}
  (8) Neutral activities

Low intensity of conflict {weight 1}
  (9) Mild verbal dismay
  (10) Strong verbal dismay, threats of retaliation

Mild intensity of conflict {weight 2}
  (11) Recall of ambassadors, mobilization.
  (12) Breaking off diplomatic relations, support for guerrilla-activities
  (13) Small-scale military actions, border incidents, blockades

---

High intensity of conflict {weight 3}
  (14) Limited war acts, mining of territorial waters, sporadic shooting
  (15) Total war, large scale invasions, bombing of civilian targets.

Note: (COPDAB scale in brackets)
    {Faber's weights in braces}

To arrive at aggregated bilateral indicators for hostile activities ($H_{ij}*$)
and co-operative activities ($C_{ij}*$), Faber's (1987, esp. p. 445—7)

method was followed.[7] He constructed a simplified weighing scheme that classifies both co-operative and conflictive behaviour into three categories according to intensity. Each category is assigned a different weight ranging from 3 ('high intensity') to 1 ('low intensity'). An additional category contains neutral activities (for example, state visits that produce neither mild verbal support nor mild verbal dismay and other 'non-events').

Faber (1987, pp. 449—55) extensively tests his weighing scheme for indicators of international behaviour and finds that the face validity is quite good, indicating that the whole set of observed policitical indicators can be described with two dimensions: co-operation and hostility. Moreover, the temporal reliability of his measurement concepts appears to be very high. Hence Faber's method seems appropriate for the present investigation.

For each country *vis-à-vis* the 39 countries the number of events with high, medium and low co-operation-intensity and conflict-intensity was established. The events were identified on the basis of *Keesings Historische Archief* which contains a subject index per country. Proper identification of an event requires the use of all potential entries, because a diplomatic interaction between, for example, Denmark and the United States may not be reported for the United States, while it is reported for Denmark. In addition the subject index enables us to work out events in international organizations and at international conferences. In a few scattered instances *Keesings Historische Archief* reported several times in one issue about the same main topic (for example, battles in the same war). This was counted as just one event.

Once an event has been identified, its relevance needs to be assessed. Based on the classification scheme of Figure 7.1 and informed by the description in *Keesings Historische Archief* the event is classified and multiplied by its appropriate weight. Finally, the weighted events are summed within the area of co-operation and within the area of conflict. So these quantitative aggregates are weighted frequencies of interactions and describe the flows of conflict and co-operation respectively, exchanged between nation-states over the period 1982—1985.

Table 7.1 Indicators for diplomatic activity (1982—1985)

	Index of aggregate co-operation	Index of aggregate hostility	Number of non-zero interactions
Argentina	6	88	17
Australia	9	16	4
Brazil	20	10	11
Canada	64	24	12
Chile	3	11	6
China	38	16	19
Czecho-Slovakia	20	12	8
Denmark	31	29	17
Egypt	37	8	14
Finland	10	17	9
France	171	48	29
Gabon	1	8	4
Germany, East	40	24	13
Germany, West	160	43	22
Ghana	9	9	5
Iceland	0	6	3
India	15	23	9
Indonesia	32	9	15
Italy	97	33	17
Japan	71	19	11
Mexico	10	9	8
Morocco	17	6	7
Nigeria	7	18	9
Norway	25	27	14
Pakistan	12	14	7
Philippines	52	8	14
Poland	28	22	13
Portugal	52	18	13
Saudi Arabia	28	10	12
South Africa	4	178	38
Soviet Union	83	184	39
Spain	134	17	20
Sudan	15	7	6
Sweden	2	19	5
Switzerland	1	8	2
Tunisia	8	6	6
Turkey	8	8	5
United Kingdom	153	108	36
United States	188	108	36
Venezuela	17	11	10
Average	*42.0*	*31.0*	*13.6*
Standard deviation	*50.8*	*42.2*	*9.7*

Table 7.1 summarizes some relevant aggregate statistics for the 40 countries which are studied in this chapter. These aggregates offer an indication of the political behaviour and relative importance of the sampled countries. The first two columns show the totals of the amounts of co-operation $\Sigma_j C_{ij}^*$ and conflict or hostility $\Sigma_j H_{ij}^*$ flowing from each country to its 39 potential trading partners. The last column shows the number of cases in which at least one indicator is positive. This happens in 522 of the 1560 cases. In 248 cases the conflict indicator exceeds the co-operation indicator; in 252 cases the co-operation indicator is larger. For the period 1982—1985 the big western market economies display a diplomatic climate in which co-operation is an important element. Conflict behaviour is especially vigorous between the superpowers and in South Africa's international relations. The Falkland crisis explains the high hostility indicator for both Argentina and the United Kingdom.

Very strong bilateral co-operation was measured between France and West Germany, between France and Spain, between the United Kingdom and the United States and between the United States and West Germany. The largest flows of hostility appeared between Argentina and the United Kingdom and in the Soviet Union's bilateral relationships with the United States, West-Germany and Sweden.

Next the indicators for bilateral political co-operation C_{ij} and bilateral political hostility H_{ij} are added to the gravity equation as additional explanatory variables. C_{ij} is defined as $1 + C_{ij}^* + C_{ji}^*$, where C_{ij}^* is the international flow of co-operative behaviour from country i to country j for 1982-1985. H_{ij} has been defined in a similar way with respect to conflict. This formulation of the political variables recognizes the fact that the measures of the diplomatic climate need to take the behaviour of both trading partners into account simultaneously.

The choice for two separate indicators for the diplomatic climate reflects Sayrs's (1990, p. 23) critique that the net conflict measure (that is conflict minus co-operation) widely used in the literature obscures differences in the trade—co-operation relation as distinct from the trade—conflict relation. A priori one might expect multicollinearity between C and H: one would expect that if conflict goes up, co-operation will go down. In general, however, no such simple relationship can be established. Some countries are more expressive than other countries implying both larger conflict indicators and larger co-operation indicators. Other countries tend to compensate conflictive behaviour by co-operation, for example if they simultaneously use the stick of negative sanctions and the carrot of positive sanctions.

Since the political variables will be included multiplicatively into the equation, a value of 1 seems appropriate in case no flow of co-operative or hostile political behaviour is measured. Hence the arbitrary transformation of the political indicators.

The extended form of the trade flow equation is also rewritten in logarithmic form for estimation purposes.

$$\ln E_{ij} = \alpha_0' + \alpha_1 \ln Y_i + \alpha_2 \ln Y_j + \alpha_3 \ln D_{ij} + \alpha_4 \ln N_i + \alpha_5 \ln N_j + \\ \alpha_6 \ln C_{ij} + \alpha_7 H_{ij} \tag{7.2}$$

with $\alpha_6 > 0$ and $\alpha_7 < 0$ and

C_{ij} = indicator of diplomatic co-operation
H_{ij} = indicator of diplomatic hostility

7.3   Empirical Results

Table 7.2 summarizes the empirical results of the restricted model (equation 7.1') and the unrestricted model (equation 7.2). The restricted model is the smaller — base — gravity model that explains trade flows by means of GDP, distance and population only. The unrestricted model includes the indicators for the diplomatic climate next to the pure economic explanatory variables.

All coefficients are significant at the 99 per cent confidence level. The signs of the coefficients conform to the theoretical a priori expectations and are highly significant. The coefficients of the continuous variables can be directly interpreted as elasticities. An improvement of the diplomatic climate, for example, that doubles the co-operation index, will increase trade on average by a good 40 per cent. The test statistics for the unrestricted model are only slightly better than the test statistics for the simple basic restricted equation.

Table 7.2 Empirical results of the OLS estimation of the gravity trade model for 40 countries in 1986

	Restricted model Equation (7.1')	Unrestricted model Equation (7.2)	
	Observed trade flows	Observed trade flows	Re-estimated*
Exporter's GDP ($\ln Y_i$)	1.40	1.36	1.58
	(30.8)	(29.1)	(34.0)
Importers's GDP ($\ln Y_j$)	1.01	0.97	1.16
	(22.5)	(21.0)	(25.1)
Geographic distance ($\ln D_{ij}$)	—0.76	—0.67	—0.86
	(—16.1)	(—14.1)	(—16.5)
Exporter's population ($\ln N_i$)	—0.79	—0.79	—0.87
	(—17.2)	(—17.6)	(—18.8)
Importer's population ($\ln N_j$)	—0.34	—0.35	—0.44
	(—7.5)	(—7.8)	(—9.6)
Co-operation index ($\ln C_{ij}$)		0.45	0.45
		(7.8)	(6.7)
Hostility index ($\ln H_{ij}$)		—0.23	—0.58
		(—3.2)	(—7.8)
Constant term	—2.2	—2.1	—3.4
	(—10.7)	(—9.4)	(—16.7)
R^2	0.605	0.624	0.664
Adjusted-R^2	0.604	0.622	0.662
F-test	340	309	438
SSR	2,627	2,546	4,211
Number of observations	1,309	1,309	1,560

Notes: *A minimal value of $ 0.5 millon has been substituted for the zero-trade flows
(t-statistics between brackets)

The F-ratio[8] for testing the hypothesis that the coefficients of the added political variables are zero is 32, well above the critical value. Hence it may be safely concluded that the added variables contribute significantly to the explanation of the dependent variable, and the unrestricted model should be chosen on statistical grounds.

It appeared from inspection of the predictions for the zero-trade flows that the majority of serious mispredictions consisted of cases with a very hostile diplomatic climate, such as the trade flows between South Africa and the Soviet Union. Hence an alternative estimation procedure was used in which an arbitrary value of $ 0.5 million was substituted for the zero flows as this is the threshold for the trade data base that was used. The results of the re-estimation of model (2) are reported in the third columns of Tables 7.2, 7.3 and 7.4. As could be expected the coefficients and empirical results are clearly influenced. R^2, adjusted-R^2 and the F-test improve if a small value is substituted for each zero trade flow. Moreover, the F-statistic for testing the hypothesis that the coefficients of the added political variables are zero increases to 47.

Both the reason for and the exact value of the zero flow are by definition unknown and the choice of the actual value that is to be substituted influences the estimated coefficients of the gravity equation. So a sensitivity check was performed in which a value q was substituted, increasing stepwise the value of q by $ 100,000 starting from $q = $ 100,000$ and ending with $q = $ 1,000,000$. Although the choice of q clearly influences the parameter estimates the overall findings do not change, as there is no reversal of signs or significance levels of the explanatory variables. Both the R^2 and the F-test are of the same order of magnitude on this interval. So essentially the parameters and the test statistics show great qualitative stability with respect to the choice of the actual value of the zero trade flows. Indeed an important conclusion from this exercise is that zero trade flows to a large extent can be explained if one takes the diplomatic climate into account.

Relative importance of the independent variables
Table 7.3 reports the so-called β-coefficients or standardized coefficients of the multiple regression model. These β-coefficients are the parameters that are obtained if all variables are measured in terms

of their estimated standard deviation (Pindyck and Rubinfeld 1991, p. 85). A β-coefficient indicates the relative contribution that the variable in question makes to the explanation of the dependent variable.

Table 7.3 Relative importance of the explanatory variables
(β-coefficients of the estimated parameters)

	Restricted model Equation (7.1')	Unrestricted model Equation (7.2)	
	Observed trade flows	Observed trade flows	Re-estimated*
Exporter's GDP ($\ln Y_i$)	0.95	0.92	0.90
Importers's GDP ($\ln Y_j$)	0.68	0.66	0.66
Geographic distance ($\ln D_{ij}$)	—0.30	—0.26	—0.26
Exporter's population ($\ln N_i$)	—0.53	—0.53	—0.49
Importer's population ($\ln N_j$)	—0.23	—0.23	—0.25
Co-operation index ($\ln C_{ij}$)		0.15	0.11
Hostility index ($\ln H_{ij}$)		—0.06	—0.12

Note: *A minimal value of $ 0.5 million has been substituted for the zero-trade flows

The diplomatic conflict constitutes a serious barrier to trade, although the absolute values of the β-coefficients for the political indicators are less than the β-coefficients for the traditional strictly economic explanatory variables of the gravity model (GDP, distance and population). Consequently, the present investigation does not offer support for Pollins's finding that the importance of bilateral political relations is as great as economic variables. The contribution of the strictly economic variables (GDP and distance) exceeds the contribution of the indicators for the bilateral diplomatic climate, and this conclusion holds if the model is re-estimated with the arbitrary value of $ 0.5 million substituted for the zero-trade flows.[9]

Predictions for the zero trade flows

Table 7.4 presents the predictions for the zero-flow cases as an additional test. It appears that both models predict the zero-flows reasonably well. The total of predictions for the zero-flow observations amounts to 1.2 per cent and 0.9 per cent of the total of the predictions for all trade flows in model (1') and model (2') respectively. The predictions of the zero-trade flows improve as expected for the re-estimated model.[10] Their total now only amounts to 0.6 per cent of the total of the predicted trade flows. Hence the present investigation is able to offer a substantial explanation with respect to the zero-flow issue.

Table 7.4 Predictions for the 251 zero-flows in 1986

	Restricted model Equation (7.1')	Unrestricted model Equation (7.2)	
	Observed trade flows	*Observed trade flows*	*Re-estimated**
	Numbers		
< $ 10 million	108	130	188
$ 10 — 50 million	101	87	47
$ 50 — 100 million	15	20	9
> $ 100 million	27	14	7
	Million US$		
Average	56	40	27
Standard Deviation	219	218	217

Note: *A minimal value of $ 0.5 million has been substituted for the zero-trade flows

7.4 Differences Between Countries

So far the discussion has focused on the general impact of diplomacy on trade. Different reaction patterns, however, between countries are to be expected. The analytic approach that was followed in Chapter 6, for example, suggests that differences are to be expected between market economies and centrally planned economies. Consequently, the coefficients of the trade equation have also been estimated on the basis of the observed trade flows for the 40 countries individually, using the same dataset. A distinction was made between the exports E_{aj} from country a to its trade partners (j) and the exports E_{ja} from the trade partners (j) to this country a. In the former case an export equation and in the latter case an import equation have been estimated.

The estimated equations are:

Export equation:
$$\ln E_{aj} = \alpha_0' + \alpha_1 \ln Y_j + \alpha_2 \ln D_{ij} + \alpha_3 \ln N_j + \alpha_4 \ln C_{ij} + \alpha_5 H_{ij} \qquad (7.3)$$

Import equation:
$$\ln E_{ja} = \alpha_0' + \alpha_1 \ln Y_j + \alpha_2 \ln D_{ij} + \alpha_3 \ln N_j + \alpha_4 \ln C_{ij} + \alpha_5 H_{ij} \qquad (7.4)$$

Table 7.5 on page 160 summarizes the coefficients C_{ij} and H_{ij} from the estimated export and import equations. In the majority of the equations countries appear to be reacting to changes in the diplomatic climate as expected; this happens in more than 75 per cent of the cases. In the export model the correct sign is found for C_{ij} 32 times, and 29 times for H_{ij}. The 40 export equations contain 18 coefficients for 15 countries that are significant at the 90 per cent level and better. None of the significant coefficients has the wrong sign. In the import model the correct sign is found for C_{ij} 29 times, and 31 times for H_{ij}. In the 40 import equations we find the only significant coefficient with a wrong sign (Argentina); 19 significant coefficients for 14 countries have the theoretically expected sign. Unexpected signs and completely 'wrong' reaction patterns are in almost all cases very insignificant. Both coefficients have the wrong (but insignificant) sign in the export equation of Venezuela and in the import equations of Chile, China, Nigeria, Norway and Turkey. Table 7.6 on page 161 lists those countries that experience a significant reduction (that is to say at the 90 per cent confidence level) in their exports or imports if the diplomatic climate deteriorates, that is if co-operation reduces and/or hostility increases.

Table 7.5 The influence of the diplomatic climate in export and import equations (1986, estimated for 40 countries individually)

	Export equation (7.3) C_{ij}	H_{ij}	Import equation (7.4) C_{ij}	H_{ij}
Argentina	—0.46	—0.34	—3.12#	—0.41
Australia	0.09	0.12	0.51	—0.84
Brazil	—0.39	—0.80#	—0.01	—1.18#
Canada	0.55#	—0.31	0.61*	—0.83#
Chile	0.53	0.11	—1.09	0.36
China	0.36	0.07	—0.34	0.74
Czechoslovakia	0.88$	—1.34#	0.94$	—0.93*
Denmark	0.26	0.04	0.54	0.29
Egypt	0.25	—0.41	0.50	—1.32
Finland	0.89*	—0.34	0.12	—0.08
France	0.49$	0.13	0.54$	0.07
Gabon	4.60	0.15	7.82#	—2.20
Germany, East	1.28$	—0.58	1.28$	0.13
Germany, West	0.14	—0.16	0.11	—0.17
Ghana	0.71	—0.27	0.64	—0.28
Iceland	N.A.	2.85	N.A.	—0.34
India	1.00	—0.09	1.08	—0.84
Indonesia	0.43	—1.27	0.36	—2.43
Italy	0.30*	—0.08	0.30*	0.01
Japan	0.27	0.01	0.11	—0.05
Mexico	0.63	—1.86	2.27	—0.70
Morocco	—0.07	—1.50	0.36	—0.48
Nigeria	4.48	—1.88	—1.34	0.47
Norway	0.01	0.14	—0.05	0.21
Pakistan	—0.54	—0.52	—0.05	—1.71#
Philippines	0.68#	1.57	0.34	—0.58
Poland	0.32	—0.52	0.84$	—1.17#
Portugal	0.47*	—1.17$	0.59#	—1.14$
Saudi Arabia	0.60	—0.67	0.67	—1.07
South Africa	—0.20	—1.45*	—0.78	—1.00
Soviet Union	0.27	—0.60	0.67#	—0.49
Spain	0.36#	—0.43	0.39*	—0.23
Sudan	1.34$	—1.83*	1.81*	—3.19
Sweden	1.32	—0.22	1.21	—0.44
Switzerland	0.76	—0.77#	0.56	—0.67
Tunisia	—0.32	—0.26	0.96	—1.62
Turkey	0.22	—0.63	—0.11	0.44
United Kingdom	0.61#	—0.28	0.51$	—0.29
United States	0.48#	—0.14	0.50	—0.72
Venezuela	—1.08	0.32	—0.26	—0.65

Notes: Significance levels: $ signals 99 per cent confidence, # signals 95 per cent confidence and * signals 90 per cent confidence level

Table 7.6 Countries that experience a significant reduction of trade when the diplomatic climate deteriorates (1986)

Export		Import	
Co-operation	*Hostility*	*Co-operation*	*Hostility*
Sudan	Portugal	Czechoslovakia	Portugal
E. Germany	Czechoslovakia	France	Poland
France	Brazil	UK	Canada
Czechoslovakia	Switzerland	Poland	Pakistan
Philippines	S. Africa	E. Germany	Brazil
Spain	Sudan	USSR	Czecho-
Canada		Gabon	slovakia
UK		Portugal	
USA		Canada	
Italy		Spain	
Portugal		Sudan	
Finland			

Note: Countries are listed in order of decreasing significance of the estimated coefficients that are at least significant at the 90 per cent confidence level.

A clear boundary between those countries for which the diplomatic climate does influence the trade flows and those for which it does not, cannot be drawn on the basis of these findings (with an exception for the Scandinavian countries where the postulated relation between trade and diplomacy was not found). The absence of a significant influence for the political indicators in the trade flow equations of the two economic superpowers Japan and West Germany is noteworthy, as is the presence of this influence for the two liberal market economies of the United States and the United Kingdom.[11]

A distinction can, however, be inferred from Table 7.6 with respect to the way trade flows are influenced by countries. Sixty per cent of the countries with one or two significant coefficients with the right sign in the export equation consist of western market economies, whereas the more centrally-planned economies appear important in the group of countries with one or two significant coefficients in the import equation. It appears that a change in the diplomatic climate leads to a change in the exports of the western economy, and a change in the imports of the centrally-planned economy. The market economy chooses its outlets on the basis of political factors; the centrally-planned economy its suppliers.

A similar pattern has been observed by Leidy (1989) with respect to the choice between import and export sanctions.[12] He argues that membership of the General Agreement on Tariffs and Trade (GATT) and the desired reversibility of export controls may have favoured the market economy's almost exclusive reliance on export controls in economic foreign policy measures. First, GATT incorporates an institutionalized bias against import controls. So the empirically established pattern may thus simply reflect the fact that some centrally-planned economies, notably the Soviet Union, East Germany and China, were not contracting parties to the GATT in 1986. Second, the principle of trade liberalization requires at least reversibility of any trade impediment. It is well known that the costs of export controls are concentrated and this will tend to generate public support for a policy reversal whereas the benefits of import controls are concentrated thus tending to effect a continuance. Hence market economies with their commitment to free trade should, according to Leidy, be expected to opt for export controls rather than import controls and this may explain the observed pattern.

7.5   Costs and Benefits of Diplomacy

Diplomatic activities may constitute a burden for society. Conflict imposes substantial costs. Enhanced reliance on sanctions, embargoes and boycotts, triggered by the greater ease with which the desired unity among nations is achieved and the greater effectiveness of threats due to the greater political linkage, also entails the hidden cost of increased trade uncertainty. Chapter 6 formally analysed the general (and possibly endogenous) trade uncertainty that results if international politics resorts to economic warfare and economic surveillance. It was argued that it may even pay to change the relative pattern of production in favour of the good in which the economy has a comparative disadvantage. The implied suboptimal allocation of factors of production is a hidden, but real cost of trade uncertainty. These costs, however, are to a large extent invisible as it is potential trade that is influenced.

Table 7.7 Impact of political uncertainty on trade

	Period	Number of countries	Elasticities of trade with respect to	
			Co-operation	Hostility
Pollins 1989a	1955—1978	6	0.01	
			0.06	
Bergeijk 1989b	1966—1970	25	0.49	—0.20
Bergeijk 1989b	1982—1985	25	0.22	—0.27
Pollins 1989b	1960—1975	25	0.04	
			0.37	
Bergeijk 1992	1985	40	0.37	—0.56
			0.44	—0.23

Table 7.7 summarizes some recent empirical findings that illustrate that trade uncertainty arising from political interactions imposes substantial costs on the world economic system. Like the findings in this chapter, these studies dealing with other periods and different countries find strictly positive and statistically significant elasticities of exports and imports with respect to diplomatic co-operation ranging up to 0.49. So, according to these studies, an improvement of the diplomatic climate by 50 per cent may on average increase trade by about 25 per cent. Moreover, additional political benefits may result from the fact that trade is an important incentive for international political co-operation.[13]

The economic costs of political trade barriers can be quite substantial indeed, as shown by the case of the case of East—West trade. The annual costs of the Cold War in terms of trade potential forgone have been estimated by Van Bergeijk and Oldersma (1990) at about 3.5 per cent of world production (slightly more than 30 per cent of world trade). They investigate the potential gains from the removal of the politically-inspired and economic-systemic barriers to trade, with a standard gravity model. To this model dummy variables have been added that capture the extent to which East—West trade relations deviate from the normal or average pattern of trade. An expected trade pattern for 49 countries in the year 1985 serves as a basis of comparison for the outcomes.[14] The investigation produces a rather good description of the world trade system in general, and of the European trade system in particular. One scenario describes the consequences of completely unresticted economic relations between East and West (the mirror image of the costs of the Cold War). This counterfactual simulation pertains to a comparison of, on the one hand a situation in which the political barriers hinder international trade and on the other hand, a situation where those barriers have been removed completely.

Table 7.8 Annual costs of Cold War (loss of export potential, 1985)

Region	Percentage of regional GDP	
Western Europe	8	
EC-12		7
EFTA		15
Eastern Europe	10	
USSR		6
central Europe		20
Asia	0.3	
Japan		1
NIEs		1
Middle East	2	
Africa	0.8	
World	3.5	

Source: Based on Van Bergeijk and Oldersma (1990)

Table 7.8 summarizes the annual costs of the Cold War. The outcome of the calculations should be seen as indications only. The increase of the trade potential has been related to country-GDP or region-GDP in order to make the changes in the trade potential comparable. Generally speaking Eastern Europe stands to gain most from *détente* and market-oriented reform. Within the OECD, Western Europe (especially the EFTA-countries) gets a better trade position. The impact on the trade flows to other continents is only marginal. Interestingly, the economic burden of the Cold War has not been shared equally, as the costs for the superpowers have been relatively small. The Soviet Union's loss of trade potential has been less than one-third of the loss suffered by the countries in central Europe. The loss of trade potential for the United States has been almost negligible. So Europe appears to have paid the brunt of the costs of the Cold War in terms of trade forgone.

These findings show with hindsight that diplomacy may impose substantial costs on the economy. However, only in exceptional cases will the costs of diplomatic accidents and structural political differences be manifested directly. Hence it is almost impossible to weigh the political gain of gestures of protest, an angry fist or strong verbal dismay, against the loss that such political 'actions' will mean for trade in the long run. Neither do the benefits of diplomatic activities aimed at co-operation directly show up in the balance of trade although they will ultimately do so. Economic research can provide better information about the costs and benefits of foreign policy. At the same time this may result in a better understanding of the actual working of the international exchange system.

Notes

1. See Brakman (1991) for a lucid review of applied trade flow modelling techniques and a critical review of the gravity analysis.
2. Isard's (1954) contribution is neglected by most students of the gravity method. This is one of many examples of primogeneity not always resulting in scientific recognition. Ethier (1993, p. 14 fn. 6) has labelled this phenomenon — which seems to be a particular nuisance in international economics — 'Gresham's Law of Names'.
3. See, for example the empirical results in Table 7.5. Checks were, however, performed on regional differences using dummy variables for COMECON, EC and EFTA membership as well as for the continents (not reported here). Although some dummy variables appeared significant, this hardly changed the results and the overall performance of the model was not significantly improved. The results in section 7.3 show the influence of the diplomatic climate under the assumption of constant parameters

across countries, while section 7.4 shows the results when this assumption has been relaxed with respect to all parameters.

4. Some of these issues have only recently and in a somewhat different context been picked up by, amongst others, Krugman (1991).

5. The overall influence of population on trade is ambiguous. Although most empirical studies find a negative sign, a number of theories have been proposed that give rise to opposite expectations.

6. This publication should be distinguished from *Keesings Historical Archives*. The source *Keesings Historische Archief* is an independent Dutch publication.

7. Other authors, such as Azar and Havener have implicitly attached about the same weights to events as has been done in Faber's 1987 article. See Faber (1987, p. 447, footnote 2).

8. The test statistic that is used here is (see, for example, Pindyck and Rubinfeld 1991, pp. 117—9):

$$F = (N\text{---}7)(SSR_{model\ (1)} \text{---} SSR_{model\ (2)})/2SSR_{model\ (2)}$$

N = Number of observations (1,309 or 1,560).

9. The impact of the choice of q can be summarized by the following ranges for estimates of the parameters for the explanatory variables (for $q = \$ 0.1$ million to $q = \$ 1$ million):

ln Y_i	1.81	1.48
ln Y_j	1.35	1.08
ln D_{ij}	—0.97	—0.81
ln N_i	—0.98	—0.82
ln N_j	—0.52	—0.41
ln C_{ij}	0.40	0.47
ln H_{ij}	—0.78	—0.50

10. Note that the results in the third column of Table 7.4 pertain to *ex post* residuals of the estimation based on 1,560 bilateral trade flows, while the other columns show out-of-sample predictions on the basis of the 1,309 non-zero trade flows. All predictions have been calculated from the observed explanatory variables using the estimated equations (7.1) and (7.2), that is Table 7.2. Note, moreover, that due to the log transformation of the multiplicative gravity equation, the constant term cannot be estimated directly and needs to be calculated so as to assure equality between the sum of predicted trade flows and the sum of observed trade flows. See, for example, Teekens and Koerts (1972, pp. 794—7).

11. The coefficients in the US import equation are significant at the 89 per cent confidence level.

12. Leidy's observations pertain especially to the United States in the 1970s where the Export Administration Acts of 1969 and 1979

constitute additional institutional considerations to restrict exports of goods and technology.

13.   See, for examples, the literature on the trade conflict relationship that was reviewed in Chapter 5.

14.   This expected trade matrix sometimes differs considerably from the observed trade matrix. For example, the bilateral trade flow between Japan and the United States is considerably underestimated.

Appendix: Data sources

This kind of investigation requires a data set that comprises both political and economic variables at the national and the international levels. INDES (Groenink, 1988) could be a source for research that deals with the 1960s and 1970s, although it covers only 25 European countries, the United States and the Soviet Union. For the present purpose of investigating the trade and diplomacy relationship in the mid-1980's a new data set had to be build. This appendix describes the sources and the details of the procedures.

From the confrontation of data sources resulted a subset of 70 countries from which Iran and Iraq were excluded because of their (total) war, which makes economic observations for them very unreliable. Singapore and Hong Kong were excluded because their trade pattern is dominated by transit trade. Belgium and the Netherlands were excluded because the data source that was used to construct the diplomatic indicators tends to be biased with respect to the diplomatic activities of these countries.

The sample of 40 countries was selected from this subset on the basis of an unweighted average ranking of the rankings for GNP per capita, GNP, export and population. The characteristic neutrality of Iceland, Sweden and Switzerland prompted their inclusion. In this selection only South Korea (rank 16) is missing from the group of 'large' countries. On the low side of the sample more potential candidates are missing such as Greece (rank 46), Israel (rank 48), Ireland (rank 49), New Zealand (rank 51), Peru (rank 52), Ecuador (rank 54) and Bolivia (rank 63).

Exports
The data set covers 80 per cent of world trade in 1986. The data on bilateral trade flows (in current US dollars) have been derived from the IMF's *Direction of Trade Statistics 1992 Yearbook*. In addition some bilateral trade flows for Comecom member countries and for trade between East and West Germany were derived from: Vienna Institute for Comparative Studies *Comecon data 1990*, (Vienna 1990, pp. 185 and 271) and Statistisches Bundesamt, *Sowjetunion*

1980—1991 Bilanz der letzten Jahren (Wiesbaden 1992, p. 87). These data have been converted into 'international' dollars of 1980 by means of the trade price data matrix for 1986 that was supplied by the Projections and Perspective Studies Branch of the Office for Development Research and Policy Analysis, Department of International Economic and Social Affairs, United Nations, New York.

Gross Domestic Product (GDP)
The data on gross national product (in 1980 US$) have been derived from a recent study by Summers and Heston (1988, Table 3, variable *RGDP1* and Table 4 variable *RGPN*, pp. 18—22). The figures for real *per capita* income have been constructed by the United Nations' International Comparisons Project (ICP). The methodology is described in Kravis, Heston and Summers (1982) and has been reviewed by amongst others Theil (1983) and Marris (1984).

It is widely recognized that comparing the gross domestic products of countries by simply converting them at market exchange rates into a common currency unit is a very unsatisfactorily method, since exchange rates do not usually reflect the relative purchasing power of the currencies.

First, the market exchange rate only applies to internationally traded goods and services and capital transactions (especially in 1985—1986 when western short-term capital flows seemed to dominate the development of the exchange rates of many currencies). As the gross domestic product also consists of non-traded and non-tradeable goods, comparing incomes converted at market exchange rates can produce misleading results. This is especially true because services (often non-traded or non-tradeables) are relatively cheap in most developing countries. Second, the official exchange rate is often a poor indication of the relative scarcity of a currency, when it is not freely convertible against other currencies, as was the case in the Centrally Planned Economies and many developing countries in 1985—1986. Finally, the big fluctuations in currency values in the mid 1980s would probably distort the econometric investigations if gross domestic products were to be converted at market exchange rates.

The ICP provides an alternative yardstick for international comparisons of gross domestic products, the so-called Purchasing Power Parity (PPP). A PPP is essentially an international price index. The gross domestic products that are used in this chapter are the PPP-converted gross domestic products per capita that are supplied in Summers and Heston and have been multiplied by the respective populations. About 90 per cent of world income in 1985 is earned by the sample of 40 countries that is being studied in this sample.

Population
The 40 counties represent about 90 per cent of the world population in 1985. Population figures have been derived from Summers and Heston (1988) Tables 3 and 4, pp. 18—22 (variable named POP).

Distances
The economic distances (that is the transportation costs) between the centres of economic gravity have been measured as the crow flies. So transportation routes have been proxied by the pure geographic distance (the length of a straight line) between the trade partners's capitals. Differences in the use of the different modes of transport (sea, air, road, rail) have not been taken into account, although transport costs certainly depend on the choice of the mode of transportation.

Distances have been calculated from the degrees of longitude and latitude of the capital cities of the trade partners, which are stated to the nearest minute in the *Oxford World Atlas*, Oxford 1983. Assume the earth to be a sphere with a circumference of 40,000 kilometres. The coordinates of a point on the unit sphere are $x = \sin\theta \cdot \cos\phi$, $y = \sin\theta \cdot \sin\phi$, $z = \cos\theta$; where θ is the normalized latitude $0 \leq \theta \leq \pi$ and ϕ is the normalized longitude $0 \leq \phi \leq 2\pi$. The angle α between the vectors $a = [x, y, z]$ and $a' = [x', y', z']$ can be obtained from $\cos\alpha = a \cdot a'$ and $\alpha < \pi$. The shortest distance between the two points is approximately $20{,}000\alpha/\pi$.

Obviously this choice of geographic distances instead of economic distances is a simplification of the routes that the goods actually have to travel. Geographic distances do not take into account the fact that natural (physical) trade barriers, such as mountains, sea currents, etc., often dictate the course of trade. The approximation, however, seems reasonable since geographic distances are good representations for flying distances and hence probably of the 'economic horizon' for the representative exporter.

Indicators for the diplomatic climate

Events and their co-operation and conflict intensities have been derived for each country *vis-à-vis* the 39 other countries for the years 1982—1985. These events have been identified on the basis of *Keesings Historische Archief* 1982, 1983, 1984, 1985 and 1986 (the 1986 volume reports on a number of events that happened in 1985). Following the identification of an event its relevance has to be ascertained. Based on the classification scheme of Figure 7.1 (see page 150) and the description of the event in *Keesings Historische Archief* the event is assigned to a category. In this process some subjectivity is unfortunately unavoidable. In any case state visits were considered as neutral activities if such visits were not amplified in *Keesings Historische Archief* (that is to say if no verbal complaints or verbal support was reported in this source).

Next the calculation of the bilateral flows of hostility and co-operation proceeds as follows. If, for example, the diplomatic behaviour of country A with respect to country B consists of two events with high conflict intensity (weight 3) and four events with low conflict intensity (weight 1), then the hostility indicator $H_{AB}{}^*$ becomes $(2 \times 3) + (4 \times 1) = 10$. The indicator for the bilateral diplomatic climate is H_{AB} $(=H_{BA})$, which equals $\ln(1 + H_{AB}{}^* + H_{BA}{}^*)$. If in the above example country B does not behave hostile in any way towards the target then H_{AB} $(=H_{BA}) = \ln(1 + 10 + 0) = \ln(11) = 2.4$. This value is used as an observation to estimate equations 7.2, 7.3 and 7.4.

Table 7.1 (page 152) and Table 7A.1 (page 172—175) report the basic indicators for the bilateral diplomatic climate for the 40 countries, that is $H_{AB}{}^* + H_{BA}{}^*$ and $C_{AB}{}^* + C_{BA}{}^*$, respectively.

Table 7A.1 Indicators for bilateral diplomacy (to the right and above the diagonal: co-operation; below and to the left: hostility)

	Can	Fra	Brd	Ita	Jap	UK	USA	Den	Fin	Nor	Swe
Canada		9	7	8	8	15	9	0	0	0	0
France	1		26	13	12	21	21	0	1	0	0
Germany (West)	1	1		12	12	23	25	0	0	2	0
Italy	1	0	1		8	15	15	0	0	0	0
Japan	0	1	1	1		12	16	0	0	0	0
United Kingdom	1	1	0	0	2		25	1	0	1	0
United States	2	7	7	4	3	7		0	0	0	0
Denmark	0	1	1	1	0	1	3		0	2	2
Finland	0	1	1	0	0	1	2	2		1	0
Norway	0	0	0	0	0	2	3	1	1		0
Sweden	0	0	0	0	0	0	1	1	0	2	
Switzerland	0	0	0	0	0	0	0	0	0	0	0
Australia	0	2	0	0	0	0	2	0	0	0	0
Iceland	0	0	0	0	0	0	1	0	0	0	0
Portugal	0	0	0	0	0	0	1	0	0	0	0
Spain	0	2	0	0	0	0	2	0	0	0	0
South Africa	3	5	2	5	5	3	2	4	4	4	4
Turkey	0	0	0	0	0	0	0	0	0	0	0
Argentina	9	8	9	10	1	28	5	5	1	3	0
Brazil	0	0	0	0	0	1	1	0	0	0	0
Chile	0	3	0	0	0	2	1	0	0	0	0
Mexico	0	0	0	0	0	1	0	0	0	0	0
Venezuela	0	0	0	0	0	1	1	0	0	0	0
Gabon	0	2	0	0	0	0	1	0	0	0	0
Nigeria	0	0	0	0	0	3	1	0	0	0	0
Egypt	0	0	0	0	0	0	1	0	0	0	0
Morocco	0	0	0	0	0	0	1	0	0	0	0
Tunisia	0	0	0	0	0	0	1	0	0	0	0
Sudan	0	0	0	0	0	0	1	0	0	0	0
Ghana	0	0	0	0	0	0	1	0	0	0	0
Saudi Arabia	0	0	0	0	0	0	3	0	0	0	0
Indonesia	0	0	0	0	0	0	0	0	0	0	0
India	0	3	0	0	0	0	3	0	0	0	0
Pakistan	0	0	0	0	0	0	0	0	0	0	0
Philippines	0	0	0	0	0	0	3	0	0	0	0
Czechoslovakia	0	0	0	0	0	0	1	0	0	0	0
Germany (East)	0	0	5	1	1	0	2	1	0	0	0
Poland	1	1	1	2	0	0	4	1	0	1	0
Soviet Union	5	8	12	7	4	9	27	7	4	10	11
China	0	1	1	0	0	2	3	0	0	0	0

Table 7A.1 continued

	Swi	Aus	Ice	Por	Spa	S-Af	Tur	Arg	Bra	Chil
Canada	0	0	0	0	2	0	0	0	2	0
France	1	0	0	7	26	0	0	0	2	0
Germany (West)	0	0	0	6	12	0	2	0	2	0
Italy	0	0	0	6	12	0	0	0	2	0
Japan	0	0	0	0	0	0	0	0	2	0
United Kingdom	0	0	0	6	14	0	0	0	2	1
United States	0	9	0	6	14	3	0	2	4	1
Denmark	0	0	0	6	12	0	0	0	0	0
Finland	0	0	0	0	0	0	0	0	0	0
Norway	0	0	0	0	6	0	0	0	0	0
Sweden	0	0	0	0	0	0	0	0	0	0
Switzerland		0	0	0	0	0	0	0	0	0
Australia	0		0	0	0	0	0	0	0	0
Iceland	0	0		0	0	0	0	0	0	0
Portugal	0	0	0		12	1	0	0	0	0
Spain	0	0	0	0		0	3	0	0	0
South Africa	0	5	4	3	4		0	0	0	0
Turkey	0	0	0	0	0	5		0	0	0
Argentina	0	0	0	0	1	6	0		1	1
Brazil	0	0	0	0	0	6	0	0		0
Chile	0	0	0	0	0	4	0	0	0	
Mexico	0	0	0	0	0	6	0	0	0	0
Venezuela	0	0	0	0	0	6	0	0	0	0
Gabon	0	0	0	0	0	4	0	0	0	0
Nigeria	0	0	0	0	0	7	0	0	0	0
Egypt	0	0	0	0	0	5	0	0	0	0
Morocco	0	0	0	0	0	4	0	0	0	0
Tunisia	0	0	0	0	0	4	0	0	0	0
Sudan	0	0	0	0	0	4	0	0	0	0
Ghana	0	0	0	0	0	5	0	0	0	0
Saudi Arabia	0	0	0	0	0	5	0	0	0	0
Indonesia	0	0	0	0	0	5	0	0	0	0
India	0	0	0	0	0	6	0	0	0	0
Pakistan	0	0	0	0	0	6	0	0	0	0
Philippines	0	0	0	0	0	4	0	0	0	0
Czechoslovakia	0	0	0	2	1	6	0	0	0	0
Germany (East)	0	0	0	2	0	6	0	0	0	0
Poland	0	0	0	3	1	4	0	0	0	0
Soviet Union	8	7	1	7	6	8	3	2	2	1
China	0	0	0	0	0	5	0	0	0	0

Table 7A.1 Indicators for bilateral diplomacy (continued, to the right and above the diagonal: cooperation; below and to the left: hostility)

	Mex	Ven	Gab	Nig	Egy	Mor	Tun	Sud	Gha	Sau
Canada	0	0	0	0	0	0	0	0	0	0
France	0	0	1	0	4	1	1	0	0	2
Germany (West)	0	0	0	0	2	0	0	0	0	0
Italy	0	0	0	0	0	0	0	0	0	0
Japan	0	0	0	0	0	0	0	0	0	0
United Kingdom	0	0	0	1	1	0	0	0	0	0
United States	1	1	0	0	5	0	0	2	0	3
Denmark	0	0	0	0	0	0	0	0	0	0
Finland	0	0	0	0	0	0	0	0	0	0
Norway	0	0	0	0	0	0	0	0	0	2
Sweden	0	0	0	0	0	0	0	0	0	0
Switzerland	0	0	0	0	0	0	0	0	0	0
Australia	0	0	0	0	0	0	0	0	0	0
Iceland	0	0	0	0	0	0	0	0	0	0
Portugal	0	0	0	0	0	0	0	0	0	0
Spain	1	1	0	0	0	8	0	0	0	0
South Africa	0	0	0	0	0	0	0	0	0	0
Turkey	0	0	0	0	0	0	0	0	0	0
Argentina	1	1	0	0	0	0	0	0	0	0
Brazil	1	0	0	0	0	0	0	0	0	0
Chile	0	0	0	0	0	0	0	0	0	0
Mexico		6	0	0	0	0	0	0	0	0
Venezuela	0		0	2	0	0	0	0	0	4
Gabon	0	0		0	0	0	0	0	0	0
Nigeria	0	1	0		0	0	0	0	1	1
Egypt	0	0	0	0		2	1	11	0	1
Morocco	0	0	0	0	0		6	0	0	0
Tunisia	0	0	0	0	0	0		0	0	0
Sudan	0	0	0	1	0	0	0		0	2
Ghana	0	0	0	2	0	0	0	0		0
Saudi Arabia	0	0	0	1	0	0	0	0	0	
Indonesia	0	0	0	0	0	0	0	0	0	0
India	0	0	0	0	0	0	0	0	0	0
Pakistan	0	0	0	0	0	0	0	0	0	0
Philippines	0	0	0	0	0	0	0	0	0	0
Czechoslovakia	0	0	0	0	0	0	0	0	0	0
Germany (East)	0	0	0	0	0	0	0	0	0	0
Poland	0	0	0	0	0	0	0	0	0	0
Soviet Union	2	2	1	2	2	1	1	1	1	1
China	0	0	0	0	0	0	0	0	0	0

Table 7A.1 Continued

	Sau	Indo	Indi	Pak	Phi	Cze	GDR	Pol	SU	Chin
Canada	0	0	0	0	0	0	0	0	4	0
France	2	4	6	3	4	0	1	0	4	1
Germany (West)	0	4	0	0	4	0	14	0	3	4
Italy	0	2	0	0	4	0	0	0	0	0
Japan	0	0	0	0	0	0	1	0	0	0
United Kingdom	0	4	0	0	4	0	0	0	3	4
United States	3	0	1	3	2	0	0	4	6	10
Denmark	0	4	0	0	4	0	0	0	0	0
Finland	0	0	0	0	0	0	0	0	8	0
Norway	2	2	0	0	4	0	0	0	5	0
Sweden	0	0	0	0	0	0	0	0	0	0
Switzerland	0	0	0	0	0	0	0	0	0	0
Australia	0	0	0	0	0	0	0	0	0	0
Iceland	0	0	0	0	0	0	0	0	0	0
Portugal	0	0	0	0	2	0	0	0	0	0
Spain	0	2	0	0	4	0	0	0	5	0
South Africa	0	0	0	0	0	0	0	0	0	0
Turkey	0	0	0	3	0	0	0	0	0	0
Argentina	0	0	0	0	0	0	0	0	0	0
Brazil	0	0	0	0	0	0	0	0	2	0
Chile	0	0	0	0	0	0	0	0	0	0
Mexico	0	0	0	0	0	0	0	0	0	0
Venezuela	4	2	0	0	0	0	0	0	0	0
Gabon	0	0	0	0	0	0	0	0	0	0
Nigeria	1	2	0	0	0	0	0	0	0	0
Egypt	1	1	2	1	0	0	0	0	4	2
Morocco	0	0	0	0	0	0	0	0	0	0
Tunisia	0	0	0	0	0	0	0	0	0	0
Sudan	2	0	0	0	0	0	0	0	0	0
Ghana	0	0	0	0	0	0	4	0	4	0
Saudi Arabia		1	1	0	11	0	0	0	0	0
Indonesia	0		0	0	4	0	0	0	0	0
India	0	0		2	0	0	0	0	3	0
Pakistan	0	0	4		0	0	0	0	0	0
Philippines	0	0	0	0		0	0	0	0	5
Czechoslovakia	0	0	1	0	0		6	8	6	0
Germany (East)	0	0	1	0	0	1		8	6	0
Poland	0	0	0	0	0	0	1		8	0
Soviet Union	1	3	5	4	1	0	3	2		12
China	0	1	0	0	0	0	0	0	3	

PART III
INSTITUTIONAL CHANGE

8. Toward a World Trade and Investment Organization

Economic realism is a powerful antidote to political enthusiasm. In the international economic arena the visions of politicians are often impressive, gestures are spectacular, and the tempo of change is assumed to be high. In reality, however, the economic scope for improvement is often small in the short term. Economic processes exhibit inertia. Consequently, economic reality often seems to lag behind political dreams. If this were all, we need not to be worried and simply let the economics prove international political statements false. However, many political gestures carry an important — although often invisible — price tag. Hence it may be efficient to seek institutional change and other ways to limit the impact of politics on trade and investment. International commercial exchange should essentially be the business of the business man, not of the diplomat.

This is especially true since politics often has difficulty in keeping up with economic realities. A clear discrepancy exists between on the one hand the globalization of production and the international economic co-operation that are almost tangible in multinational corporations, and on the other hand, world politics where the colour of one's passport completely dominates affairs. Too many problems are still being dealt with from a national — and all too often nationalistic — point of view. Remedies are mainly sought in domestic policies which in many cases distort international exchange. Globalization, however, is rendering domestically oriented policies increasingly impotent. Modern communication technologies, new modes of transportation and the liberalization of international capital flows have reduced transportation costs and have made many firms geographically mobile. This implies that firms have the opportunity to exploit a 'new' solution to problems that are posed by government-induced distortions, namely to leave the country. Often this aggrevates the problems for which the domestic distortion was meant to provide a solution. The mirror image is of course that policies that in the past could rightly be considered as purely domestic, such as government procurement, may now generate external effects on other countries and possibly lead to international conflicts (see, for example, Kindleberger 1986, pp. 9—10 on the neglect of international repercussions in domestic policy-making). Such frictions may pose a significant challenge to conflict resolution in the framework of a New World Order.

In this chapter we will be looking for potential improvements of trade institutions that may enable the world community to internalize both the political externalities of international trade and investment and the economic externalities of modern diplomacy. The discussion starts with a description of some long-term trends and recent developments in the international economic system. Next the history of the plans for an International Trade Organization is discussed briefly, as the multilateral trade system and its guardian GATT have grown from this background. In the 1980s discomfort grew with the functioning of the rules and procedures of the multilateral trading system. In addition new political demands have put pressure on GATT. Accordingly, many authors have proposed changes to the GATT rules and suggested ways to strengthen its role in the world economy. In December 1993 an encouraging step has been made with the adoption of the Final Act of the Uruguay Round. A further strengthening of the institutional framework for international trade and investment, however, is needed and some suggestions are made.

8.1   The Global Trade System

Products are increasingly being produced and distributed within corporate networks. Many products have become international composites. Hence international exchange especially pertains to research, design, marketing, advertising, financing and routine components and services.[1] An example is the production of cars in the US by General Motors. Even for a typical American car like the Pontiac Le Mans more than 60 per cent of value is produced by other countries (see Table 8.1). This suggests that internationally traded goods as well as 'domestic' goods that contain substantial foreign inputs characterize modern consumption and production patterns.

Table 8.1 Production of a Pontiac Le Mans (value added by country)

Country	Value added in per cent	Economic activity
United States	38	Basic design and co-ordination
South Korea	30	Routine labour and assembly
Japan, Asian NIEs	21	Advanced and small components
Germany, England	10	Styling, marketing
Ireland, Barbados	1	Data processing

Source: Reich (1991), p. 113

Globalization of both consumption and production has clear benefits that are not always fully recognized in the political decision-making processes. International exchange enhances efficiency both because comparative advantages and economies of scale can be exploited more fully and because international competition is an important incentive for firms to minimize costs and to innovate products and production techniques. In addition interdependence and the mutual benefits that derive from international exchange are important economic incentives to reduce international political and military conflicts in the long run. Usually, however, only the short-term political costs and benefits are considered.

Economic sanctions, for example, may influence the behaviour of other countries, as shown in Part I of this book. The affirmative answer, however, on the positive theoretical question of whether sanctions can become effective instruments in foreign policy-making is of little significance for normative policy dilemmas concerning the utility and the desirability of the actual implementation of a boycott or an embargo in a specific case. Indeed, the use of sanctions as an instrument of foreign policy often comes down to fighting a political conflict by trampling on consumers and firms that have relatively little outstanding with the political differences of opinion. Economic sanctions are essentially the heaviest non-military instrument in international conflict resolution. Their use should be restricted to those exceptional cases where other, possibly more appropriate, diplomatic measures have been exhausted. In reality, however, political decision-making often neglects other options such as formal protests at high political levels, recalling of ambassadors and other non-economic sanctions. The bias towards economic sanctions is particularly worrying since resorting to economic warfare and economic surveillance more often, increases trade uncertainty and this yields a suboptimal allocation of factors of production. Such hidden, but real costs of international diplomacy are generally not considered in the discussions about a New World Order. In general those discussions focus only on ways to reap the so-called peace dividend.

Since the costs and benefits of diplomatic relationships are not expressed properly to decision-makers, the actual outcome of the 'market' where diplomatic co-operation and diplomatic hostility are being 'traded' is inefficient. Supply of diplomatic hostility is too large since the costs of hostile exchange are largely unknown and, consequently, underestimated. At the same time too little economic co-operation is supplied as the benefits are underestimated. This lack of transparancy and proper information suggests that substantial diplomatic barriers to trade hinder the proper functioning of the world trade system and this constitutes an important economic burden for the New World Order.

In many other fields too, the achievements of liberal trade policy are threatened so that it becomes very difficult to reap the trade dividend of improving diplomatic relationships and free exchange of people and products. A lot of unproductive activity occurs that frustrates the international exchange of goods, services, capital and labour. Interest groups are quite successful in putting pressure on trade officials and politicians to 'correct' international economic relations so as to foster their own interests. Bhagwati and Srinivasan (1982) have coined these activities Directly Unproductive Profit-seeking (DUP) activities. Essentially DUP activities generate shifts in income and profit at the expense of productive inputs: DUP activities dupe. Lobbying for protectionist measures is a clear example of a DUP activity that reduces the welfare for all in order to achieve larger incomes for the few. Agriculture provides another example of the difficulties that liberal trade encounters. Despite more than two centuries of economists arguing for free trade, the edifices of protectionism and managed trade are still very visible. In Europe the Common Agricultural Policy contributes importantly to the Fortress

Europe image. In the US the so-called Bumper amendment prohibits international development assistance if agricultural aid enables Third World farmers to increase the commercial production of meat and crops such as maize and palm oil (Thompson 1992).

The pervasion of managed trade and protectionism has even led some observers to consider the free trade paradigm as an ideology only (see, for example, Ruigrok and Van Tulder 1993). Fortunately, multilateral rules rather than bilateral bargaining and threats still constitute the motive force of the world trade system. Indeed, outside agriculture, the simple paradigm of free trade fits reality rather well and serves policy-makers best (Baneth 1993). GATT membership is growing, multilateral trade negotiation is high on the agenda all around the world and the Uruguay Round has successfully been ended. Indeed, outspoken critics of traditional trade theory admit that one may plausibly argue that 'among the set of efficient policies free trade would be uniquely easy to define and would thus stand out as the focal point for negotiation' (Krugman 1993, p. 364).

Two developments since the early 1980s have necessitated a strengthening of the open multilateral trade system. The first development is the objectionable reasoning that relates disappointing trade performance to unfair practices by other countries even before looking at home for possible causes. This sentiment has been fed particularly by Japan's strong trade position at a time when the United States has lost hegemony. The US trade deficit since the 1980s, however, was mainly caused by its unbalanced economic fiscal policy as well as lagging American productivity (Sato and Rizzo 1988). It is common economic knowledge that a strive to regulate bilateral trade flows simply cannot work. Reducing one's trade deficit *vis-à-vis* a specific trade partner influences other countries both directly and indirectly. Ultimately bilateral actions will reduce demand for the products that are being exported by the country that is trying to regulate its foreign trade. The Americans, however, failed to grasp this simple logic and reached a wrong conclusion. Consequently, they felt cheated and US demands for conditional and strategic protection became louder. In several cases the resulting political pressure led to incorrect application and flaunting of trade policy rules and GATT-conform trade regulating instruments.[2] The second threat to the open multilateral trading system stems from the UN's unexpected decisiveness and the world community's economic achievements in imposing severe and effective sanctions against a number of countries in the 1990s. Economic sanctions have not been quite as successful politically — and the New World Order has yet to come into being — but it is not far-fetched at all to assume increasing political demand to use economic sanctions and other diplomatic trade barriers, as was argued in Chapter 1.

All in all, an important challenge in the 1990s is to reduce the scope for discretion in trade and investment policy as discretion enables political motives to play an increasingly large role in this traditional field of 'low politics'. Given the economic and political costs of diplomatic barriers to trade that have been investigated in Part II, the next sections will deal with the institutional changes that aim at preserving free trade as a viable policy option.

8.2   A Starting Point: Free Trade

During the Second World War institutional arrangements were proposed to safeguard the post-war economy. These institutions aimed at a world order that could prevent a repetition of the depression of the 1930s that was aggrevated by (in so far as it did not result from) a wave of protectionism and beggar-thy-neighbour policies. The crucial point of departure for the new post-war international economic order was the 1944 conference on the world monetary system in Bretton Woods. Here the International Monetary Fund and the International Bank for Reconstruction and Development (the World Bank) were created. Also proposals about an International Trade Organization (ITO) were discussed. The Bretton Woods view of the global economy is a system that rested on three organizations that were to secure:

- a stable and healthy international monetary system (IMF);
- the reconstruction and development of national economies (World Bank);
- free international economic exchange (ITO).

Unfortunately, this structure supported by three pillars, did not come into being, mainly because politicians did not want to hand over their autonomy and policy discretion in the field of international economic relations. The 1948 United Nations Conference on Trade and Employment in Havana drew up a shopping list for the ITO which covered many trade related subjects such as employment, reconstruction, development, restrictive business practices, as well as specific topics in trade policy such as basic principles (transparancy, non-discrimination and reciprocity), conflict settlement procedures, international commodity agreements and the structure and working programme of the ITO. The US Congress, however, refused to ratify the ITO Charter. Hence an interim agreement, the General Agreement on Tariffs and Trade (GATT), was made and remained in the place of the ITO.[3] So an agreement (with a small secretariat) came into being instead of an organization that should have been the equal of the IMF and the World Bank. Consequently, GATT had to do without the instruments that were needed both to enforce free trade rules and to discourage from undesired trade policies.

Although essentially understaffed, GATT has been quite successful. Periodical multilateral trade negotiations have been initiated that have resulted in a general reduction of import tariffs in the industrialized countries from more than 40 per cent in 1947 to about 5 per cent in the 1990s and this is the main reason behind the tenfold increase in the world trade volume since the 1950s. Many of the items on the 1948 ITO shopping list have been brought within multilateral trade negotiations. The scope of the GATT negotiations has substantially increased over the years. Since the Kennedy Round (1963—1967) non-tariff barriers have become an important topic on the agenda. In the Tokyo Round (1975—1978), for example, government purchases, quality restrictions and import permits were discussed. The Uruguay Round negotiations (1986—1993) were complicated by new issues such as Trade-related Intellectual Property Rights (TRIPs), Trade-related Investment Measures (TRIMs) and the extension of the liberalizing process to international trade in services.[4] The idea of a specialized international trade organization had an unexpected sequel in the Uruguay Round, when the 1991 draft accord of the Uruguay Round (the so-called Dunkel Paper) proposed the creation of a Multilateral Trade Organization (MTO).

The idea of a 'second-best' world trade organization is not new. Jackson (1989), for example, has proposed a new structure for

GATT. His proposal is not as far reaching as the original ITO proposals as it is essentially aimed at solving some of the legal problems of the multilateral trade negotiation, such as the fact that GATT is an interim agreement, the troubled relationship — if any — between GATT and the domestic legislation of the contracting parties and the less than optimal conflict settlement procedures. Others, for example the Atlantic Council (1976), have sought to restore GATT's credibility and to increase its standing and impact by creating a 'GATT-plus' with different decision-making procedures. In GATT decision-making is based on the principle of one country one vote. Giving the larger countries a larger share in the vote (for example in accordance with their share in world GDP or world trade) would perhaps bring the benefit of greater GATT conformity to the trade policies of the major countries (as they would be in a better position to change the rules of the game). At the same time it would to a much larger extent bring economic power diplomacy in multilateral trade negotiation. If the sovereign equality of states is to be the backbone of both the New World Order and world trade system (as it should be since bilateral and discriminatory arrangements are inefficient from a global perspective), then only multilateralism offers a way for trade liberalization through negotiation.[5]

In sum the main arguments for the creation of a world trade institution are:

●   to create a legal and more permanent framework for multilateral trade monitoring and negotiation;
●   to cover more fully the interrelated problems encountered by international trade and services;
●   to provide for an institutionalized international burden-sharing.

An additional reason is provided by the economic argument that efficiency gains could be reaped if the international organizations would specialize in accordance with their respective comparative advantages. For example, the major statistical data source on world trade flows, the *Direction of Trade Flows*, is presently being prepared and published by the IMF. This task could perhaps better be performed by a specialized trade institution. Moreover, the GATT secretariat is already publishing its own assessments of exchange in the international economic systems. Another example is the fact that GATT allows for balance of payments safeguards, while the IMF's balance of payments adjustment programmes could provide for the necessary conditionality if this particular exceptional provision is to be invoked. In this case the IMF's competence clearly supersedes. In order to achieve synergy and to benefit from specialization, some funds and manpower have to be reallocated from IMF and World Bank to the newly established organization, but this restructuring will not entail additional costs for the world community.

The creation of a formal international organization that deals with international trade and trade-related issues took 45 years. In December 1993 the 117 GATT member countries reached consensus on the content of the Final Act of the Uruguay Round of multilateral trade negotiations under the auspices of the GATT, thereby creating a World Trade Organization. The World Trade Organization serves as the institutional framework that encompasses the GATT and other results of the Uruguay Round related to, for example, liberalization of industrial products, agricultural products and services; intellectual property; technical trade barriers; anti-dumping rulings and government procurement, etc. GATT Director and Chairman of the Uruguay Round, Peter Sutherland, claimed that the success of the Uruguay Round implied that 'the world has chosen openness and co-operation instead of uncertainty and conflict'.[6] It is, however, still much too early to accept that the 'newly born' can offer a cure against protectionism and the rise of political barriers to trade. Indeed, nationalistic attitudes made progress in the Uruguay Round often very difficult. Consequently, it is more likely that the World Trade Organization that resulted from the negotiations is rather an impotent compromise, than a *panacea*. Moreover, a trade institution is a necessary condition for openness and co-operation at best, but certainly not a sufficient condition. The 'old' GATT already provided a considerable number of rules and procedures aimed at restricting economic 'power diplomacy' with respect to international trade. Specified procedures and regularized criteria set the rules of the games played in the international economic exchange system and provide a framework for conflict resolution and dispute settlement.

Unfortunately, the problem in the present international context is that the application of many trade remedies that are allowed in GATT (anti-dumping, countervailing duties, etc.) has increasingly come in the realm of national sovereignty. Finger and Dhar (1992) argue that particularly in the 1980s, the development and application of GATT rules by nation states has been an exercise in the application of economic and political power. GATT's success in limiting the use of tariffs and quotas may have led countries to seek the use of fair trading laws to remedy their economic woes. The corresponding rise of administered protection has been most evident in countervailing duties and in anti-dumping measures. Major problems in this respect have always been the arbitrariness and the increase in the frequency of anti-dumping measures.[7] Dumping originally referred to the selling of a product on a foreign market at a price that yields on average less net revenue than comparable sales in a firm's home market. The extension of the concept of dumping to 'imports not priced at full costs' significantly increased administrative discretion and expanded the power and scope of the anti-dumping instrument. In the early 1960s only about 40 to 50 anti-dumping decrees were in force (incidentally concentrated in South Africa); at the beginning of the 1990s more than 500 anti-dumping actions were in force.[8] According to Finger and Dhar (1992), this increase in the use of trade policy instruments has been largely driven by endogenous factors such as the facts that trade intervention became an important vehicle for constituent service in the United States and that the European Commission could develop anti-dumping into a powerful community instrument at its discretion.[9] The increase in anti-dumping measures as well as the growing political and administrative discretion in trade policy represent increases in both exogenous and endogenous trade uncertainty and will most probably lead to political frictions. Multilateral trade negotiation has not been able to produce quick results in these fields, although political demands have often been very explicit.

The Uruguay Round's Final Act does not provide a solution for the problem posed by the resort to trade remedies. The Final Act provides more detailed rules for establishing dumping as well as a stricter interpretation of the causality of the petitioner's damage. However, during the last decade it has become increasingly recognized that both GATT's lack of power to enforce rules and procedures and the more frequent use of anti-dumping and countervailing duties derive from a lack of knowledge of the costs of protection and from the fact that anti-dumping investigations can only consider the injury of dumping caused to the petitioners's sales, profit, employment, etc. This means that those domestic interest groups that bear the costs of protectionist measures (mainly consumers and user industries) are generally not taken into account. In fact, it is this neglect of the domestic losers from trade impediments that is at the root of both the anti-dumping problem and the detoriation of GATT's standing in the 1980s. So a first-best solution to the present trade problems should seek to reform the domestic formulation of trade policy by the contracting parties so as to take injuries to non-petitioners into account as well. This should lead to stricter procedures and purer interpretation of trade rules. The lesson from history, however, is that an important force against free trade derives from protectionist interpretation of agreed rules and procedures. So more is needed than the provision of more detailed and more sophisticated rules of the game. Making the costs of protection more transparent and more widely known to the public in general, seems the best way to strengthen the case of international economic exchange. Only greater transparency will provide a climate in which free trade can develop and flourish.

8.3 Upgrading the World Trade Organization

These important threats to the proper functioning of the world system could be countered by a strengthening of the trade and investment institution both in an organizational sense and with respect to the instruments that are made available to it. This final section draws up a list of suggestions.

Monitor the world trade system
A first option that is presently being pursued is to let the GATT secretariat periodically review the trade policies of its members. This is in line with the OECD's Economic Development Review Committee which annually reviews its members' economic developments, prospects and policies. The findings of these reviews are made readily available to the general public in the OECD's *Economic Surveys* series. In 1989 GATT's Trade Policy Review

Mechanism was introduced which reviews the trade policies of the major countries on a regular basis. Objective information on the costs and benefits of trade policy measures provided by a relative outsider will clarify many debates on international trade. So the Trade Policy Review Mechanism may become an essential input in multilateral trade negotiation and may improve on trade policy decisions around the world. This is so because protection in general carries an efficiency cost and a welfare loss, and because a connection is apparent between protectionist trade demands and cartel behaviour. For example, about a quarter of EC anti-dumping actions concern firms and products that will eventually be investigated for restrictive business practices (Montagnon 1990, pp. 79—81).

The newly set-up World Trade Organization can play an important role in uncovering the costs of protectionist measures and other politically inspired trade distortions. A fresh start with a new organization can help Trade to shrug off the inheritance of a decade of criticism on GATT, thus possibly generating the necessary political momentum that is needed to solve the major issues related to international trade and investment. The creation of a new international organization will certainly help to solve some of the legal problems related to GATT. The present move toward an explicit general monitoring system, however, has several drawbacks. Curzon Prince (1991) points out three defects. First, the secretariat has no authority to qualify measures as being GATT-legal or GATT-illegal. Second, the reports are a rather descriptive catalogue of trade policy measures, while an analytical approach is necessary if the costs of such measures are to be exposed.[10] Third, the reports are not easily digestable so that it is difficult to communicate to the public the main findings about the negative repercussions of trade and investment impediments.

Cover investment more fully
It is definitely a disadvantage that the interrelated issues of trade and investment cannot be handled in a comprehensive way by the new international organization. Julius (1991) points out that although foreign direct investment is very important to trade (especially in services), investment still is the 'neglected twin of trade'. Trade policy, she argues, must become 'trade and investment policy'. The

need to extend the activities of the World Trade Organization to international investment are obvious. Harris (1993) shows that since the early 1980s the quantitative importance of foreign direct investment in the world economic system has increased much quicker than the importance of international trade. Foreign direct investment often exposes sheltered parts of the host economy to international competitive forces, expanding the tradeables sector at the expense of previously protected activities. Governments will on the one hand experience the trade-substitution and trade-diverting effects of foreign direct investment that can be detrimental to their economy. On the other hand they will be tempted to attract foreign capital through tax incentives and favourable investment conditions in order to reap the benefits of both trade-complementing investment and offshore operations that produce for the international market. Equally challenging is the question of how to deal with the process of globalization of production as this may force governments to negotiate directly with multinational corporations over the conditions to locate their core operations within their jurisdictions (Schott 1993). Hence, as Petersmann (1993) points out, the proper functioning of the world economic system requires competition rules for governments.

Examine dumping

If the secretariat of the World Trade Organization were explicitly instructed to examine dumping and other unhealthy trade practices many of the present threats to the international economic system could perhaps be redeemed. The objective assessment of an act of dumping will put anti-dumping measures beyond any doubt thus restraining anti-dumping to those cases where trade practices are unfair indeed. And already the possibility of a negative ruling by the World Trade (and Investment) Organization may significantly influence trade policies around the world. This would in an *ex ante* sense support the open multilateral trade system. Such authoritative judgements could, moreover, be the international sanctions that are needed to provide against the free-riding that would otherwise plague the international public good provided by an open multilateral trading system.[11] Economies to scale in information costs could be reaped, thus enabling the provision of the public good of trade monitoring at lower costs.

Deal with regional trade iniatitives

A serious drawback of GATT has been its inability to deal with the increase in regional trade arrangements and programmes such as Europe's Internal Market, the European Economic Space and North and Latin America's free trade agreements NAFTA and LAFTA). Those exceptions to the GATT most-favoured-nation rule have in the past been allowed because regional integration was assumed to be favourable to the world trade system since trade creation would exceed trade diversion.[12] Experience, however, often contradicted theoretical expectations, while sectoral exceptions (for example in agriculture and textiles) and discriminatory treatment have created political frictions. This could be remedied if the World Trade (and Investment) Organization were to track regional co-operation initiatives after they are signed. Schott points out that 'The challenge is to close the loopholes in the trading rules to ensure that regional pacts do not compromise or undermine the commitment to the multilateral trading system' (Schott 1993, p. 19).

Solve the resource constraint

A financial injection is needed if these shortcomings are to be put right. Admittedly, the matter of the authority is essentially a legal question that could be solved without any increase in budgets. It would, however, in practice be as efficient a constraint on the general monitoring system if the World Trade (and Investment) Organization's legal competence were to be extended while the funds for the necessary increase in legal manpower were not made available. Resource constraints are also major impediments for a more analytical approach and the public relations side of the relevant findings of the Trade Policy Review Mechanism. So far the funding of sound trade policy research has been an important problem, while the international scientific community seems to have been too much involved in the theoretical debate on the fundamentals of the 'new' trade theory to be able to fill the gap in our knowledge about these practical issues.[13] The World Trade (and Investment) Organization can play an important role in generating and channeling the necessary funds.

An important benefit of the institutional strengthening of the world trade system would be its protection of small and medium-sized countries, as only the large economies can benefit from strategic trade policies and economic warfare, while the rest of the world is the victim. Ultimately, however, unilateral trade policies will reduce world demand for the products of the country that is trying to regulate its foreign trade. Hence in the long-run an open multilateral trade system is in the interest of all countries.

It is the multilateral approach that offers a first line of defence against increasing bilateralism and protectionism and against power politics of other economies. In this capacity a World Trade and Investment Organization could provide an important instrument to support the New World Order as well as create the institutional and economic background against which the trade and the peace dividends can be reconciled.

Notes

1. Porter (1990) is one of the most outspoken proponents of globalization. See, however, Ruigrok and Van Tulder (1993) for a contrary opinion on the internationalization of modern corporations, especially with respect to the location of headquarters and the composition of the boards of directors.
2. See Bhagwati (1992) for a lucid discussion of these and related issues.
3. GATT derives from chapter IV of the Havanna Charter, *Final Act and Related Documents: the Second Sesssion of the Prepatory Committee*. See also Karsdorp (1992) for a Dutch perspective on the issues surrounding the ITO.
4. See on these new issues in the Uruguay Round, for example, De C. Grey (1990) and Greenaway and Sapir (1992).
5. See the summer 1992 issue of *International Organization* for an informed discussion of many issues related to multilateralism.
6. *GATT Focus* No. 140, December 1993, p.1.
7. A related problem is multiple jeopardy in the application of measures by a specific country: a petitioner may continue to petition untill he finds a legal ground that is accepted (see Finger and Dhar 1992). In international procedures 'forum shopping' may become a serious threat if international trade and investment related questions are going to be dealt with in different organizations.

8.   In addition, many antidumping petitions are withdrawn before the final verdict. Prusa (1992) presents data for the United States in the period 1980-1985. About a third of the petitions was rejected and in about a quarter of the cases antidumping duties were imposed. So in about half the cases petitions are withdrawn. As a withdrawal does not signal that the domestic industry's case has failed, but rather indicates out-of-court settlement, in these cases tacit collusion is to be expected. The evidence suggests that the impact of settlement in the average case of a withdrawn petition is comparable to the case where duties are imposed. Since only about 50 per cent of the withdrawn cases involve agreements, the restraint of trade that is implied by an out-of-court settlement may be much larger than the explicit trade barrier of the antidumping duties. Moreover, it is often argued that firms might use antidumping law as an offensive strategic weapon (see Prusa 1992 and Webb 1992).

9.   Moore (1992), for example, finds systematic evidence that petitions involving constituencies of members of the US Senate's Oversight Committee may be systematically favoured in US antidumping decisions. In addition his empirical investigation indicates that these decisions are biased against developing countries, possibly because of a lack of retaliatory power. See, however, Devault (1993) for a contrary opinion and Thakaran (1991) for a European perspective.

10. Note, however, that even where and when an analytical approach is possible, the specific evaluation method may often be quite vulnerable to theoretical and practical criticism. This makes it often rather difficult to quantify the welfare costs of protection unambiguously.

11. In addition, Schott (1993, p. 20) argues that the IMF and GATT should enter into a strategic alliance, because the IMF's programmes may provide for the necessary conditionality for trade and investment policy as well. In practice this stick, however, would seem to be too short to hit the industrialized countries as they hardly make an appeal to the Fund's funds. Moreover, countries that run a current account surplus are quite invulnerable to such IMF- sanctions.

12. That is to say that regional integration would increase world trade more than it would redirect its trade from non-members to the members of the regional integration scheme.

13. Transparency can also be produced by domestic organizations (both public and private) that strive for liberal trade. Examples are consumer organizations and user industries. See Spriggs (1991) for a review of the extensive literature on the relative merits of domestic versus international transparency institutions.

References

Adler-Karlsson, G., 1982, 'Instruments of Economic Coercion and Their Use' in: F.A.M. Alting von Geusau and J. Pelkmans (eds.), *National Economic Security: Perceptions, Threats and Policies*, Tilburg: John F. Kennedy Institute, pp. 160—82.

Amemiya, T., 1981, 'Qualitative Response Models: A Survey', *Journal of Economic Literature*, **29** (4), pp. 1483—536.

Anderson, K. and R. Blackhurst, 1992, *The Greening of World Trade Issues*, New York: Harvester Wheatsheaf.

Anderson, K. and H. Norheim, 1993, 'From Imperial to Regional Trade Preferences: Its Effect on Europe's Intra- and Extra-regional Trade', *Weltwirtschaftliches Archiv 129* (1), pp. 78—102.

Arad, R.W. and A.L. Hillman, 1979, 'Embargo Threat, Learning and Departure from Comparative Advantage', *Journal of International Economics*, **9**, pp. 265—75.

Aspin, L., 1991, 'The Aspin Papers: Sanctions, Diplomacy, and War in the Persian Gulf, *Significant Issues Series* **13** (2), Washington D.C.: Center for Strategic and International Studies.

Atlantic Council, 1976, *GATT Plus: A Proposal for Trade Reform*, Washington D.C.

Azar, E.E., 1980, 'The Conflict and Peace Data Bank (COPDAB) Project', *Journal of Conflict Resolution*, **24** (1), pp. 143—52.

Bailey, N.A. and C. Lord, 1988, 'On Strategic Economics', *Comparative Strategy*, **7**, pp. 93—7.

Balassa, B. and L. Bauwens, 1988, *Changing Trade Patterns in Manufactured Goods: An Econometric Investigation*, North-Holland: Amsterdam.

Baldry, J.C. and B. E. Dollery, 1992, 'Investment and Trade Sanctions Against South Africa in a Model of Apartheid' *UNE Working Papers in Economics*, 1.

Baldwin, D.A., 1971, 'The Power of Positive Sanctions', *World Politics*, **24** (1), pp. 19—38.

Baldwin, D.A., 1985, *Economic Statecraft*, Princeton: Princeton University Press.

Baldwin, R.E., 1992, 'Are Economists' Traditional Trade Policy Views Still Valid?', *Journal of Economic Literature* **30**, pp. 804—29.

Balkan, E.M., 1992, 'Political Instability, Country Risk and Probability of Default', *Applied Economics* **24** (9), pp. 999—1008.

Baneth, J., 1993, 'Fortress Europe and Other Myths Concerning Trade, *World Bank WPS Working Papers* WPS 1098, World Bank: Washington D.C.

Bayard, T.O., J. Pelzman and J.F. Perez-Lopez, 1983, 'An Economic Model of United States and Western Controls on Exports to the Soviet Union and Eastern Europe', in: Joint Economic Committee Congress of the United States, *Soviet Economy in the 1980s: Problems and Prospects*, Washington D.C., pp. 507—55.

Bergeijk, P.A.G. van, 1987, 'A Formal Treatment of Threats: A Note on the Economics of Deterrence', *De Economist*, **135** (3), pp. 298—315.

Bergeijk, P.A.G. van, 1989a, 'Success and Failure of Economic Sanctions', *Kyklos* **42** (3), pp. 385—404.

Bergeijk, P.A.G. van, 1989b, 'Trade and Diplomacy: An Extension of the Gravity Model in International Trade Theory', Institute of Economic Research Memorandum No. 320, Groningen: University of Groningen.

Bergeijk, P.A.G. van, 1990, *Handel en diplomatie*, [Trade and Diplomacy], Groningen: University of Groningen.

Bergeijk, P.A.G. van, 1991, 'International Trade and the Environmental Challenge', *Journal of World Trade* **25** (6), pp. 105—15.

Bergeijk, P.A.G. van, 1992, 'Diplomatic Barriers to Trade', *De Economist* **140** (1), pp. 44—63.

Bergeijk, P.A.G. van, 1994, 'A Note on the Accuracy of International Economic Observations: Tribute to Oskar Morgenstern', *Bulletin of Economic Research* [in print].

Bergeijk, P.A.G. van, R.C.G. Haffner and P.M. Waasdorp, 1993, 'Measuring the Speed of the Invisible Hand: The Macroeconomic Costs of Market Inertia', *Kyklos* **46** (4), pp. 529—44.

Bergeijk, P.A.G. van and D.L. Kabel, 1993, 'Strategic Trade Theory and Trade Policy', *Journal of World Trade* **27** (6), pp. 175—86.

Bergeijk, P.A.G. van and R. Lensink, 1993, 'Trade, Capital, and the Transition of Central-Europe', *Applied Economics* **25** (6), pp. 891—903.

Bergeijk, P.A.G. van and C. van Marrewijk, 1993, 'Why Do Sanctions Need Some Time to Work? Adjustment Versus Learning by the Target', *TRACE discussion paper* TI 93—27, Rotterdam: Tinbergen Institute.

Bergeijk, P.A.G. van and C. van Marrewijk, 1994, 'Hidden Costs of the New World Order', in: M. Chatterji, A. Rima and H. Jager (eds.) *Economics of International Security. Essays in Honor of Jan Tinbergen*, London: Macmillan, 168—82.

Bergeijk, P.A.G. van and H. Oldersma, 1990, 'Détente, Market-oriented Reform and German Unification, Potential Consequences for the World Trade System,' *Kyklos* **42** (3), pp. 599—609.

Bergstrand, J.H., 1985, 'The Gravity Equation in International Trade: Some Microeconomic Foundations and Empirical Evidence', *Review of Economics and Statistics*, **67** (1), pp. 474—81.

Bergstrand, J.H., 1989, 'The Generalized Gravity Equation, Monopolistic Competition, and the Factor-proportions Theory in International Trade,' *Review of Economics and Statistics* **71**, pp. 143—52.

Bergström, C., G.C. Loury and M. Persson, 1985, 'Embargo Threats and the Management of Emergency Reserves', *Journal of Political Economy*, **93**, pp. 26—42.

Bhagwati, J.N., 1989, 'Is Free Trade Passé After All?', *Weltwirtschaftliches Archiv* **125** (1), pp. 17—44.

Bhagwati, J.N., 1991, *Political Economy and International Economics*, Cambridge (Mass.): MIT Press.

Bhagwati, J.N., 1992, 'The Threats to the World Trading System', *World Economy* **15** (4), pp. 443—56.

Bhagwati, J.N. and T.N. Srinivasan, 1976, 'Optimal Trade Policy and Compensation Under Endogenous Uncertainty: The Phenomenon of Market Disruption', *Journal of International Economics*, **6**, pp. 317—36.

Bhagwati, J.N. and T.N. Srinivasan, 1982, 'The Welfare Consequences of Directly-unproductive Profit-seeking (DUP) Lobbying Activities: Price *Versus* Quantity Distortions', *Journal of International Economics* **13** (1), pp. 33—44.

Biessen, G., 1991, 'Is the Impact of Central Planning on the Level of Foreign Trade Really Negative?', *Journal of Comparative Economics* **15** (1), pp. 22—44.

Bikker, J.A., 1982, *Vraag-aanbodmodellen voor stelsels van geografisch gespreide markten toegepast op internationale handel en op ziekenhuisopnamen in Noord-Nederland*, Amsterdam: VU University Press.

Bikker, J.A., 1987, 'An International Trade Flow Model With Substitution: An Extension of the Gravity Model', *Kyklos*, **40**, pp. 315—37.

Bikker, J.A., 1992, 'Internal and External Trade Liberalization in the EEC: An Econometric Analysis of International Trade Flows', *Economie Appliquée* **45** (3), pp. 91—119.

Black, P.A. and J.H. Cooper, 1989, 'Economic Sanctions and Interest Group Analysis: Some Reservations', *South African Journal of Economics* **57** (2), 188—93.

Bonetti, S., 1991, 'Sanctions and Statistics: Reconsidering *Economic Sanctions Reconsidered*', University of St. Andrews Department of Economics Discussion Paper 9103, St. Andrews.

Bonetti, S., 1993, 'The Persistence and Frequency of Economic Sanctions', in: M. Chatterji, A. Rima and H. Jager (eds.), *Economics of International Security. Essays in Honor of Jan Tinbergen*, London: Macmillan [in print].

Bornstein, M., 1968, 'Economic Sanctions and Rewards in Support of Arms Control Agreements,' *American Economic Review* **58** (2), Papers & Proceedings, 417—27.

Boulding, K.E., 1962, *Conflict and Defense - A General Theory*, New York: Harper.

Brady, L.J., 1987, 'The Utility of Economic Sanctions as a Policy Instrument', in: D. Leyton-Brown (ed.), *The Utility of International Economic Sanctions*, New York: St. Martins Press, pp. 297—302.

Brakman, S., 1991, *International Trade Modeling: Decomposition Analyses*, Groningen: Wolters Noordhoff.

Bremer, S.A. (ed.), 1987, *The Globus Model. Computer Simulation of Worldwide Political and Economic Developments*, Frankfürt am Main: Campus Verlag.

Bull, H., 1984, 'Economic Sanctions and Foreign Policy', *The World Economy* 7 (1), pp. 218—22.

Carbaugh, R.J., 1989, *International Economics*, 3rd edition, Wadsworth: Belmont.

Carter, B.E., 1988, *International Economic Sanctions: Improving the Haphazard U.S. Legal System*, Cambridge (Mass.): Cambridge University Press.

Cataquet, H., 1985, 'Country Risk Analysis: Art, Science and Sorcery?', in: H.J. Krümmel (ed.) *Internationales Bankgeschäft* Beihefte zu Kredit und Kapital H8, Berlin.

Centre for Economic Policy Research (CEPR), 1990, *Monitoring European Integration: The Impact of Eastern Europe*, London: CEPR.

Citron, J. and G. Nickelsburg, 1987, 'Country Risk and Political Instability', *Journal of Development Economics* 25, pp. 385—92.

Clausewitz, C. von, 1988, *On War*, Harmondsworth: Penguin. (First published 1832).

Cohen, S.I., F.W. van Tongeren and H.J. Boehlé, 1992, 'Modelling the Restructuring of Economic Systems in the GLOBUS Framework', in: W.-D. Eberwein, *Transformation Processes in Eastern Europe: Perspectives from the Modelling Laboratory,* Frankfurt am Main, Peter Lang, pp. 145—60.

Collini, S., D. Winch and J. Burrow, 1983, *That Noble Science of Politics, A Study in Nineteenth-Century Intellectual History*, London: Cambridge University Press.

Committee on Science, Engineering, and Public Policy of the Panel for the Future Design and Implementation of U.S. National Security Export Controls, 1991, *Finding Common Ground: U.S. export Controls in a Changed Global Environment*, Washington D.C.: National Academy Press.

Cooper, H., 1986, 'The Welfare Effects of Sanctions', *Journal of Studies in Economics and Econometrics*, (25), pp. 3—11.

Cooper, R.N., 1987, 'Trade Policy as Foreign Policy', in: R.M. Stern (ed.), *U.S. Trade Policies in a Changing World Economy*, Cambridge (Mass.): MIT Press, pp. 291—322.

Curzon Prince, V. 1991, 'GATT's New Trade Policy Review Mechanism', *World Economy* **14** (2), pp. 227—38.

Daoudi, M.S. and M.S. Dajani, 1983, *Economic Sanctions: Ideals and Experience*, Boston: Routledge & Kegan.

Deardorff, A.V., 1984, 'Testing Trade Theories and Predicting Trade Flows', in: R.W. Jones and P.B. Keenen (eds.), *Handbook of International Economics*, Vol. 1, Amsterdam: North Holland, pp. 467—517.

Dekker, P.G., 1973, 'Economische oorlogvoering: Enige opmerkingen over boycot en embargo', [Economic Warfare: A Note on Boycott and Embargo] *De Economist* **121** (4), 387—402.

Denters, E. and J. Klijn, 1991, *Economic Aspects of a Political Settlement in the Middle East: The Dynamics of Self-determination*, Amsterdam: VU University Press.

Devault, J.M., 1993, 'Economics and the International Trade Commission' *Southern Economic Journal* **60** (2), pp. 463—78.

Diamond, P.A., 1967, 'The Role of a Stock Market in a General Equilibrium Model with Technological Uncertainty', *American Ecnomic Review* **57** (1), pp. 171—9.

Döhrn, R. and A.R. Milton, 1991, 'Zur künftigen Einbindung der osteuropäischen Reformländer in die Weltwirtschaft', *RWI—Mitteilungen* **43**, pp. 19—40.

Dollery, B., 1992, 'Financial and Trade Sanctions Against South Africa: A General Equilibrium Analytical Framework', Faculty of Economic Studies No. 47, Armidale: University of New England.

Doxey, M., 1982, 'The Application of International Sanctions', in: F.A.M. Alting von Geusau and J. Pelkmans (eds.), *National Economic Security: Perceptions, Threats and Policies*, Tilburg: John F. Kennedy Institute, pp. 143—59.

Duyne, C. van, 1975, 'Commodity Cartels and the Theory of Derived Demand', *Kyklos* **28** (3), pp. 597—612.

Eaton, J. and M. Engers, 1992, 'Sanctions', *Journal of Political Economy* **100** (5), pp. 899—928.

Eaton, J. and G. Grossman, 1986, 'Optimal Trade and Industrial Policy under Oligopoly', *Quarterly Journal of Economics* **101**, pp. 383—406.

Eggleston, R.C., 1987, 'Determinants of the Levels and Distribution of PL 480 Food Aid: 1955—79', *World Development* **15** (6), pp. 797—808.

Erickson, B.H., 1975, *International Networks: The Structured Webs of Diplomacy and Trade*, Sage professional papers in international studies 02—036, Beverly Hills and London: Sage.

Ethier, W.J., E. Helpman and J.P. Neary (eds.), 1993, *Theory, Policy and Dynamics in International Trade: Essays in Honor of Ronald W. Jones*, Cambridge (Mass.): Cambridge University Press.

Eymann, A. and L. Schuknecht, 1991, 'Anti-dumping Enforcement in the European Community', *World Bank PRE Working Papers Series* WPS 743, Washington D.C.: World Bank.

Ezran, R., C. Holmes and R. Safadi, 1992, 'How Changes in the CMEA Area May Affect International Trade in Manufactures', *World Bank PRIT Working Papers Series* WPS 973, Washington D.C.: World Bank.

Faber, J., 1987, 'Measuring Cooperation, Conflict and the Social Network of Nations', *Journal of Conflict Resolution*, **21** (3), pp. 438—64.

Finger, J.M. and S. Dhar, 1992, 'Do Rules Control Power? GATT Articles and Arrangements in the Uruguay Round', *World Bank WPS Working Papers Series* WPS 818, Washington D.C.: World Bank.

Fischer, D., 1984, *Preventing War in the Nuclear Age*, Totowa: Rowman & Allanheld.

Fisher, F.M., 1989, 'Games Economists Play: A Noncooperative View', *RAND Journal of Economics* **20**, pp. 113—24.

Folmer, H., P. van Mouche and S. Ragland, 1993, 'Interconnected Games and International Environmental Problems', *Environmental and Resource Economics* **3** (4), pp. 313—35.

Fontanel, J., 1994, 'Disarmament for Development in Favour of Developing Countries', in: M. Chatterji, A. Rima and H. Jager (eds.) *Economics of International Security. Essays in Honor of Jan Tinbergen*, London: Macmillan [in print].

Frey, B.S., 1974, 'Subventionierung der Abrüstung', *Annuaire Suisse de Sience Politique* **14**, pp. 57—68.

Frey, B.S., 1984, *International Political Economics*, Oxford: Basil Blackwell.

Frey, B.S. and F. Schneider, 1986, 'Competing Models of International Lending Activity', *Journal of Development Economics* **20**, 225—45.

Friedman M. and R. Friedman, 1980, *Free to Choose: A Personal Statement*, Harcourt Brace Jovanovich: New York.

Gasiorowski, M.J., 1986, 'Economic Interdependence and International Conflict: Some Cross-national Evidence', *International Studies Quarterly*, **30**, pp. 23-38.

Geraci, V.J. and W. Prewo, 1977, 'Bilateral Trade Flows and Transport Costs', *Review of Economics and Statistics* **69** (1), pp. 67—73.

Ghoshal, A., 1983, 'Going Against the Grain: Lessons from the 1980 Embargo', *The World Economy* **6** (1), pp. 183—93.

Good, I.J., 1983, *Good Thinking: The Foundations of Probability and Its Applications*, Minneapolis: University of Minnesota Press.

Grampp, D., 1987, 'Peace and Trade: The Classical vs. the Marxian View', in: H. Visser and E. Schoorl (eds.) *Trade in Transit*, Dordrecht: Kluwer, pp. 17—31.

Greenaway, D. and A. Sapir, 1992, 'New Issues in the Uruguay Round: Services, TRIMs and TRIPs', *European Economic Review* **36** (2/3), pp. 509—18.

Grey, R. de C., 1990, *Concepts of Trade Diplomacy and Trade in Services*, London: Trade Policy Research Centre.

Griffin, K. and J. Gurley, 1985, 'Radical Analysis of Imperialism, the Third World, and the Transition to Socialism: A Survey Article', *Journal of Economic Literature* **23** (3), pp. 1089—1143.

Groenink, R.J. (ed.) 1988, *Data on Europe, 1945—1980*, Bilthoven: Prime Press.

Guttentag, J.M. and R.J. Herring, 1986, 'Disaster Myopia in International Banking', *Essays in International Finance 164*, Princeton University Press: Princeton.

Hahn, F., 1990, 'On Some Economic Limits in Politics' in: J. Dunn, (ed.), *The Economic Limits to Modern Politics*, Cambridge: Cambridge University Press, pp. 142—64.

Ham, P. van, 1992, *Western Doctrines on East-West Trade: Theory, History and Policy*, London: Macmillan.

Hamilton, C.B. and L.A. Winters, 1992, 'Opening Up International Trade with Eastern Europe', *Economic Policy* **14**, pp. 77—116.

Haney, P.J., R.Q. Herzberg and R.K. Wilson, 1992, 'Advice and Consent: Unitary Actors, Advisory Models, and Experimental Tests', *Journal of Conflict Resolution* **36** (4), pp. 603—33.

Hanlon, J. and R. Omond, 1987, *The Sanctions Handbook*, Harmondsworth: Penguin.

Harris, P.B., 1968, 'Rhodesia: Sanctions and Politics', *Rhodesian Journal of Economics*, **2**, pp. 5—20.

Harris, R.G., 1993, 'Globalization, Trade and Income', *Canadian Journal of Economics*, **26** (4), 755—76

Havrylyshyn, O. and L. Pritchett, 1991, 'European Trade Patterns After the Transition', *World Bank PRE Working Papers Series* WPS 748, Washington D.C.: World Bank.

Hayes, J.P., 1987, *Economic Effects of Sanctions on Southern Africa*, London: Trade Policy Research Centre.

Hayes, J.P., 1988, 'Divided Opinions on Sanctions against South Africa', *The World Economy*, **11** (2), pp. 267—80.

Helpman, E., 1987, 'Comment on "The National Defense Argument for Government Intervention in Foreign Trade"', in: R.M. Stern (ed.) *U.S. Trade Policies in a Changing World Economy*, Cambridge: MIT Press, pp. 370—3.

204   *Economic Diplomacy, Trade and Commercial Policy*

Helpman, E. and A. Razin, 1978, *A Theory of International Trade under Uncertainty*, London: Academic Press.
Henderson, J.M. and R.E. Quandt, 1971, *Microeconomic Theory: A Mathematical Approach*, 2nd edition, New York: McGraw—Hill.
Hermele, K. and B. Odén, 1988, *Sanctions Dilemmas. Some implications of economic sanctions against South Africa*, Discussion Paper 1, Scandinavian Institute of African Studies, Uppsala.
Hirsch, S., 1981, 'Peace Making and Economic Interdependence', *The World Economy*, **4**, pp. 407—17.
Hirschman, A.O., 1980, *National Power and the Structure of Foreign Trade*, expanded edition, Los Angeles: University of California Press. (First published in 1945).
Hobson, J.A., 1988, *Imperialism. A Study*, 3rd edition, London: Allen & Unwin. (First published in 1902).
Hont, I., 1990, 'Free Trade and the Economic Limits to National Politics: Neo-Machiavellian Political Economy Reconsidered', in: J. Dunn, *The Economic Limits to Modern Politics*, Cambridge: Cambridge University Press, pp. 41—121.
Hout, W., 1985, 'Economie en oorlog', *Economisch Statistische Berichten* **70**, pp. 400—2.
Hower, G., 1988, 'The Effects of Cooperation on Crisis Outcome', paper at the IIIrd world congress of the Peace Science Society (International), University of Maryland.
Hufbauer, G.C. and J.J. Schott, 1985, *Economic Sanctions Reconsidered: History and Current Policy*, Washington D.C.: Institute for International Economics.
Hufbauer, G.C., J.J. Schott and K.A. Elliott, 1990, *Economic Sanctions Reconsidered: History and Current Policy*, 2nd edition, 2 volumes, Washington D.C.: Institute for International Economics.
Hughes Hallett, A.J. and A.S. Brandsma, 1983, 'How Effective Could Sanctions Against the Soviet Union Be?', *Weltwirtschaftliches Archiv* **119**, pp. 498—522.
Hutchison, T., 1988, *Before Adam Smith. The Emergence of Political Economy 1662—1776*, Oxford: Basil Blackwell.

Hyrkkanen, M., 1987, 'Free Trade and Contract as Alternatives to Imperialism and the Arms Race: The Case of Eduard Bernstein', in: V. Harle (ed.), *Essays in Peace Studies*, Aldershot: Avebury, pp. 167—80.

International Monetary Fund (IMF), 1983, 'Statistical Asymmetry in Global Current Account Balances' in: *World Economic Outlook*, IMF: Washington 1983, pp. 161—7.

International Monetary Fund (IMF), 1987, *Report on the World Current Account Discrepancy*, IMF: Washington D.C., 1987.

International Monetary Fund (IMF), 1990, *World Economic Outlook*, Washington D.C.: IMF.

International Monetary Fund (IMF), 1992a, *Issues and Developments in International Trade Policy*, Washington D.C.: IMF.

International Monetary Fund (IMF), 1992b, *Report on the Measurement of International Capital Flows*, IMF: Washington D.C., 1992.

Intrilligator, M.D., 1987, 'Comment on "The National Defense Argument for Government Intervention in Foreign Trade"', in: R.M. Stern (ed.) *U.S. Trade Policies in a Changing World Economy*, Cambridge, pp. 364—9.

Isard, W., 1954, 'Location Theory and Trade Theory: Short—run Analysis', *Quarterly Journal of Economics* **68** (2), pp. 305—20.

Isard, W., 1988, *Arms Races, Arms Control and Conflic Analysis. Contributions from Peace Science and Peace Economics*, Cambridge: Cambridge University Press.

Jepma, C.J. et al., 1992, *LDC Financial Requirements*, Aldershot: Avebury.

Jackson, J.H., 1989, *Restructuring the GATT System*, London: Royal Institute of International Affairs.

Julius, D., 1991, 'Foreign Direct Investment: The Neglected Twin of Trade', *Occasional Papers 33*, Washington D.C.: Group of Thirty.

Just, R.E. and D. Zilberman, 1979, 'Asymmetry of Taxes and Subsidies In Regulating Stochastic Mishap', *Quarterly Journal of Economics* **93** (1), pp. 139—48.

Kaempfer, W.H. and A.D. Lowenberg, 1986, 'A Model of the Political Economy of International Investment Sanctions: The Case of South Africa', *Kyklos*, **39** (3), pp. 377—96.

Kaempfer, W.H. and A.D. Lowenberg, 1988, 'The Theory of International Economic Sanctions: A Public Choice Approach', *American Economic Review*, **78** (4), pp. 786—93.

Kaempfer, W.H. and A.D. Lowenberg, 1992, *International Economic Sanctions: A Public Choice Perspective*, Westview: Boulder.

Kaempfer, W.H. and A.D. Lowenberg, 1993, *Transnational Externalities, Sanctions and Domestic Interest Group Influence*, mimeo, University of Colorado.

Kaempfer, W.H., A.D. Lowenberg, H. N. Mocan and K. Topyan, 1993, 'International Sanctions and Anti-Apartheid Politics in South Africa', *OCFEB Discussion Papers Series*, Rotterdam: Erasmus University.

Kaplow, L., 1990, 'A Note on the Optimal Use of Nonmonetary Sanctions,' *Journal of Public Economics* **42**, pp. 245—47.

Karsdorp, P.A., 1992, 'Naar een nieuwe wereldhandelsorganisatie' (Toward a New International Trade Organization; in Dutch), Den Haag: Directorate General for International Economic Relations.

Kemp, M.C., 1964, *The Pure Theory of International Trade*, Englewood Cliffs: Prentice Hall.

Kendall, M. and A. Stuart, 1977, *The Advanced Theory of Statistics*, 4th edition, Vol. 1, London: Griffin and Company.

Kennedy, P.M., 1989, *The Rise and Fall of the Great Powers. Economic Change and Military Conflict from 1500 to 2000*, New York: Vintage.

Keohane, R.O. and J.S. Nye, 1977, *Power and Interdependence*, Boston: Little Brown.

Keynes, J.M., 1984, *The Economic Consequences of the Peace*, Collected Writings II, Macmillan: London. (First published in 1919).

Keynes, J.M., 1986, *The General Theory of Employment, Interest and Money*, Collected Writings VII, Macmillan: London. (First published in 1936).

Khan, H.A., 1988, 'Impact of Trade Sanctions on South Africa: A Social Accounting Matrix Approach', *Contemporary Policy Issues* **6**, pp. 130—40.

Kindleberger, C.P., 1970, *Power and Money: The Economics of International Politics and the Politics of International Economics*, New York: Basic Books.

Kindleberger, C.P., 1986, 'International Public Goods without International Government', *American Economic Review* **76** (1), pp. 1—13.

Klein, L.R., 1994, 'Development and Disarmament: The Meaning', in: M. Chatterji, A. Rima and H. Jager (eds.) *Economics of International Security. Essays in Honor of Jan Tinbergen*, London: Macmillan [in print].

Klir, G.J., 1969, *An Approach to General Systems Theory*, New York: Van Nostrand Reinhold.

Knight, F.H., 1939, *Risk, Uncertainty and Profit*, London. (First published in 1921).

Knorr, K., 1975, *The Power of Nations: The Political Economy of International Relations*, New York: Basic Books.

Kravis, I.B., A. Heston and R. Summers, 1982, *World Product and Income: International Comparisons of Real Gross Product. United Nations International Comparison Project Phase III*, Baltimore: John Hopkins University Press.

Krugman, P.R. (ed.), 1986, *Strategic Trade Policy and the New International Economics*, Cambridge (Mass): MIT Press.

Krugman, P.R., 1991, *Geography and Trade*, London: MIT Press.

Krugman, P.R., 1993, 'The Narrow and Broad Arguments for Free Trade', *American Economic Review* **83** (2), 362—6.

Lawson, F.H., 1983, 'Using Positive Sanctions to End International Conflicts: Iran and the Arab Gulf Countries', *Journal of Peace Research*, **20** (4), pp. 311—28.

Leamer, E.E. and R.M. Stern, 1970, *Quantitative International Economics*, Boston: Allyn and Bacon.

Leidy, M.P., 1989, 'The Theory of International Economic Sanctions — A Public Choice Approach: Comment', *American Economic Review* **79** (5), pp. 1300—3.

Leitzel, J., 1987, 'Hufbauer, G.C. and Schott, J.J.: Economic Sanctions Reconsidered: History and Current Policy' (review), *Kyklos* **40** (1), pp. 286—8.

Lenin, V.I., 1967, 'Report on Concessions Delivered to the R.C.P. [B] Group at the Eighth Congress of Soviets [December 21, 1920]', in: C. Leiteisen (ed.), *Lenin on Peaceful Coexistence*, Moskow: Progress Publishers, pp. 72—95.

Lensink, R., 1993, *External Finance and Development,* Groningen: Wolters Noordhoff.

Lensink, R. and P.A.G. van Bergeijk, 1991, 'The Determinants of Developing Countries' Access to the International Capital Market', *Journal of Development Studies* **28** (1), pp. 86—103.

Levine, R. 1988, 'Trade vs. National security: Section 232 Cases', *Comparative Strategy* **7**, 133—141.

Leyton-Brown, D. (ed.), 1987, *The Utility of International Economic Sanctions*, New York: St. Martin's Press.

Lindsay, J.M., 1986, 'Trade Sanctions as Policy Instruments: A Re-examination', *International Studies Quarterly*, **30**, pp. 153—73.

Linnemann, H., 1966, *An Econometric Study of International Trade Flows*, Amsterdam: North-Holland.

Linnemann, H. and H. Verbruggen, 1991, 'GSTP Tariff Reduction and Its Effects on South-South Trade in Manufactures', *World Development* **19** (5), pp. 539—52.

Losman, D.L., 1972, 'The Effects of Economic Boycotts', *Lloyds Bank Review*, No 106, pp. 27—41.

Lundahl, M., 1984, 'Economic Effects of a Trade and Investment Boycott Against South Africa', *Scandinavian Journal of Economics* **86** (1), pp. 68—83.

Lundborg, P., 1987, *The Economics of Export Embargoes: The Case of the US-Soviet Grain Suspension*, London: Croom Helm.

Lundborg, P., 1988, 'Voting with the US or the USSR in the United Nations: A Logistic Approach,' Paper Third World Peace Science Congress, 30 May—3 June 1988, University of Maryland [mimeo].

Maclean, J., 1988, 'Marxism and International Relations: A Strange Case of Mutual Neglect', *Millennium* **17**, pp. 295—319.

Maizels, A. and M. K. Nissanke, 1984, 'Motivations for Aid to Developing Countries', *World Development*, **12** (1), pp. 879—900.

Maizels, A. and M.K. Nissanke, 1986, 'The Determinants of Military Expenditures in Developing Countries', *World Development* **14** (9), pp. 1125—40.

Marer, P., 1985, *Dollar GNPs of the USSR and Eastern Europe*, Baltimore.

Marrewijk, C. van, 1990, 'Boycotts, Private Production, Optimal Production, the Choice of the Numéraire and Exact Indexation', *Institute for Economic Research Discussion Paper Series* 9008/G, Rotterdam: Erasmus University.

Marrewijk, C. van, 1992, 'Trade Uncertainty and the Two-Step Procedure: The Choice of Numéraire and Exact Indexation', *De Economist* **140** (3), pp. 317—27.

Marrewijk, C. van and P.A.G. van Bergeijk, 1990, 'Trade Uncertainty and Specialization: Social versus Private Planning", *De Economist* **138** (1), pp. 15—32.

Marrewijk, C. van and P.A.G. van Bergeijk, 1993, 'Endogenous Trade Uncertainty: Why Countries May Specialize Against Comparative Advantage', *Regional Science and Urban Economics*, **23** (4), pp. 681—94.

Marris, R., 1984, 'Comparing the Incomes of Nations: A Critique of the International Comparison Project', *Journal of Economic Literature*, **22**, pp. 40—57.

Marshall, A., 1965, *Money, Credit and Commerce,* New York: Reprints of Economic Classics. (First Published in 1923).

Martin, L.L., 1992, *Coercive Cooperation: Explaining Multilateral Economic Sanctions*, Princeton: Princeton University Press

Marx, K. and F. Engels, 1928, *Das Kommunistische Manifest*, 5th edition, Vienna. (First published in 1848).

Mayer, W., 1977, 'The National Defense Tariff Argument Reconsidered', *Journal of International Economics* **7**, pp. 363—77.

McKenna, C.J., 1986, *The Economics of Uncertainty*, Brighton: Wheatsheaf.

Menkveld, P.A., 1991, *Origin and Role of the European Bank for Reconstruction and Development*, London: Graham & Trotman.

Mill, J.S., 1968, *Principles of Political Economy With Some of Their Applications to Social Philosophy*, Collected Works II, London: Routledge. (First published in 1840).

Mintz, A. and R. Stevenson, 1992, 'Defense Expenitures, Economic Growth and the "Peace Divicend": A Longitudinal Analysis', paper presented at the Economics of International Security conference, The Hague, May 21—23, 1992.

Montagnon, P. (ed.), 1990, *European Competition Policy*, London: Royal Institute of International Affairs.

Moore, M.O., 1992, 'Rules or Politics?: An Empirical Analysis of ITC Anti-dumping Decisions', *Economic Inquiry* **30** (3), pp. 449—66.

Morgenstern, O., 1950, *On The Accuracy of Economic Observations*, Princeton: Princeton University Press.

Murphy, J.A., 1992, 'An Analysis of Terms of Trade Problems', *Economic Systems* **14**, 149—59.

Neumann, J. von and O. Morgenstern, 1980, *Theory of Games and Economic Behavior*, Princeton: Princeton University Press. (First published in 1944).

Nossal, K.R., 1989, 'International Sanctions as International Punishment', *International Organization* **43**, pp. 301—22.

Olson, R.S., 1979, 'Economic Coercion in World Politics. With A Focus on North—South Relations', *World Politics*, **31** (4), pp. 471—94.

Organization for Economic Co-operation and Development (OECD), 1991, *OECD Economic Surveys 1990/1991: Germany*, Paris: OECD.

Organization for Economic Co-operation and Development (OECD), 1993, *Economic Outlook 53*, Paris: OECD.

Paarlberg, R.L., 1980, 'Some Lessons of the Grain Embargo', *Foreign Affairs* **59** (1), pp. 144—162.

Page, S., 1991, 'Europe 1992: Views of Developing Countries', *Economic Journal*, **101**, 1553—66.

Pen, J., 1967, *A Primer on International Trade*, New York: Random House.

Petersmann, E.-U., 1991, 'Trade Policy, Environmental Policy and GATT: Why Trade Rules and Environmental Rules Should Be Consistent', *Außenwirtschaft* **44**, 197—221.

Petersmann, E.-U., 1993, 'International Competition Rules for the GATT—MTO World Trade and Legal System', *Journal of World Trade* **27** (6), 35—86.

Pindyck, R.S. and D.J. Rubinfeld, 1991, *Econometric Models and Economic Forecasts*, Singapore, 2nd edition, New York: McGraw Hill.

Polachek, S.W., 1980, 'Conflict and Trade', *Journal of Conflict Resolution*, **24** (1), pp. 55—78.

Polachek, S.W., 1992, 'Conflict and Trade: An Economic Approach to Political International Interactions,' in: W. Isard and C.H. Anderton (eds), *Economics of Arms Reduction and the Peace Process*, Amsterdam: Elsevier, pp. 89—120.

Polachek, S.W. and J.A. McDonald, 1992, 'Strategic Trade and Incentives for Cooperation', in: M. Chatterji and L.R. Forcey (eds.), *Disarmament, Economic Conversion, and the Management of Peace*, Praeger: Westport, pp. 273—84.

Pollins, B.M., 1989a, 'Does Trade Still Follow the Flag?', *American Political Science Review*, **85**, pp. 465—80.

Pollins, B.M., 1989b, 'Conflict, Cooperation, and Commerce: The Effect of International Political Interactions on Bilateral Trade Flows', *American Journal of Political Science* **33**, pp. 737—61.

Pomery, J., 1984, 'Uncertainty in Trade Models', in: R.W. Jones and P.B. Kenen (eds.), *Handbook of International Economics*, Amsterdam: North-Holland, pp. 419—65.

Porter, M.E., 1990, *The Competitive Advantage of Nations*, New York: Free Press.

Porter, R.C., 1979, 'International Trade and Investment Sanctions: Potential Impact on the South African Economy', *Journal of Conflict Resolution* **23** (4), pp. 579—612.

Potters, J. 1992, *Lobbying and Pressure: Theory and Experiments*, Amsterdam: Tinbergen Institute and Thesis Publishers.

Prusa, T.J., 1992, 'Why Are So Many Antidumping Petitions Withdrawn?', *Journal of International Economics* **33** (1), pp. 1—20.

Reekie, D., 1987, 'The Economics of Apartheid Politics', *Economic Affairs*, **7**, pp. 10—13.

Reich, R.B., 1991, *The Work of Nations: Preparing Ourselves for 21st-Century Capitalism*, New York: Vintage Books.

Renner, M., 1993, 'Preparing for Peace', in: L.R. Brown (ed.) *State of the World 1993*, New York: Norton, pp. 139—57.

Rhodes, C., 1989, 'Reciprocity in Trade: The Utility of a Bargaining Strategy', *International Organizaton* **43**, pp. 273—99.

Ricardo, D., 1962, *The Principles of Political Economy and Taxation*, London: Everyman's Library. (First published in 1817).

Richardson, L.F., 1960, *Arms and Insecurity. A Mathematical Study of the Causes and Origins of War*, London: Atlantic Books.

Richardson, N.R., 1978, *Foreign Policy and Economic Dependence*, Austin: University of Texas Press.

Roemer, J.E., 1977, 'The Effect of Sphere of Influence and Economic Distance on The Commodity Composition of Trade in Manufactures', *Review of Economics and Statistics*, **59**, pp. 318—27.

Roodbeen, H., 1992, *Trading the Jewel of Great Value: The Participation of The Netherlands, Belgium, Switzerland and Austria in the Strategic Western Embargo*, Leiden: Leyden University.

Rosa, D.A. de, 1992, 'Protection and Export Performance in Subsaharan Africa', *Weltwirtschaftliches Archiv* **128** (1), 88—124.

Rosecrane, R., 1986, *The Rise of the Trading State. Commerce and Conquest in the Modern World*, New York: Basic Books.

Ruffin, R.J., 1974, 'International Trade Under Uncertainty', *Journal of International Economics* **4**, 243—59.

Ruigrok, W.M. and R.J.M. van Tulder, 1993, *The Ideology of Interdependence: The Link between Restructuring, Internationalisation and International Trade*, Ph. D. Thesis Leyden University.

Sandler, T., 1992, *Collective Action: Theory and Applications*, Brighton: Harvester Wheatsheaf.

Sanso, M., R., Cuairan and F. Sanz, 1993, 'Bilateral Trade Flows, the Gravity Equation, and Functional Form', *Review of Economics and Statistics* **75**, 266—75.

Sato, R. and J.A. Rizzo (eds.), 1988, *Unkept Promises, Unclear Consequences*, Cambridge: Cambridge University Press.

Sayrs, L.W., 1987, 'Trade Reciprocity and Peace', University of Iowa Political Science Occasional Paper Series 63.

Sayrs, L.W., 1988a, 'Reconsidering Trade and Conflict. A Qualitative Response Model With Censoring', *Conflict Management and Peace Science*, **10** (1), pp. 1—19.

Sayrs, L.W., 1988b 'New Issues in Trade and Conflict', University of Iowa Political Science Occasional Papers Series 79.

Sayrs, L.W., 1990, 'Expected Utility and Peace Science: An Assessment of Trade and Conflict', *Conflict Management and Peace Science* **11** (1), pp. 17—44.

Schelling, T.C., 1980, *The Strategy of Conflict*, Harvard: Harvard University Press. (First published in 1960).

Schiavo-Campo, S., 1978, *International Economics. An Introduction to Theory and Policy*, Cambridge (Mass): Winthrop.

Schneider, F. and B.S. Frey, 1985, 'Economic and Political Determinants of Foreign Direct Investment', *World Development* **13** (2), 161—75.

Schott, J.J., 1993, 'Reassessing the World Trading System', *International Economic Insights* **4** (5), pp. 17—20.

Schrödt, P.A., 1985, 'Adaptive Precedent-Based Logic and Rational Choice; A Comparision of Two Approaches to the Modeling of International Behavior', in: U. Luterbacher and M.D. Ward (eds), *Dynamic Models of International Conflict*, Boulder (Colorado): Lynne Rienner, pp. 373—400.

Schulz, C.E., 1989, 'On the Rationality of Economic Sanctions', [mimeo] Oslo: Norwegian Institute of International Affairs.

Schumpeter, J.A., 1954, *History of Economic Analysis*, London: Allen & Unwin.

Schumpeter, J.A., 1966, *Capitalism, Socialism, and Democracy*, 2nd edition, London: Unwin. (First published in 1943.)

Schweinberger, A.G., 1993, 'Procompetitive Gains from Trade and Competitive Advantage', Paper European Workshop on International Trade (ERWIT 93), Rotterdam, 11 june.

Scolnick, J.M., 1988, 'How Governments Utilize Foreign Threats', *Conflict* **8**, pp. 12—21.

Seeler, H.J., 1982, 'Wirtschaftssanktionen als zweifelhaftes Instrument der Außenpolitik', *Europa-Archiv*, **20**, pp. 611—8.

Shipping Research Bureau, 1989, *Newsletter on the Oil Embargo against South Africa*, Nr. 15/16.

Shone, R., 1981, *Applications in Intermediate Microeconomics*, Oxford: Martin Robertson.

Simon, J.L., 1989, 'Lebensraum: Paradoxically, Population Growth May Eventually End Wars', *Journal of Conflict Resolution* **33** (1), pp. 164—80.

Smeets, M., 1990, 'Economic Sanctions Against Iraq: The Ideal Case?', *Journal of World Trade* **24** (6), pp. 105—20.

Smeets, M., 1992, 'Efficacy of Economic Sanctions, with special reference to Iraq and Yugoslavia', paper presented at the Tinbergen Institutes Congress 'Economics on International Security', The Hague, May 22.

Smeets, M., 1994, 'Economic Sanctions Against Iraq', Chapter 3 in: H.H. Blumberg en C.C. French (eds), *The Persian Gulf War: Views from the Social and Behavioural Sciences*, University Press of America: Lanham (in print)

Smith, Adam, 1976, *An Inquiry into the Nature and Causes of the Wealth of Nations,* Canna's edition, Claredon Press: Oxford. (First published in 1776).

Smith, Alasdair, 1986, 'East West Trade, Embargoes and Expectations', CEPR Discussion Paper 139, CEPR: Londen.

Södersten, B., 1980, *International Economics*, 2nd edition, Macmillan: London.

Sorsa, P., 1992, 'GATT and Environment,' *The World Economy* **15**, pp. 115—33.

Spero, J. (J. Edelman-Spero), 1977, *The Politics of International Economic Relations,* London: Allen & Unwin.

Spriggs, J., 1991, 'Towards an International Transparency Institution: Australian Style', *World Economy* **14** (2), 165—80.

Srinivasan, T.N., 1987, 'The National Defense Argument for Government Intervention in Foreign Trade', in: R.M. Stern (ed.) *U.S. Trade Policies in a Changing World Economy*, Cambridge: MIT Press, pp. 337-63 and 374—5.

Stegemann, K., 1989, 'Policy Rivalry Among Industrial States: What Can We Learn from Models of Strategic Trade Policy?', *International Organization* **43** (1), 73—100.

Stoeckel, A. et al., 1990, *Western Trade Blocks: Game, Set or Match for Asia, Pacific and The World?*, Canberra: Centre for International Economics.

Subramanian, A., 1992, 'Trade Measures for Environment,' *The World Economy* **15**, pp. 135—52.

Summary, R.M., 1989, 'A Political-Economic Model of U.S. Bilateral Trade', *Review of Economics and Statistics*, **71** (1), pp. 179-82.

Summers, R. and A. Heston, 1988, 'A New Set of International Comparisons of Real Product and Prices: Estimates for 130 Countries, 1950—1985', *Review of Income and Wealth*, **34** (1), pp. 1—25 (and on diskette).

Teekens, R. and J. Koerts, 1972, 'Some Statistical Implications of the Log Transformation of Multiplicative Models', *Econometrica* **40** (5), pp. 793—813.

Tharakan, P.K.M., 1991, 'The Political Economy of Anti-dumping Undertakings in the European Communities', *European Economic Review* **35** (6), pp. 1341—59.

Theil, H., 1983, 'World Product and Income: A Review Article', *Journal of Political Economy* **91**, pp. 505—17.

Thompson, P.B., 1992, *The Ethics of Aid and Trade: U.S. Food Policy, Foreign Competition, and the Social Contract*, Cambridge: Cambridge University Press.

Tinbergen, J., 1962, *Shaping the World Economy - Suggestions for an International Economic Policy*, New York: Twentieth Century Fund.

Tinbergen, J., 1985, 'De economie van de oorlog', [Economics of peace and war] *Economisch Statistische Berichten* **70**, 172—5.

Tolley, G.S. and J.D. Wilman, 1977, 'The Foreign Dependence Question', *Journal of Political Economy*, **85**, pp. 323—47.

Tsebelis, G., 1989, 'The Abuse of Probability in Political Analysis: The Rubinson Crusoe Fallacy', *American Political Science Review* **83**, pp. 77—91.

Tsebelis, G., 1990, 'Are Sanctions Effective. A Game Theoretic Analysis', *Journal of Conflict Resolution* **34** (1), pp. 3—28.

Ungar, S.J. and P. Vale, 1985/86,'South Africa: Why Constructive Engagement Failed', *Foreign Affairs*, **64**, pp. 234—58.

Waltzer, M., 1977, *Just and Unjust Wars*, New York.

Wang, Z.K. and L.A. Winters, 1991, 'The Trading Potential of Eastern Europe', *CEPR Discussion Paper Series* 610, London: CEPR.

WCED (World Commission on Environment and Development), 1987, *Our Common Future,* Oxford University Press: Oxford.

Webb, M., 1992, 'The Ambiguous Consequences of Anti-dumping Laws', *Economic Inquiry* **30** (3), pp. 437—48.

Weck-Hannemann, H. and B.S. Frey, 1992, 'The Contribution of Public Choice Theory to International Political Economy', in: C. Polychroniou (ed.), *Perspectives and Issues in International Political Economy*, Westport: Praeger, 38—58.

Welfens, P.J.J., 1989, 'The Economics of Military and Peacekeeping: An Emerging Field', in: *Jahrbuch für Sozialwissenschaft* **40** (3), pp. 358—85.

Welfens, P.J.J., 1992, *Market-oriented Systemic Transformations in Eastern Europe*, Springer Verlag.

Wilde, J.H. de, 1991, *Saved from Oblivion: Interdependence Theories in the First Half of the 20th Century*, Dartmouth: Aldershot.

Wolf, T.A., 1983, 'Choosing a U.S. Trade Stategy Towards the Soviet Union', in: Joint Economic Committee Congress of the United States, *Soviet Economy in the 1980s: Problems and Prospects*, Washington D.C., pp. 400—18.

World Bank, 1991, *World Development Report 1991*, World Bank: Washington D.C.

Yeats, A.J., 1990, 'On the Accuracy of Economic Observations. Do Sub-Saharan Trade Statistics Mean Anything?', *World Bank Economic Review* **4**, 135-156.

Yeats, A.J., 1992, 'Can a Manufactured Good Cease to be a Manufactured Good Mereley by Crossing a National Frontier?', *Bulletin of Economic Research* **44** (3), 199—219.

Author Index

Subject Index